12

W9-BKJ-471

DON'T SAY I DO!

DON'T SAY I DO!

Why Women Should Stay Single

Orna Gadish, MSc

NEW HORIZON PRESS
Far Hills, NJ

Copyright © 2012 by Orna Gadish

All rights reserved. No portion of this book may be reproduced or transmitted in any form whatsoever, including electronic, mechanical or any information storage or retrieval system, except as may be expressly permitted in the 1976 Copyright Act or in writing from the publisher.

Requests for permission should be addressed to:

New Horizon Press
P.O. Box 669
Far Hills, NJ 07931

Gadish, Orna
        Don't Say I Do!: Why Women Should Stay Single

Cover design: Wendy Bass
Interior design: Scribe Inc.

Library of Congress Control Number: 2011928851
ISBN 13: 978-0-88282-382-9

New Horizon Press

Manufactured in the U.S.A.

16   15   14   13   12   1   2   3   4   5

Author's Note

This book is based on the author's research, personal experiences and clients' real life experiences. In order to protect privacy, names have been changed and identifying characteristics have been altered except for contributing experts.

For purposes of simplifying usage, the pronouns his/her and he/she are sometimes used interchangeably. The information contained herein is not meant to be a substitute for professional evaluation and therapy with mental health professionals.

Contents

Introduction

Many women in modern society are not buying into the notion that they need to be married, remarried or in a relationship in order to lead happy, meaningful lives. In *Don't Say I Do!* we will focus on the new movement among women maintaining that there is absolutely nothing a single woman cannot do that a married woman can; on the contrary, single women have the freedom and the time to do everything they want, plus a whole lot more. More women have started owning the single status, recognizing it for the wonderful opportunity that it is.

In the past, the majority of women thoughtlessly bought into the idea that singlehood must automatically relegate one to a life of dissatisfaction and unfulfilled dreams, deplete of meaning, with images of a depressed woman curled up on the couch with a tub of ice cream and a pile of chick flicks, trying to wash away her fears and discontent and waiting until Prince Charming comes along to make all of her dreams come true.

The good thing is that, if you choose, you too can let go of those confining and destructive ideas, stereotypes and stigmas and become free to live the best years of your life as a single and unmarried woman. You can lead the rest of your life liberated and empowered. Being single, unmarried, divorced or even widowed is negative only if you *let* it be negative.

If you choose to think of your time as a single woman as a blessing and use your time and money wisely to ensure your personal happiness, amazing opportunities will arise to be profoundly yourself and you are bound to find single life fulfilling. The motivational speaker Les Brown accurately observed, "You are the only real obstacle in your path to a fulfilling life."[1] It's definitely time to start getting out of your own way.

There are always many options for how you choose to see any given situation in life. Many women become consumed with focusing heavily on the disadvantages of being single, unmarried or divorced. What is the point of this, other than to waste precious time and energy that could be used for personal growth and enjoying life to the fullest?

Look at all of the examples of gorgeous, smart, successful women who choose to stay single, unmarried or happily divorced, because they value themselves enough to put themselves first. Choose to be optimistic about being single and soon you may be the envy of many of your married friends. Expect nothing less than a wonderful situation and you will begin to create and see just that.

Too many women make the mistake of thinking that they need a special someone in their lives in order to be happy and fulfilled; that happiness comes from an external source, such as a walk down the wedding aisle with a man whose job (that you project on him) is to make all of your dreams come true. I believe this line of thought plays against women, because you and only you can be responsible for your own contentment in life. The sooner you recognize that, the sooner you will be on a better path.

If you feel that you're "not worth anything" unless you are part of a couple, then you won't be. On the other hand, if you decide that your time and status as a single woman is a great opportunity to be yourself and make yourself happy, you'll find single life much more fulfilling. An optimistic and take-charge approach is the key to creating lasting and authentic happiness in being a single, unmarried or divorced woman today.

We live in a world where the number of marriages is declining. Many people around the world now believe that marriage is not the epitome of a happy life. In fact, the percentage of young adults (ages twenty-five to thirty-four) who have never married is at an all-time high of 46.3 percent, with sharp increases in the number of single people in big cities in the United States and throughout the industrialized world.[2] This is the first time that the number of unmarried young adults exceeds the number of those who are married.

More and more women are shunning the institution of marriage. With more women in the workforce and sharp increases in cohabitation, single parenthood and out-of-wedlock childbirths, along with increasing divorce rates, fewer women than ever opt to tie the knot. The decline of marriage is happening now.

Don't Say I Do! is the product of five years of exhaustive research into the subject of why women should choose the single life. During that time, I examined articles, essays, books and films about the collapse of marriage. As part of the research, I interviewed fifty-five single, unmarried and divorced women, as well as unhappily married women between the ages of eighteen and seventy-five, from various sociocultural backgrounds in the United States, Europe and around the Western world. These women agreed to share their stories of searching for and finding fulfilling careers and personal lives in which their own desires and goals are paramount, whether they choose marriage or opt out of it. Stories that are a testament to the waning of marriage were embedded in the narrative of this book.

The breakdown of marriage, as shown in the number of couples never tying the knot or severing the knot with divorce, is a burning sociocultural and international phenomenon. With society producing more single and unmarried people than ever, it is important to understand why large numbers of women are electing not to marry—why many of us are single by choice and loving every moment!

Forget about old-fashioned patterns, molds and rules of past generations that are no longer relevant. It's time to be aware of all of the new choices, options and opportunities available to single, unmarried or divorced women today. Recognize and embrace all the amazing alternatives you have in moving forward with your relationships, family and career matters as a liberated and self-reliant woman.

There are plenty of relationship possibilities for unmarried women, various alternative family structures, options to conceive and become a mother, ways to raise children alone and so many other alternatives for those staying single by choice. You can and should live your life to the fullest right now, without regretting anything or apologizing to anyone.

The rules of the game have been changed forever. I strongly believe that, by remaining single, not only won't you miss out, but also you have won the game! Now, more than ever, you can take charge of your life and steer it toward your own desires. As you do, you will be amazed at the exciting options open to you to live your life freely and on your own terms!

For women living in the postmodern era, traditional marriage and its derivatives—nuclear, monogamous, heterosexual and even homosexual families—are choices but no longer prerequisites for living with a partner, sharing finances, having sex or even having or raising children. Times have changed; people have changed. This book may be the harbinger.

UNMARRIED WOMEN IN RELATIONSHIPS

Your status is that you have a sexual partner, but you are reluctant to marry him. You may cohabit with your partner and share expenses or reside apart in a Living Apart Together (LAT) dwelling arrangement, where each keeps his or her own place and maintains separate finances.

While sexual relations are at the heart of many bonds, cohabitation, shared finances and a marital contract are certainly not inherent components to such bonds. Marriage appears to me to be an artificial social and cultural phenomenon. As an unmarried woman in a relationship, this book will help you understand how you can benefit from your unmarried state without proceeding toward marriage as expected by traditional society.

UNMARRIED WOMEN IN UNHAPPY RELATIONSHIPS

If you are an unmarried woman who is currently disappointed in your "unofficial" commitment but are reluctant to break up with him for various reasons, such as those related to social pressure, obligations to extended family or community or, alternatively, financial, physical or emotional dependence on your partner, you should definitely reconsider. You will find in this book some timely commentary and suggestions that can be relevant to your bewildering state. I encourage you to stop deliberating and make the choice to be happy without this destructive relationship.

SINGLE WOMEN NOT IN RELATIONSHIPS

The population of single women is growing at an aggressive rate, with millions of single women around the world. Statistics show that just over 50 percent of American women are unmarried and more women remain single at a later age.[3] This is true for many other countries around the industrialized Western world, including Australia, New Zealand, Canada and Mexico. It strongly applies to women in European countries, especially prosperous ones (that are also affected by lower birth rates): Britain, France, Germany, Austria, Italy, Spain, Portugal, the Netherlands, Bulgaria, Romania, Latvia, Estonia, the Czech Republic, Hungary, Poland, Croatia, Greece, Slovenia, Romania, Turkey, Malta and Luxembourg. It is very relevant to the Nordic countries (Denmark, Sweden, Finland, Norway and Iceland) where women tend to live with partners without marrying, to Far East nations such as China and Japan, which have high rates of singles, and, to a lesser extent, to Eastern European countries, such as Russia and Ukraine. Being single is an international trend.

Similarly to many Western countries, the percentage of single women in Israel is growing. According to the Central Bureau of Statistics of Israel, the highest percentage of unmarried women is currently in big cities with over one hundred thousand inhabitants. For example, 53 percent of women in Tel-Aviv (and 72 percent of men) between the ages of twenty-five and thirty-four are unmarried. However, the percentage of those unmarried decreases in typically Orthodox cities, such as Bnei-Brak, with only 18 percent of women unmarried (and 22 percent of men).[4]

Many single women are taking part in the lively "singles scene," particularly in big cities around the world. Thanks to women's liberation achievements, technology and science, more women than ever pursue studies and establish professional careers before thinking about having families and children. Even for those women who want children, they do not necessarily see marriage as part of their plans.

As a woman in this group, in this book you will find support and inspiration for the self-reliant choice you have made or may make to remain single. You will also be introduced to some of the postmodern alternatives to traditional marriage, empowering you to carve your independent path in life without leaning on a man.

DIVORCED WOMEN

You are a woman who has been married once or more than once and currently you are divorced. Statistics show that today 40 percent of all marriages in the United States end in divorce and, throughout the industrialized Western world, divorce statistics are not significantly different. In Israel, around 30 couples divorce for every 100 couples who marry. Most married couples tend to break up after their second, third or fourth year of marriage at an average age of 38.1.[5]

This book will give you sound advice that will encourage and stimulate you to stay single, if that is what you want. You will understand the benefits of your decision to divorce and you will be motivated to take the next step to stay unmarried, either within a new relationship or not.

UNHAPPILY MARRIED WOMEN

As a woman who is in an unhappy marriage, disappointed with marriage, contemplating divorce, on the verge of divorce or in a "cooling period" before divorce, you will find some chapters in this book that will be beneficial and inspiring to you. You will learn that getting a divorce and staying in an unmarried state is not the end of your world and can actually be its very beginning!

Unfortunately, many fearful women continue to suffer in impaired marriages, either physically or emotionally. As Leo Tolstoy put it in his timeless novel *Anna Karenina*, "Happy families are all alike; every unhappy family is unhappy in its own way." Many women endure miserable marriages but remain in them, nonetheless. Some of them talk about it, some of them do not. If you are ready to face and change your unhappy situation in marriage, you will find advice in this book that will encourage you to stop putting up with the pain and to start over, this time without marriage.

If you belong to one of the groups focused on in *Don't Say I Do!*, I present practical advice that will guide you through your situation and toward making the best decision, without wavering or being afraid of change. Even if that change seems impossible at first, you owe it to yourself to consider new possibilities.

For thousands of years, marriage was nothing more than a fairly straightforward business partnership. Marriage was a way to make alliances, pay off debts and pass along wealth and an attempt to control sexuality in a patriarchal world. Most marriages were arranged to capitalize on these points as much as possible and nowhere in the equation entered the notion of love.

So why in modern times do so many people, especially women, thoughtlessly yet enthusiastically buy into the idea of marriage as the ultimate expression of love or faithfulness? Women in today's society have more options and freedom than ever before and modern women certainly do not need to sign a piece of paper to guarantee themselves financial security, business or familial alliances or a sexual partner. I strongly believe a truly empowered woman is liberated and knows beyond any doubt that she can make the conscious choice to enjoy profound relationships rooted in an unconditional love, while side-stepping all of the legal hassle and constrictive implications of the archaic institution of marriage. While she may enjoy the company of men, she never needs one. If she makes the choice to be single, she can do so confidently, knowing that she is already a complete and fulfilled being with much to offer to the world on her own.

Women around the world are choosing short-term partners in relationships and marriages. Many believe that marriage has become obsolete.[6] Also, there are plenty of substitutes for marriage today and alternative families are becoming more common and acceptable in American society and around the Western world. A woman does not have to walk down the aisle and have a ring on her finger in order to have a family today.

We'll discuss in the next chapters why such sociocultural transformation in the way the family unit is defined and perceived makes it necessary to think outside the constraints of marriage. However, you need to make your own decisions in a world that in many ways is still governed by the interests of men. The *Don't Say I Do!* project stands for single women's independence and liberation in the global arena. The sooner we're aware of the cultural change and the endless options the change brings about, the better, stronger and prouder we will become as individuals.

We'll take a close look at new options, choices and alternatives to marriage for postmodern women: the new roles that women can play, the new relationship options available to them, the newly accepted family structures that were unimaginable just a few decades ago, the large leaps in education, workplace and career and the endless opportunities to live life happily ever after as a single, modern woman.

Part I
Married Women

Chapter 1

Pros and Cons of Marriage

Are you thinking about getting married or are you already married? Many women around the world accept the ideal of marriage, only to discover later that the reality of married life falls short of their expectations. Younger and older women find themselves struggling to redefine marriage for the twenty-first century lifestyle.

There is so much we admire about married life, but unfortunately many believe, as I do, that it is an archaic ideal that is out of touch with reality and, in many cases, totally unsuitable for how women imagine themselves living today. But marriage, for all kinds of reasons, remains a pressing concern—one that has the tendency to polarize even the most balanced and like-minded of individuals.

Conversation about the pros and cons of marriage frequently reveals our own deeply personal agendas and biases. Few life events possess the same capacity to unravel the best of us. And so, strong, fearless and confident women who usually proceed without questioning or second-guessing their actions can be caught off-guard by the marriage issue. The very thought of matrimony seems to cause some women to embrace their own personal bliss fervently, while others turn pale with fright. Marriage is not an easy topic to debate.

Some women desire to be happily married above all else and devote a great deal of their time and energy to that end. Others detest the idea of giving up their freedom and independence just to tie the knot with another person and will actively resist going in that direction. Some are confused about marriage and prefer to ignore the whole issue. Chances are, we've all experienced some doubts and hesitations during the process of figuring out where we fit in the marriage puzzle.

We are all familiar with the "happily unmarried and very comfortable staying that way" individuals in our close circle of friends; likewise, we know starry-eyed romantics who want to believe that true love can do no wrong. Then there are women who find themselves torn between wanting to get married, because they feel they should, and feeling enormous anxiety about losing their freedom, sense of self and individuality.

Sometimes the marriage question arrives in the form of a jubilant exclamation, while at other times it resembles a nagging query in the back of one's mind. Some may feel a creeping sense of alarm as time passes without marrying. While some women see marriage as an inconvenient hurdle to maneuver around, others are trying to be true to themselves without disappointing their parents and families, who may still hold rigid views on sex and marriage. The topic of marriage creates much difference of opinion and family discord.

But what is it about marriage that causes so much excitement on the one hand and apparent distress and disillusionment on the other?

There are good things about married life as well as some not-so-good things. While most women have no problem listing the pros, there is a tendency to push the less desirable aspects of marriage out of the way and pretend they don't exist. Unfortunately, this kind of denial of their disillusionment with marriage can produce serious complications later on, especially when women harbor unrealistic expectations.

The attraction of marriage exerts considerable influence over many women today. Many women have grown up with an image of having a fairy-tale wedding, endlessly making them want to get hitched. Even those women who think they are immune to the lure of marriage may find themselves caught up in wedding ceremonies, attracted by the theatrical show and overt expression of love. Women might seek marriage for many different reasons, but most commonly it is in order to have "a dream come true."

The greatest plus of all related to marriage is the discovery of the person with whom you wish to spend "the rest of your life." Women are believed to be biologically primed for this long-term attachment, so it is little wonder that there is excitement and satisfaction when two people do connect with each other and fall in love.

Marriage involves so much more than just the pleasure of finding someone with whom to share our precious time on this Earth. The act of marrying someone goes hand in hand with a strong level of commitment. Yet more marriages break up due to reasons such as infidelity and irreconcilable differences than ever before. The challenge lies in maintaining married relationships that are meaningful for both parties; relationships that respect individual needs as well as the common goals of the people involved. It is virtually impossible to meet everyone's needs equally at all times.

The major problem with many married relationships—and a key reason why many women choose to forsake marriage—is when one person's requirements start to overshadow everything else. This may occur when one individual starts to exert more control over the direction of goals. Soon the other partner feels ignored and betrayed. Therefore, a main drawback to marriage is the reality that it is not possible to attend to two individual agendas at the same time.

While we may find ourselves surprised at the number of conflicting viewpoints and cultural idiosyncrasies about the question of marriage, there is no doubt that marriage remains an important decision in the lives of most women. Some women view marriage as a good choice, while others regard it as something to be avoided. Like it or not, most women will eventually find themselves struggling with the issue.

But the general attitude is as though women are reaching out for something they can't quite control. They know and understand the rules, but they are either unable or unwilling to follow those rules. I believe the reason is that the old rules don't work anymore.

BEING UNMARRIED IN A MARRIAGE-CENTERED WORLD

In many countries, women are no longer bound by the same societal values as their parents. Strong, empowered, confident women are now revered and respected. Each woman is successful in her own right and women proudly define themselves by their goals, talents and abilities, not by the people with whom they choose to live "happily ever after."

Most women cling to their freedom and independence as an indisputable right. Modern women are absolutely capable of providing for themselves on every level, whether physically, emotionally or financially. Many feel strongly that they don't require a man for the purpose of defining themselves nor to act in the role of "head of the family." Women don't need to be married in order to be considered successful. Some of the most accomplished women in the world are single and proud of it.

While this is so, we may still find it difficult to completely ignore the underlying traditional values that permeate American and Western European cultures. Never before has there been such a deep divide between the way women are expected to live their lives (joining in binding partnership with another person) and the individual qualities that celebrate success and independence.

The qualities that prompt respect and admiration concern women's selves. But the celebration of the self and individuality is hardly the blueprint for successful relationship building and thus self-oriented women may find themselves being labeled "self-centered" when in reality they are trying to fulfill their aspirations and make their goals reality. Many married women who are so dedicated to care-giving might be unable or unwilling to look after their own needs and are often hard-hit by unreasonable social expectations.

Thus, women find themselves hard-pressed to please every-one, even when they know that this is not a healthy lifestyle. People in many cultures have redefined the family, only to find themselves somewhat alienated within the very structure that they created.

I believe, by its very nature, traditional married life is incompat-ible with the brave new ideals advanced by modern and postmodern society, which has changed dramatically and drastically during the past decade and completely transformed the family definition and real-life structures. Today more and more people choose the alterna-tive of independent lifestyles over marriage—lifestyles with or with-out a family, with or without children.

Nevertheless, within the same changing society the rules of mar-riage are still in place. And while some families encourage their daugh-ters to aspire to self-determination, others do so while continuing to sanctify marriage. It appears that the autonomy and freedom for women that is attained through strength and determination, more often than not, contradicts the archaic norms of the institution of marriage; norms where spouses' interests, rights and obligations are far from being equally split and in most cases, women's interests and aspirations are considered secondary.

It is true that single women can be selfish without any ill will, whereas married women are often expected to put their partners' needs first. No wonder many women struggle to hold onto their own personal needs and desires while in a married relationship. The ideals of married life and personal fulfillment are diametrically opposed.

The nature of family in many cultures has changed dramatically in the past few decades. Divorce, separation and cohabitation have resulted in a myriad of different living combinations, such as single parents, gay, lesbian and transgender couples, blended families and the thousands of women who choose to live common-law, live long-distance or "Live Apart Together" (LAT). It appears that variety is the rule rather than the exception when it comes to the way women choose their partners and live. So why does society sill place so much emphasis on getting and staying married the traditional way?

Today, women, especially in America and Western Europe, have more relationship options available than ever before. Women owe it to themselves to break free from relationship practices and old-fashioned rules that are no longer relevant for the way they desire to live their lives. Single women do not have to make excuses for wanting to live autonomously. Without the bonds of marriage holding them down, women are free to please themselves, whether through following career goals, traveling the world or dating more than one person.

More women than ever before realize that trying to fit themselves into a role that is hopelessly outmoded and outdated may be a losing proposition. It might take a bit longer to digest the fact, but marriage has become obsolete.

KEEPING IT TOGETHER OR NOT

One main concern about marriage is whether the relationship is going to last. Separation and divorce have impacted so many marital relationships that today roughly 40 percent of marriages don't endure.[1] In American and other cultures, women are quick to marry and equally quick to divorce and remarry. Second and third marriages are common today, leaving us to question the point: why bother to marry in the first place, when the couple is just going to split up a few years later?

No woman wants to enter into an uncertain union that could end in dissension and heartbreak. At the same time, many women are enticed by social pressure, glossy magazine pictures and popular culture to wed. What is it about marriage that makes it appear so attractive to some women? Is it possible to consider alternative partnership arrangements that allow us to experience all the good things that marriage has to offer but without the stress of having to pick up the pieces when things don't work out the way we expect?

Many women decide to move in with their partners. Cohabitation has become acceptable for many women in America and the Western world, with millions preferring this option to marriage itself. According to recent demographic trends, living together without marrying is seen as good or neither good nor bad by 55 percent of the American public.[2] This is a clear move away from marriage. The figures are likely to increase as time goes on and as the older population is replaced by a more liberal-thinking younger generation.

It seems that marriage has the potential to create much uncertainty for those women who are trying to come to terms with their life's ambitions, anxious not to miss out on their dreams. Some women describe their discomfort with marriage as a large question mark that hangs precariously over their heads. For others, trepidation over the issue of marriage may make its presence known in more subtle ways. Many women who are uncomfortable with traditional married life may find themselves exploring other exciting relationship options.

According to statistics, cohabitation is the living arrangement of choice for over six million households in a year.[3] More and more couples choose to live together before getting married. By doing this, they hope to resolve any major relationship difficulties before the wedding and maybe even save some money while waiting for the right moment to commit to marriage. Cohabitation offers couples a taste of day-to-day partnership without the actual worry of signing a contract. However, many couples in this sort of living arrangement may be unaware of their legal rights and responsibilities and it pays to find out the facts before entering a cohabiting relationship.

Same-sex couples face even greater challenges as they cope with the marriage issue. Since the year 2000, same-sex households have increased by 80 percent, indicating that gay, lesbian, bisexual and transgender (GLBT) relationships are here to stay. According to revised figures from the 2010 census, it is estimated that the number of households in the United States with same-sex couples is around 650,000.[4] According to Joseph Chamie and Barry Mirkin's study "Same-Sex Marriage: A Global Perspective," "32 countries—representing 15%

of the world population—legally recognize same-sex couples."[5] Many brave individuals who are not afraid to present their true selves to the world are to be admired for leading and championing this life-style option. Gay marriage is becoming recognized and legal in many countries, as it is in different states across America, although it is still banned in many others.

Frequently, marriage is considered to be the ultimate culmination of love between two people. But that is not necessarily true. In the whole process of finding love, which is mistakenly connected with finding a partner, it is troubling that there appears to be little concern for what happens after the ceremony.

Married life, after the wedding ritual is completed, represents the greatest amount of time together. But some women are in such a hurry to be able to declare themselves married that they often forget to examine the huge implications of this major lifestyle change.

On the other side of the aisle, there is the fact that marriage does offer relative stability if a woman is searching for life in a committed relationship. Some women value the perceived security of marriage and the knowledge that they can face life's challenges together with their spouses. These couples value teamwork. While there is no guarantee that a relationship will last, many women still believe this to be the best environment for raising a family.

The biggest challenge for married couples is keeping the relationship fresh and alive, especially after many years together. Some long-term relationships become strained and with looser commitment after decades of marriage. It becomes more and more difficult to revive the original spontaneity and excitement that attracted the spouses to each other in the first place. The battle of coping with the daily grind can turn into a war of attrition as the ever-increasing pressures of life take their toll.

At this point, many marriages succumb to cheating or boredom or a combination of the two. "You get to a point where you already know so much about your partner that saving the relationship seems useless," says Mellissa, a married account executive. "I already put in so many hours at work. When I get home, I'm exhausted. I just don't have the energy to commit extra hours to a relationship which is sinking fast anyway." The reality is that the work required to save a failing marriage is very difficult and many couples split up because of waning passion, lack of shared interests and different needs and desires.

This is not to say that there are no benefits to getting married. For some of us, marriage is the right option. Some couples manage to operate successful, happy marriages in which the needs and individual rights of each partner are valued and respected. But I maintain in this book that today these vitally important relationship qualities can be successfully attained without traditional marriage.

DATING GAMES

Visions of marriage produce rather mixed memories for some women. We have all had our share of good and bad relationships and married couples are not immune to the challenges of getting along with each other. Married life has a tendency to highlight the very best as well as the very worst in compatibility issues. Without marriage, there would be no divorce. However, the issue here is more than finding a well-suited partner of similar temperament and motivation. Long-term relationships are especially challenging.

No one wishes to appear desperate to find a marriage partner, yet that is exactly what happens when women convince themselves that they are less than whole without a man. Some women believe that the longer they are removed from the dating scene, the less likely they will be to find true love. This places women in an especially vulnerable position, creating an unnecessary sense of urgency to find a marriage partner. These same women would never consider rushing into other important life decisions. So why are they so pressured to marry?

There are a number of reasons behind this peculiar rush to walk down the aisle. Even though most women pride themselves on their independence and individualism, women in many societies are still expected to get married.[6] While the nuclear family of the 1950s is no longer an appropriate fit for the twenty-first century woman, there is still tremendous cultural pressure on women to find suitable matches, marry and start families. The idea of a traditional wedding is often planted in girls' minds from a very early age. Women's opinions can be swayed by romantic childhood stories, the desire to uphold family tradition or seeing their peers exchange marital vows.

But even if an old-fashioned wedding is not uppermost in some women's thoughts, chances are that they are pressured into marriage in order to appease their relatives. Remember, things can get remarkably complicated when a woman finds herself torn between her own needs and the vicarious desires of various family members. It takes a great deal of courage to sort out your own priorities under these challenging circumstances. However, in the end it is the woman who has to bear the consequences of her relationship choices, not her family or friends.

Some might believe that a marriage proposal may present unbridled joy for women seeking solutions to their aching loneliness or insecurity. Indeed, getting married may provide a means to silence the critics who cling to the old-fashioned belief that marriage epitomizes fulfillment of a woman's purpose in life. Some women might still listen to their well-meaning relatives reminding them that cohabitation is tantamount to living in sin. It is demoralizing to cope with such outmoded perspectives which tarnish personal relationship choices.

While a few married women are relieved about their release from the "shackles" of the dating scene, it has been noted that some of their problems could have been spared by avoiding the pervasive industry of matchmaking which exists today. In 2002, there were 904 dating services in America, employing nearly 4,300 people.[7] One can only imagine the economic impact of an industry that capitalizes upon the affairs of the heart today.

I believe it is a rather sad statement of our current system of values when people feel the need to hand over money in order to find "true love." In some ways, society hasn't moved very far from the days of arranged marriages and dowries; the only difference is that this time around, women are the ones asking for potential suitors and the money goes to the company instead of the bride.

However, many women enjoy the dating scene and find the thought of settling for one lifetime partner to be limiting and quite boring. These are women who, for one reason or another, do not want to settle down with one person. They enjoy the stimulation of meeting new people and love the fact that they are free to go out with whomever they want. These same women will happily admit that they do not want a committed relationship—not now and probably not in the future. They are too busy enjoying their independent paths in life to consider this level of relationship commitment.

THE FAIRY-TALE VISION OF MARRIAGE

Some single women are still enamored by the concept of marriage. Some soak up information about celebrity weddings and immerse themselves in the personal histories of reality television brides. Some are fascinated by behind-the-scene glimpses of marriage preparation—from wedding cakes to bridal gowns to the bride and groom. Most of all, some women view the traditional wedding ceremony as an important rite of passage, fully believing that one day they too will have their very own traditional weddings.

When it comes to lavish wedding preparations, television specials seldom lack for viewers. Women's fascination seems to know no bounds when wedding extravagance is combined with a handsome prince and beautiful princess about to be united in holy matrimony. For those entranced with the fairy-tale ideal, it is all the better when one of them is a commoner. The recent royal wedding in England of Prince William, Duke of Cambridge, and Catherine Middleton garnered over twenty-three million viewers in the United States alone and many millions worldwide.[8] In my opinion, it has much less to do with the English monarchy than with the cultural ideal of marriage perfection.

Royal and celebrity weddings seem to ignite daydreams in some women who view their wedding days as chances to be real-life princesses. Others confess to a secret desire to be a "celebrity for a day." Many women grew up listening to fairy tales as children in which a young woman falls in love, overcomes the odds and marries a prince. Unfortunately, some women are still raised with this delusive expectation. Many women admit that the images of their own traditional weddings already exist in their minds, long before the arrival of their prospective mates.

Can there still be anything magical about this fairy-tale wedding? The answer is yes. Some women are still moved by the sight of a traditional wedding party, complete with the bride wearing a full length, white-beaded gown, lace veil and white gloves and holding a bouquet. The rest of the entourage, in full costume with pretty bridesmaids, handsome groomsmen and all the opulent trappings, reinforces the show. Surely for a woman who chooses marriage, her wedding day is considered to be one of the most important days of her life and nothing should stop her from enjoying it to the fullest. However, many women today do not find such visions enchanting but rather unrealistic.

In fact, that type of white wedding ceremony is relatively new. In Victorian times, a white wedding dress provided evidence of wealth, a fashion started in England by Queen Victoria.[9] Before her trend-setting event, weddings were much less grandiose affairs and, at times, the bride even wore black, which was considered to be a much more practical color to keep clean. Today, the choice of a white wedding dress signifies what the fashion industry markets as the "right" bridal attire. But the original symbolism of white representing sexual purity has long since been replaced for many by the marital concept of love and joy above all. Many brides today are neither virgins nor even first-time brides.

Nevertheless, some women equate a costly wedding ceremony and special occasion with a display of personal affluence. But money does not guarantee togetherness in the high-stakes game of marriage and many marriages in numerous countries end in divorce. Second and third marriages fare even worse statistically and perhaps this is why modern women in many countries from America to China are choosing single lives.

Cultural expectations aside, women should not take part in traditional wedding ceremonies unless that is truly what they want. For those who wish to get married but prefer a simpler solution, there is always the option of a quiet civil ceremony or a marriage chapel, Las Vegas style. Although some may see these plainer alternatives as watered-down versions of large traditional ceremonies, the focus on the couple rather than on the event can be refreshing.

It is a mistake to believe that a decision to choose being single precludes women from enjoying many of the trappings of a marriage ceremony. Women can certainly dance at their friends' wedding celebrations, eat the cake and have it too—you can definitely stay single, unmarried and/or happily divorced by choice.

Creativity knows no bounds and you can create your own celebration with or without a man by your side. Many women are incredibly content with remaining single and do not feel that something is missing just because they "missed out" on the big and expensive event. Remember, one of the great positives of remaining single is the ability to decide to live the life that you want. So if your fun includes dancing at your best friend's wedding party, go on and dance. If your fun includes throwing your own sleek, gourmet single-by-choice or divorce party with friends, go for it and enjoy.

SEARCHING FOR STABILITY BUT ENDING IN DIVORCE

With more relationship options available than ever before, many women find themselves facing apprehension regarding their future well-being and happiness. Undoubtedly, no one wants to make a mistake with something as serious as "commitment for life" and even the best of intentions can get out of control in the search for perfection or for a marriage partner to fill the gap. With the added pressure of various well-meaning friends and relatives all offering their versions of what's best, it is perfectly understandable that many women feel overwhelmed and frustrated with the marriage concept. There are few feelings more unsettling than the uncomfortable realization that you are sharing your life with the wrong person.

Amy's Story

A stormy romance and marriage when she was only twenty-five left Amy feeling tied down and frustrated. The marriage quickly dissolved into petty arguments, followed by Amy's realization that her husband had been unfaithful to her. Both mutually agreed to separate and divorce. "Thinking of it, I'm not even sure why I got married," Amy said to me at the age of thirty-three. "It felt like it was the right thing to do at the time. Almost like it was expected that we would get married." But the destructive relationship left Amy feeling shaken and betrayed. "We should never have gotten married," she stated emphatically. "We were both so young and, really, just good friends. There was no benefit to getting married at all."

Many women share Amy's opinion on marriage. They view marriage as an unnecessary convention, an obstacle that restricts women's choices and offers no real advantages over remaining single. Many modern women believe it is better to remain single or unmarried and stay on friendly terms with one's partner rather than to risk everything in a marriage that may feel like a poor fit just a few years later.

Men are not the only ones who stray when it comes to cheating in marriage. Author Michelle Langley explores some of the reasons why a large number of women cheat on their husbands in her book, *Women's Infidelity*. Many of the interviewed women express feeling tremendous guilt following their indiscretions. The troubling feelings within their married relationships intensified when they attempted to resume "normal" day-to-day activities with their spouses.[10]

Maintaining "good chemistry" between two individuals over a long period of time requires proactive strategies and, contrary to popular belief, a number of women do not gain much satisfaction from the tedious and uninspiring repetition that often comes with daily married life. This is one of the reasons why married women and men cheat.

Instead of the longed-for familiarity, commitment and stability in marriage, real life is often routine and banal, absent of interesting and exciting experiences that offer stimulating variety and carefree encounters. In this respect, I believe, married life cannot compare to staying single. There are few women who are not attracted to the idea of time alone combined with strong, meaningful relationships. This is the very hallmark of life as a single woman.

Especially telling is the fact that currently 70 to 75 percent of all divorces are initiated by women.[11] Women have different emotional and physical requirements from men and married life may not be the best means to meet these needs. Women who feel they are trapped in unresponsive marital relationships due to cheating or for other reasons are miserable company, both for themselves and for others. Our life energy is too precious to waste, whether it be blaming others or sinking into depression. Women owe it to themselves to ensure that they care for themselves within an environment that allows them to achieve the very best they can.

BEING HAPPILY DIVORCED

Many divorced women likely find themselves considering a second marriage or even a third. Cultural expectations may lead them to rationalize the merits of matrimony when they're trying to reestablish some much-needed stability in their lives. The problem is that although most women are older and wiser by the time of a second or third marriage, they are still vulnerable to the same human frailties that tripped them up the first time.

American women are more likely to engage in numerous short relationships than women in any other country in the Western hemisphere.[12] Women truly want these relationships to work and when things go wrong, they tend to react with a quick-fix mentality. Thus, the probability of divorced women in America remarrying within five years of their previous marriages is 54 percent. Unfortunately, the likelihood of these second marriages lasting is not good: 23 percent are doomed to end in separation or divorce after five years and the number swells to 39 percent after ten years.[13]

Divorced women are especially susceptible to remarrying for economic reasons, the same reasons some women consider a benefit of married life.[14] Since, unfortunately, equality in the workplace is still only a dream for many women, remarriage may appear to be a viable solution—a "cost-effective" partnership on the road to success. This worldview better suits past generations, but such considerations are still dominant today in many ways. In addition, some single mothers may view marriage or remarriage as a way to cope with inflexible work schedules that leave them scrambling to find affordable childcare options. As noted by Heather Boushey in her essay, *The New Breadwinners*, many couples, caught in the trap of lower-paid employment, resort to "tag-team parenting."[15] This sad reality is an unlikely formula for romance and togetherness; therefore it is not surprising that often these marital unions dissolve quickly.

Even divorced women who are relatively well-off financially can fall prey to the belief that they can jump into brand new marriages without changing anything that led to the demises of their first marriages. What a mistake.

The truth is that some people are just not suited for the institution of marriage. Just as it is unfair to expect a partner to change into something he or she is not, it is equally unreasonable to believe that we will be able to undergo metamorphosis and transform into somebody different who is more suitable marriage material. Anyone who is tempted to believe that her subsequent marriage will be effortless and trouble-free should take time for a period of reflection and introspection and possibly professional counseling before leaping into another marriage commitment.

Relationship problems which occurred in a first marriage are likely to reappear in a second marriage unless women put in some pretty hard work. Remember, marital breakdown occurs because of an inability to mesh the needs of two individuals. Remarrying has little effect on a woman's personality traits and preferences, not to mention her intrinsic values and desires. If, generally speaking, a woman is not content to give and take, which actually means giving up her needs or taking away someone else's, she should consider whether marriage is the right thing for her. Women need to consider truly and honestly whether they wish to overhaul themselves for the benefit of their partners in order to make marriage work.

Often, divorced women who consider remarriage face additional pitfalls, such as emotional baggage from previous marital relationships. The failure of a previous marriage is rarely a happy occasion and most divorced women will do everything in their power to prevent it from happening again. It is human nature to want to compare; it is almost impossible to remain detached and unbiased when weighing the merits of one marriage partner against another and even small indiscretions can rock a relationship to its core.

Emotional baggage can arise at the most inappropriate moments, such as during sexual intimacy. Who is truly able to control the urge to evaluate a situation based upon past experiences? However, it is the day-to-day act of living with another person which presents the greatest challenge for most women. But the question that needs to be asked is: Why marry for that?

Many women today are still ready to leap into yet another marriage with little consideration of the alternatives. But an overwhelmingly large number of women are just not well-suited for marriage. This is not a character flaw, but rather a part of nature and modern culture—unique and individual personality traits that combine to make women who they are in the postmodern environment.

Women owe it to themselves to make sure that they don't enter another turbulent marriage in order to satisfy some outdated ideals. For a large number of wonderfully strong-willed and self-determined women, romantic marriage is an old-fashioned fantasy, ill-suited to the way women live in modern society.

Perhaps divorce needs to be seen as less of a failure and more of a realization that two people should never have gotten married. Perhaps this is the reasoning behind the so-called no-fault divorce involving irreconcilable differences. Few unions of two young people in their teens or early twenties remain based on the same set of values when those individuals reach midlife. So the questions remain the same: Why tie yourself to a person through marriage? Why not just be friends?

FINANCIAL CONSIDERATIONS

Financially successful women may worry more about losing their independence and hard-earned prosperity than finding a "permanent" partner in marriage. But marriage is not kind to those who enter into the commitment based on a wavering emotional attraction to another human being. Many women are unaware of how much they have to lose, both financially and emotionally.

While modern society admires strong, capable, self-reliant women, many men may be uneasy sharing their lives with someone who embodies many of the characteristics to which they themselves may aspire. It takes a very special sort of man not to feel threatened under such circumstances and it places an enormous strain on the marital bond that cements relationships.

Denise's Story

Denise, a self-reliant thirty-six-year-old woman who purchased her home several years ago, enjoys the benefits of an LAT relationship. When she first met Kenny she had already been successful in her own right. Denise was committed in her love for Kenny but unwilling to risk her financial security in a marriage which could potentially fail. She had already seen the consequences of bitter, acrimonious divorces among her friends and was determined that things would be different between her and Kenny.

Denise explained to me that part of the reason she opted for the LAT relationship was because she wanted a partnership based on love and respect rather than on ill-conceived security and dependence. In other words, she wanted to preserve her hard-earned financial status and retain full and independent ownership of her properties. At the same time, she recognized that Kenny was a very important part of her life and saw no reason why they couldn't continue to enjoy a loving relationship from separate home bases. It was the best of both worlds for them.

For women considering marriage, be aware there is more to consider than just the act of getting married. For example, can you handle losing your high credit rating if your partner has a problem with debt? In order to avoid this pitfall, some couples opt for individual, rather than joint, accounts. In the United States, the law requires that the credit ratings of both individuals be examined in order for a married couple to obtain a loan. This can present considerable hardship if one partner is mired in debt while the other has worked hard all her life to maintain good standing. It is no wonder why financial stress is one of the top reasons marriages fail in the United States, Australia and many other countries.[16]

For most married couples, money is a major issue and a highly emotional topic. Each partner's history with money, comfort regarding credit and loans and willingness to save can all impact a marriage badly. One of the great advantages of staying single lies in one's ability to control one's finances autonomously, with no fear of adverse repercussions from a spouse with different financial priorities.

Single women feel a tremendous sense of satisfaction in knowing that they are not dependent upon anyone but themselves. There is enormous relief that comes from being self-sufficient and in knowing that you alone control your financial destiny. Consider how great it is to have the means to determine how to spend your money without having to account for anything to anyone.

INDEPENDENCE, SPONTANEITY AND LOVE

Women in America and Europe pride themselves on being resourceful and independent. They feel fulfilled when they achieve their goals and most of all, they value their self-sufficiency. Empowered women are confident and self-assured and have no difficulty tackling life's difficult issues. These women need to maintain their feelings of autonomy. To settle for anything less is the equivalent of turning their backs on themselves.

Unfortunately, marital conflict over matters such as family goals and priorities can become vicious, especially when one partner has been culturally conditioned to believe that his agenda should be given top priority. While we would like to believe that outright sexism no longer exists in relationships in modern society, there are more unexpected ways that women find themselves at a disadvantage. It takes a strong-willed and self-assured woman to make a stand against unfair treatment that may be directed at her decisions and to place her own needs above those of her spouse.

Marriage is a bit like a car, inasmuch as you can only have one person driving at a time. No matter how loud the protests, nor even how reasonable the suggestions from other passengers, it is ultimately the responsibility of the driver to steer the vehicle in the right direction. Within a marital relationship, the proper course may be perceived very differently by each person. Everyone has a unique route in mind for his or her journey through life and conflict is unavoidable when a woman finds her partner leading her in another direction. Many married women feel resentful when they are unable to fulfill their hopes and aspirations.

Even those marriages in which both parties are actively working toward the same educational or career goals can experience discrimination toward the woman. For example, Monty and Sarah Don, an extremely successful couple in the jewelry business, found themselves in the peculiar position of having to explain that they were both equally involved in the design and fabrication of their pieces of jewelry. Without considerable explanation, the public came to the inevitable conclusion that Monty was the main inspirational source and Sarah his assistant.[17] This sexist thinking happens more often than we would like to believe.

Modern women have more opportunities than ever before to enjoy independent and self-fulfilled lives. They can choose to take advantage of mutually satisfying close relationships, unhindered education and career opportunities and even the joys of pregnancy and motherhood. These options become more accessible when women make the bold decision to remain single and unattached.

Despite marriage partners sharing responsibilities more equally today, men don't face the same pressures as women to fragment themselves. It is difficult for most women to maintain their marriages while simultaneously meeting the requirements of their demanding career or caretaking for their children.

Single women are free to do what they want, when they want. If a woman wishes to build her career, there is nobody to stop her. Single, unattached women can travel the world, work weekends and spend time visiting their friends and relatives. Single women don't have to make excuses for their personal choices and they alone are responsible for their decisions, good and bad. They can concentrate their efforts on numerous and diverse important issues in their lives. Can you imagine inventing something, starting a challenging new business or earning a graduate degree?

An enormous amount of time and energy is required for a successful marital relationship. No one should enter into marriage without being prepared to give him or herself over to the needs of the relationship as necessary. It would be unfair to oneself and one's partner to consider any other set of priorities. Some women are not prepared to work this hard in order to be "successfully" married. Others realize that they have underestimated the commitment involved and may look for alternatives.

Being single allows women to explore life and experience new things without inhibition. Remaining single presents women with so many of the good things they associate with marriage while doing away with unnecessary encumbrances! They can enjoy the companionship of good friends, sexual relationships should they desire them or the possibility of choosing to become a single parent without being tied down in a long-term marital relationship which may be filled with disagreements.

With so many different lifestyles emerging in mainstream America and other countries around the world, I believe it's only a matter of time before marriage is seen as merely one of a variety of lifestyle alternatives. For many women, marriage has already become obsolete. Single women who may have once felt compelled to marry now may be anxious to avoid being trapped in what they feel is a constricting and irrelevant tradition. Finally single women are able to follow their own destinies rather than please someone else. Strive to attain this degree of comfort within yourself. You deserve to be free.

Chapter 2

Why Women and Men Cheat

Cheating is often both glamorized and criminalized by the media. Real-life celebrities like Tiger Woods or politicians like John Edwards or Eliot Spitzer who cheat may be portrayed in a negative light. However, on television shows like *Desperate Housewives*, cheating is typically shown as more acceptable. A study by the Parents Television Council found that references to adultery outnumbered references to marital sex three to one in prime-time broadcast television. Even when marital sex is referenced, it is often in a negative manner: The sex is depicted to be unsatisfying or burdensome.[1]

Television shows often glamorize cheating. On the drama *Grey's Anatomy*, brain surgeon Derek agrees to work things out with his successful neonatal surgeon wife Addison after a short separation. Then he sleeps with surgical intern Meredith. When Derek's boss accuses Derek of having an affair, Derek breaks up with his wife to convince himself that Meredith is more than an affair. Because of these actions, Derek is depicted as having integrity and strong values. In the reality show *Jersey Shore*, Ronnie has a past of cheating on his girlfriend Sammi. She sometimes ignores the evidence in front of her and always takes him back. Meanwhile, Ronnie is portrayed as a tough guy who can just pick up another girl if Sammi doesn't want to stay with him. On *Desperate Housewives*, Gabrielle's affair with her gardener satisfies

31

her needs for respect and emotional support that her husband does not provide. Her affair is depicted as passionate, fun and self-fulfilling.

It is quite possible that women become desensitized to cheating because of the constant stream of glamorized media coverage. Adultery seems to have become a popular recreational activity, but it's not just fictional characters, celebrities or politicians who are guilty. While there's no exact figure telling how many married people are engaging in cheating, estimates range from 26 to 70 percent for women and 33 to 75 percent for men.[2]

THE NATURE OF CHEATING

Mating is universal among humans, but lifelong mating doesn't seem to be a modern era norm. In about 80 percent of societies around the world, polygamy or having multiple wives or mistresses is considered acceptable. In the United States, where monogamy is stressed, divorce rates remain around 40 percent. Many experts and others feel that keeping one partner for life isn't realistic, especially not for modern couples. In general, humans have spent more overall evolutionary time pursuing short-term mates than they have looking for monogamous relationships.[3]

Historically, society has been more tolerant of the misdeeds of men than those of women. While many think the urge is hardwired in males, there are also men who don't cheat on their wives or girlfriends and there are women who do. Indeed, whether infidelity is curable is a good question. But the fact is more men use infidelity to solve their relationship woes.

There are certain strategies that each gender, whether consciously or subconsciously, follows when searching for short-term mates, which I believe relates to natural selection. Species compete amongst themselves to have the highest number of healthy offspring and to ensure the more desirable traits are passed on. Short-term relationships increase the chances for offspring; however, they also increase the odds of getting a sexually transmitted disease along with the odds of cheating.

It would be counterproductive for men to invest time and resources in women who are not sexually accessible to them. Promiscuity, which would be undesirable in a long-term mate, may be viewed as the most desirable trait for a short-term mate. Desirable traits in long-term mates, such as conservative behavior and sexual inexperience, are to be avoided when looking for something short-term.[4]

There is a difference between fertility and reproductive value. Fertility is a woman's chances to reproduce right away, while reproductive value is the number of children she can conceive in the future. A woman in her mid-thirties would have a good fertile value, but a twenty-something female would have a higher reproductive value since she is younger and has many years of fertility ahead of her. Research shows that women with high fertility are the best short-term mates, whereas women with high reproductive values make good long-term mates.[5]

The final problem many men face when looking for short-term mates is avoiding women who want commitment. The more a man invests in one woman, the less he can invest in multiple women and a woman who wants a lengthy commitment tends to tie up the man in a very unwanted way.[6]

It seems that many of the biological strategies men have for pursuing short-term mates are similar to tactics that modern men actually use. Anybody who has lived on a college campus or in a city with a lively nightlife can attest to these strategies. Large numbers of young men are on a constant prowl for women to sleep with, women with whom they expect zero commitment.

However, women have their own strategies when pursuing short-term mates. Like men, they must also beware of sexually transmitted diseases and the risk of getting a poor reputation due to "promiscuity." Women tend to receive more severe repercussions due to a poor reputation than men. Being known as promiscuous is a difficult thing to make others forget where women are concerned.

When looking for a short-term mate, women need to maximize their immediate resource extraction. In some societies, men are expected to bring their mistresses gifts. If they don't, the women are free to refuse sex. Prostitution is also common in many cultures around the world and there the gift translates to money. But in the United States and Western Europe, most women expect men to take them on a few dates before they agree to copulate.[7]

Strangely enough, some women also use short-term mating to assess which men are good candidates for a long-term mate. Does he have characteristics that are desired in a long-term mate? Is he hard-working, reliable and a good provider? Will he be searching for a long-term mate in the near future? Another factor women sometimes consider in a short-term mate is if the man can protect her from other men who might try to force themselves on her sexually. Or, in today's society, a woman might desire a man who can protect her from a mugger or even just from men who try to hit on her in a crowded venue.[8]

But it appears that men put far more effort into finding short-term mates than most women do. Women appear to be more selective whereas men are most eager and competitive in finding short-term mates. Men seem to want to have sex with lots of women, while women seem to need less rotation than men do. But while men may struggle against the commitment aspect, they ultimately have to give in to a woman's terms since she has the power to withhold sex.

According to research, men tend to be more willing to find a short-term mate in someone they do not know well. Women seem less fond of this preference. In one study on a college campus, directed by psychology professors Russell Clark and Elaine Hatfield, an attractive man or woman approached students and asked one of three randomly chosen questions: 1) Would you go out with me tonight? 2) Would you come over to my apartment tonight? 3) Would you go to bed with me tonight? About 50 percent of women agreed to the date, 6 percent agreed to go to the apartment and not one woman consented to going to bed with the stranger. Of all the men questioned, about 50 percent agreed to the date, 69 percent agreed to go to the apartment and 75 percent agreed to go with her to bed.[9]

Regarding cheating in relation to biology, men and women have different primary concerns. Since fertilization is an internal bodily occurrence—that is, it occurs inside of the woman—a man can't be completely sure if the child the woman has is his. Most women, however, are sure of the paternity of their offspring, so their biggest concern is whether their long-term mates will start directing resources to another woman.[10] This is the point where women are affected severely by their mates' infidelity.

HOW CHEATING STARTS

People in good and bad relationships alike tend to cheat. It is not always because one partner is seeking thrills or is bored with the current relationship. Sometimes two people form a deep connection before they even realize that they've crossed boundaries. While it is easy to place blame on the cheating partner, the reasoning behind the affair isn't simple. Even in well-functioning relationships, extramarital activities can sneak up on one partner and remain unrecognized until it is too late. In other words, a woman might find herself betraying personal beliefs and values as well as the person she loves without having the original intention to do so.

Opportunity is a primary factor and contributes to cheating in an otherwise happy relationship.[11] Most people think that something has to be wrong in the relationship for one partner to "stray"; that the cheater has to be inconsiderate and self-centered, while the faithful partner is inadequate in bed or not as attractive looking as he or she used to be. Or maybe the husband spends too much time at work, leaving his wife to deal with the children and the household issues and feeling lonely and ignored. But in reality, situations like these don't always have to be present for cheating to take place.

In earlier eras, predominantly men cheated, but that is changing now. Women today are more sexually experienced than ever before. They also find themselves with more power, wealth and social status, because they are working in fields that were previously male-dominated. Financial and intellectual independence also brings more opportunities to have affairs. Statistics from a study by psychologist Shirley Glass show that about 46 percent of women and 62 percent of men who cheated on their spouses did so with a person they met at work. The women with the most lenient marital attitudes and behaviors have traditionally male professions, such as legal and corporate jobs.[12]

Working closely together to meet deadlines may fuel chemistry between two coworkers, even if one or both of them are in happy relationships or marriages. They look forward to seeing each other at work, meeting for coffee breaks or working on projects together. After some time, they make a point to chat every day and the conversations become more intimate and start to include their relationship issues or their hopes and dreams. The attraction may be unintentional at first and it can happen to people who have been in happy marriages for long periods of time. Men who get involved in workplace affairs often have been married for longer than men who find their affair partners in other settings. One study shows that of men who cheated for the first time after nine years of marriage, 56 percent had a workplace affair and only 27 percent had an affair outside of the workplace.[13]

Friends or neighbors are also common partners for cheating spouses. It makes sense that two people who already have a friendship could become romantic: they know each other's pasts, it is easy to talk to each other and they already enjoy each other's company. About 16 percent of cheating husbands and 29 percent of cheating wives had affairs with a friend or neighbor.[14] Additionally, friendships progress into romantic or sexual relationships when there becomes a level of secrecy between the friends. The guilty partner often hides the feelings of attraction and doesn't mention every encounter with the friend to his or her spouse.

In unhappy relationships, oftentimes an affair begins because emotional needs are not being met between the partners. While a partner who is cheating might feel ignored and underappreciated, it is not solely the fault of the spouse. The cheating partner is responsible for being dishonest about his or her lack of interest in the ongoing relationship and not telling the truth about feelings for another person. The cheater is probably also to blame for a certain level of emotional neglect. The spouse who is being betrayed contributes to the affair by not meeting the emotional needs of his or her partner. Maybe he or she was working too much, not paying enough attention to the partner or not listening to what the partner had to say. Whatever the reason, the result is that the partner did not feel completely satisfied in the relationship. The lover is to be blamed for forming an emotional or sexual relationship with a person in a committed relationship. The lover is also guilty of helping the cheating partner with his or her emotional needs and being a more reliable figure than the spouse.[15]

Indeed, the urge to have an emotional need fulfilled can be a driving force behind cheating. An emotional need is like a craving. When it is satisfied, you feel happy and content. For example, minor emotional needs can be sated by eating chocolate, seeing a movie starring your favorite actor, going shopping or gossiping with friends. Bigger emotional needs may lead people to risk their current relationships.

Typically, there are ten emotional needs that tend to be important to most people: admiration, affection, conversation, domestic support, family commitment, financial support, honesty and openness, physical attraction, recreational companionship and sexual fulfillment. When ranked in order of least to most important, the emotional needs that women rate highest get the lowest ratings from men. This could explain the gap in communication and the different "wiring" of men. While men or women might try what they would appreciate the most in a relationship, it is not necessarily what their partners want or need.[16] For example, a man might place a high value on financial support and work extra hard to be successful in his job. The sacrifice is that he spends less time at home with his partner. His wife, however, may not think that money is more important than spending time at home. When a man is trying to do what he thinks is best for his relationship or family, he actually may be falling short from his partner's point of view.

An open line of communication can solve many of the problems that fuel affairs. However, it is difficult for many people to admit to emotional connections with someone outside of their primary relationships. For example, a man might worry about hurting his spouse's feelings, so he doesn't mention his attraction to another woman. Often, lack of communication is the reason that a person begins cheating. A woman may try to tell her boyfriend that she feels underappreciated, but he shrugs her off, because there is a football game on television. When she meets a man who makes her feel appreciated and listens to what she says, she probably won't tell her boyfriend about him.

Tom and Danni's Story

Tom and Danni were a young couple who had been engaged for several months. They lived in an apartment together and Tom paid most of the bills, because Danni was in graduate school. Danni was deeply in love with Tom and appreciated everything her fiancé did for her. But because of her demanding class and work schedule, she did not have a lot of extra time to spend with Tom.

Tom had not gone to college, but he successfully maintained a full-time job. He could not understand why Danni was always so busy studying and writing papers. He began to feel neglected and underappreciated in their relationship. He also became jealous, because he believed she was a great catch. Tom thought for sure that Danni would not want to be with him after she graduated and started a successful career. But Danni had no idea that Tom was thinking these things, because he never told her.

While Tom normally worked weekdays, Danni usually worked late on weekends. On Friday and Saturday nights, Tom frequently went out with his friends. Soon Tom's friend Sophie started paying closer attention to him. She was always sure to invite him when their friends made plans. Because he saw her so frequently, they grew closer. Sophie was always willing to listen to what Tom had to say. She was sympathetic when he wanted to talk about how Danni did not have time for him.

The calls and texts between Sophie and Tom increased and they began spending time together several days a week. Tom was becoming more dependent on Sophie, because she filled his emotional gaps. While the time he spent with Danni was filled with discussions about the bills that needed to be paid, the deadlines that were coming up and the errands that needed to be done, his time with Sophie was filled with laughter and mutual joy.

After one night of drinking, Sophie gave Tom a ride back to his apartment. Before he got out of the car, she leaned over and kissed him. He was confused at first, as he walked into his apartment. Danni, who had just gotten home from work, was disappointed when she saw that Tom was drunk. Immediately Tom felt justified for what had happened between him and Sophie.

Tom and Sophie continued to see each other and eventually began a sexual relationship. Tom was convinced that he loved both Sophie and Danni. He knew that Danni would be better for him in the long term, because she was smart, on the verge of a successful career and offered a stable relationship. But Sophie was fun to be with. The cheating went on for three months before Danni discovered Tom's sexual texts and e-mails to Sophie.

At this point, Tom and Danni tried to work things out. But Danni was upset about his lying. She wanted to get revenge so she cheated on Tom with a guy from one of her classes. This only tore their relationship apart further. They both felt betrayed and emotionally worn down.

Finally Danni and Tom decided to break up. Danni moved to a smaller apartment and became a successful businesswoman after receiving her MBA, but she never shook her fear of being cheated on in a relationship. Tom tried to keep seeing Sophie, but he missed the stability with Danni. Eventually he found a new girlfriend, but he never stopped regretting what he did to Danni.

PHYSICAL VERSUS EMOTIONAL AFFAIRS

There are two types of affairs: physical and emotional. An affair that is purely emotional is void of sexual contact, but the effects can be just as devastating to a relationship. A purely physical affair is sex without a greater affection between the two parties involved. However, most affairs tend to overlap into both realms. When it's both physical and emotional, that is where the excitement hits and where most problems to the current relationships appear.

However, physical affairs often generate a different reaction than emotional affairs do. Men are more likely to be upset if their spouses have a physical affair rather than an emotional affair. Women are the opposite: they are more upset if they discover that their spouses have an emotional connection to another woman than if they have a purely physical relationship.[17] Why is this?

One explanation is that men, by nature, are more "physical creatures" than women. They associate proximity with availability. Men think that because a woman is physically available, she must also be sexually and emotionally available. While women know that this is untrue, it could explain a number of misunderstandings in relationships. Men think in physical terms, in notions related to territory first and consider emotions only as an afterthought. When a man's partner has sex with someone else, he considers it a violation of his territory.[18]

On the other hand, women consider emotions to be more important. They are far more likely to feel a physical attraction after an emotional connection has already been established. Most women understand that men are more physical, so they have to work hard to get men to feel emotions as well. This is why women get more upset when their partners have emotional affairs. In most cases, it does not take a lot of effort to get a man's attention in a physical sense, but it does take a lot of effort to get an emotional investment from him.[19]

Most people who get into an emotional affair are looking for something that they are not getting out of their current relationships. They want more love, attention or respect. They might even want less of something: criticism, demands or negativity.[20] Once they find a person who is willing to listen to what they say and offer comfort and respect, it can become quite difficult to walk away.

Therefore, in a relationship it is important that both partners praise each other for the things they are doing well. If there is not enough praise, it is easy for a partner to feel neglected, which can lead to one or both partners being underappreciated. The situation gets worse once an affair starts. There is more criticism and less praise. Partners can feel even more desperate for acceptance.[21]

Some people have emotional affairs because they don't feel they have enough freedom. Maybe a partner gets tired of all the responsibilities, has surly teenagers or misses the easy-going lifestyle of his or her twenties. When being in a relationship becomes too demanding and time consuming, the committed partner can get blamed for all the obligations that the cheating partner entered into willingly.[22]

Sometimes a relationship seems too predictable. While it is nice to make routines together and know each other's favorite foods, some spark and novelty needs to exist to keep the relationship feeling fresh. Life can get too repetitive if a couple always goes to the same movie theater, eats at the same restaurant and makes love the same way. A break from a routine and monotonous relationship is another hole an affair seems to fill.

Emotional intensity is another valuable factor in any relationship. Some people have a great desire for intensity, while others prefer to be calm all the time. Often, after the initial courtship is over and there is no rush of emotions or a constant stream of new experiences, the intensity seeker is left dissatisfied. In this case, an affair provides a level of secrecy that makes life more exciting. Even getting caught in an affair can cause the primary relationship to get more dramatic.[23]

While these are all reasons to have an emotional affair, they are also reasons to have a physical affair. Spouses are not giving the necessary emotional support but someone else is. The cheating partner might live in a fantasy land with his or her new partner: they don't have to pay bills together or pick up the children from extracurricular activities. There is nothing major to argue about, so life seems to be blissful. Also, it is easy for emotional cheating to segue into physical affairs as well. Two-thirds of husbands and wives who have sex outside of their marriages believe that falling in love justifies cheating.[24]

There are several stages of physical cheating. The "red light" stage occurs when both partners are fully committed to each other. They firmly believe that it is unacceptable to cheat in any form. The "yellow light" stage is when the couple is still together, but one partner is cheating on the other. The cheating partner might feel as if he or she is allowed to cheat as long as he or she doesn't leave his or her partner. He or she believes him or herself still committed to the relationship. The cheating partner might think that as long as he or she does not have sex with another person or does not fall in love with another person, he or she is not violating the terms of the current relationship. The "green light" stage is when an affair completely takes over. The cheaters are falling in love and/or having sex with each other joyfully. In most cases, the cheaters tend to rationalize their actions in a way that makes cheating look and feel deserved. They don't think that they are having a standard affair. They think that they have something much more special than that.[25]

Additionally, women who cheat go through a set of stages over the course of their relationships or marriages. The first stage of this cycle begins with the loss of sexual desire. Initially, women push for commitment from their spouses and they tend to get what they want. Eventually, women don't feel as happy in their relationships as they did previously. It feels as though something is missing. Sex turns into a chore, like buying groceries or washing the car, mechanical and routine. Women avoid sex by making up excuses. Women who report having too many headaches at night, especially before sex, are the ones who appear to be concerned about their spouses' fidelity.

The second stage involves a reawakening of desire, fueled by someone other than the regular partner. After losing interest in sex with her current partner, the woman finds someone else who makes her feel happier. This encounter could be platonic or sexual and it is given a high emotional significance by the parties. Guilt may set in and women try to be more attentive or appreciative to their original spouses or partners. But eventually there is a feeling of justification. It was something a spouse was doing or not doing that set these feelings into motion. Cheating often follows.

In the third stage, women are having affairs, ending affairs or considering divorces. After the cheating begins, women become resentful toward their spouses and may need time apart. They may blame their spouses for their bad behavior.[26] Cheating women may live in limbo for several years, wondering if they should stay married or get divorced. If a woman is still involved in an affair, she might believe that she has found her soulmate. At this time, her original partner might be making attempts to make her happy. Nevertheless, she might initiate a separation with the hope that it will clear the confusion she is feeling. Regardless, at this stage women often want to keep the excitement and passion of an affair without losing the security of marriage.[27]

The fourth stage is when a woman makes the decision to stay married and continue the affair or get divorced. Women who stay married believe that they can continue the affairs without disrupting their primary relationships. The women who divorce, on the other hand, feel they have made a brave decision.

With regard to men, when they feel the urge to cheat, it may be a way to escape their relationships or marriages. Since many divorces happen because of cheating, it might be a man's way of saying he is done with the relationship. Lying and secrets only make a marriage seem worse to a man. Things become corrupt when there are aspects of each spouse's life that are not clear. Even if the husband is the one who made the relationship complicated, he might stop seeing the value in the relationship. Men are especially likely to stop seeing the benefits they get from being married. Additionally, they also tend to "overestimate their ability to do well outside of marriage. Women seem to do much better outside of marriage than men do."[28]

SOCIAL NETWORKING AND CHEATING

In our digital age, there has been an increase in the amount of people using social networking sites to connect with potential affair partners. In the past five years, 81 percent of divorce attorneys have seen an increase in the number of cases using social networking sites as evidence of an extramarital affair. In one survey, over 5,000 attorneys said that Facebook was specifically mentioned in 20 percent of divorce cases.[29]

But social networking sites can hardly deserve all the blame that is due in an affair. If cheating is going to happen in a relationship, it will probably happen with or without social networking sites. These sites are more of a modern tool for affairs, though they might intensify an affair. Since these sites are used to reconnect with old friends, many people may rediscover a boyfriend or girlfriend from high school or college. The feelings of youth and long-lost love can take over and make men and women in relationships do something out of character.

Using technology to cheat, however, is not a new phenomenon. In the 1990s, cell phones were the primary venue for affairs. Many affairs could be discovered by reviewing a partner's phone bill and identifying an oft-called phone number. By the late 1990s, e-mail became popular to use for cheating and logging into a partner's e-mail account could provide evidence of an affair. While some people will have an affair with or without technology and social networks, others are unlikely to cheat without an extra push. That extra push might come in the form of "friending" a cute coworker or getting a flirty message from an old crush. Spouses or partners who consider themselves to be "teeterers"—those who wouldn't necessarily have an affair without that push—might want to reconsider setting up a social networking account.[30]

There is also a network of Web sites committed to helping spouses who want to cheat. One popular site for married cheaters has over twice as many male members as female. Not all people using these sites necessarily want to have physical affairs. They may just want to find someone who will pay attention to them, take them out to lunch or talk about what's wrong in their current commitments.

Online relationships can be outlets for what is lacking emotionally in a primary relationship. The use of profiles and avatars on social networking sites is a way to sort out who has similar interests and beliefs. If someone seems incompatible, the user can just click to the next person. When two people who have similar interests do find each other, it is a new source of mental and intellectual stimulation to both A woman's husband might be too tired after work to have deep conversations, but the new man she met online may have plenty of time to discuss politics, literature and art.

However, people pursing online relationships are not always looking to leave their current relationships. They may want to add more human connections, more interest and, perhaps, more emotion. Women especially want to feel sexy, appreciated, smart and irresistible. But until their committed partners start noticing them, they may fill their needs in other places.

With the absence of the physical aspect, can cybersex really be considered cheating? It depends on each person's standards. Many men believe that they are only cheating if they take part in sexual intercourse.[31] Others believe that it is wrong to do anything they would not feel comfortable having their spouses know about. Regardless, most spouses would be upset if they knew their committed partners were having sexual or emotional chats with strangers online.

Often, online relationships do not extend further than the computer screen. Having sexual or emotional conversations with strangers online falls into the "grey category" for many, because there is no physical interaction, though it might fill an emotional craving. But there is evidence that online cheating can lead to real-life physical encounters.

Sociologists Diane Kholos Wysocki and Cheryl Childers used a survey on a popular marriage infidelity site to learn the effects of technology on relationships and infidelity. Their survey revealed that "women were more likely than men to engage in [online or virtual sexual] behaviors. Over two-thirds of the respondents had cheated online while in a serious relationship and over three-quarters had cheated in real life. Women and men were just as likely to have cheated both online and in real-life." Respondents also admitted to having a higher priority of finding people to have as real-life dating and sex partners than of finding someone to be an online partner only.[32]

No matter if the intention is to keep the flirtations online or bring them into real life, it can be difficult to admit to what is going on. Often, the investments put into the online sex or online relationship take away from the real-life relationship. All the emotions, thoughts and sexual drive are focused on someone other than the primary spouse. This will not bring any closure to the current relationship and might be a warning sign for the betrayed spouse to end the current bond. In today's world, cheating via social networking sites can be a difficult thing to avoid, especially for the tech savvy.

AFTER CHEATING

The real trouble begins after a cheating spouse has been discovered. The partner that remained faithful often feels betrayed, put down and maybe even depressed. The cheating spouse may admit to what he or she did, but it is unlikely he or she is going to sever the ties with his or her lover right away. After the double life is exposed, the other partner will see the signs of the cheating partner's relationship with his or her lover. The cheating partner will probably still come home from work late, make private phone calls and sneak away from the house. This is especially painful for the betrayed partner, because now he or she knows what is going on but cannot really do anything to stop it.

At this juncture, there are also many concerns that need to be addressed before moving forward. Each partner needs to evaluate the relationship and determine if it is worth staying. Consider whether it would be possible to be happy together, once again, after all the damage. With the loss of trust and feelings of not being loved, it is necessary to reflect on the relationship prior to the affair. Was it happy and intimate? Or was it full of disappointment, emotional neglect and heartache?[33]

The next step is to ascertain if the partners can rebuild the trust. Is the cheating partner only expressing remorse because he or she got caught? Does the cheating partner have a history of lying? Was it the only time he or she cheated during the relationship or has it happened before? Does the cheating partner understand the pain that he or she has caused? If the cheating partner has a history of lying and cheating, it is likely that he or she will go back to a double life when things in the main relationship seem to be settled.

Next, determine if the positive changes that are being made are permanent. A cheating partner may feel guilty and suddenly start spending more time with the children, taking up mutual hobbies and helping out around the house more. It is similar to when a man first starts dating a woman and he makes a real effort to win her over. Once she is his, he usually lessens the amount of effort. If the partners are considering staying together, examine whether these new changes are going to endure or if they are just temporary gestures.

Question if the cheating spouse really misses the relationship or if he or she just needs it to hold his or her life together for some time. Does the cheating partner want the other partner or does he or she just want the "package" of being a couple? Perhaps the cheating partner does not want to lose custody of the children, a certain kind of lifestyle or a mate to take care of him or her.

The partners must make sure they have good, rational reasons for staying together. It is a legitimate concern whether a partner can support him or herself financially and emotionally. After the first year of divorce, most women's living standards decrease by over one third.[34] Some are overwhelmed with the idea of moving out and starting over.

Another concern to address is the issue of the children. Many fractured relationships tend to continue with the "for the kids" excuse. Should a person stay together with a cheating partner for the sake of the children? The answer is no. Consider the amount of conflict that goes on at home. Research shows that it's better for children to be exposed to few household conflicts and be in a divorced family than to be in an environment of constant conflict and be in an "intact" family. Both parents need to maintain stable emotional connections with their children if they want the children to stay psychologically healthy and that is often difficult if one of the partners has cheated.

The partner who has been loyal might feel like his or her spouse could not possibly have loved him or her because of the fact he or she cheated. In an affair, the loyal spouse's self-esteem is often damaged. When you are the loyal spouse, you might think you are not worth being loved or appreciated. Other times, the affair is so enraging that you can think only of revenge. For instance, you might want to have your own affair so he can see how it feels.

If you are the one doing the cheating, you might feel like you should spend more time with your lover to figure out where the relationship is heading. However, by doing this, it is unlikely that you will learn anything new about your primary relationship. You'll probably feel more intensity toward the affair, but that may be your intention.

These are all valid considerations, but they are not the only concerns. Each relationship will have different matters that need to be addressed depending on the context of the cheating. These are the situations that need to be sorted out before deciding to stay or leave. If partners make a decision to stay together, there will be additional work and compromise needed. It will be a long and painful recovery.

When spouses decide to stay together, the first step is that the cheating partner must dissolve the relationship with his or her lover. There are certain rules that are beneficial to making a clean break from a lover. However, most people don't do what it takes to make a clean break.[35]

Be aware that when the cheating spouse severs ties with his or her lover, there's a period of withdrawal, including feelings of anxiety, depression and anger. The feelings of depression may be overwhelming and it may seem nothing can be done to make him or her happy. If you are the faithful spouse, you have to be present as often as possible during this time. If you are not present, it is likely that your partner will call his or her ex-lover in an effort to ease the pain. The most intense withdrawal feelings are known to last for about three weeks, but it takes about six months for them to fade completely. If there is a slip-up and contact is made with the ex-lover, the scenario may begin again.[36]

The cheating partner may have to change jobs or relocate. Changing jobs may be necessary if the affair was work-related. Sometimes a couple wants to relocate, because the reminders of the affair seem to be everywhere they look. However, changing jobs and relocating will likely be a costly and mentally and emotionally draining event for the family. But without taking these territorial precautions, the risk of the affair reigniting remains.[37]

The next precaution is to block all communication with the lover. Sometimes, after months of being apart, all it takes to restart the affair is a simple e-mail, text or phone call. Then the cheating may start again, perhaps more discreetly than before. Phone numbers and e-mails must be changed.

The next issue is to account for time. It is of the utmost importance that the unfaithful partner be available to be contacted by his or her mate at any point in time. Any change in pre-established plans should be discussed and confirmed.

One of the most difficult precautions is accounting for money spent. Having an affair can cost a lot of money—there may be money spent on nice restaurants, hotel rooms, gifts and occasional weekend getaways. For many people, accounting for money seems like a punishment, especially if they are the partners who bring in the greater income. It is necessary, though, because examinations of the financial record can indicate suspicious activity.

The last measure to implement is spending more leisure time together. It is a good idea to have meals together during the day and to spend evenings with each other. If the cheating spouse has to go on an overnight business trip, the loyal partner may want to accompany him or her. While this can get expensive, it might be necessary to ensure that another fling will not happen.

These are just some precautions that might be necessary to make a clean break from a lover. Many cheaters will not agree to take these precautions, saying it feels too much like they are in jail or are being babysat like infants.[38] It's not any easier for the faithful spouse. In addition to responsibilities with the children, work and household duties, loyal partners now have to be watchful of their partners. Undoubtedly, it will add a lot of strain to an already stressful situation.

Additionally, the partner who was cheated on will go through a variety of painful emotions. Normal occurrences, such as hearing love songs on the radio, watching romantic scenes in movies or even encountering everyday objects might trigger traumatic memories of the affair. A betrayed partner may even become obsessive and replay memories of the painful discovery of the affair. The partner may develop a fixation that makes him or her unable to focus or think about anything else.[39] In some cases, a betrayed partner may be consumed with developing memories that do not reflect reality.

Concerning the emotional distress that cheating causes, the cheating partner normally suppresses the guilt while the betrayed partner obsesses over the memories. The cheater tries to downplay his or her wrongdoings and make it seem as if his or her actions were not a big deal. But the obsessed partner frequently replays all the feelings of humiliation and anger. Suppressing fuels the obsessing and vice versa.[40]

While partners can learn to control obsessive thoughts to a certain degree, flashbacks are involuntary. They can be triggered by a conscious or subconscious cue, such as sight, smell, sound or physical touch. Such cues are connected in some way to the affair. They induce a sense of fear, panic and rage.[41]

Constriction can involve thoughts and feelings that inhibit the cheated party. It can consist of a feeling of numbness. While in the constricted state, one might pull away from the friends and activities one once loved and suppress emotions. This is a coping mechanism for events that may seem too painful to handle. While it might be a relief to feel numb from the emotional trauma, most often it is only a temporary state.[42]

It is also possible to go into a state of hyper-arousal after betrayal. In such a case, the betrayed partner becomes alert and over-sensitive. The physiological hyper-arousal manifests in the form of disordered sleep, intense overreactions, loss of appetite or being startled by loud noises. Emotional hyper-arousal may be in the form of expressing emotions in an out-of-control manner. It happens when a person magnifies his or her emotions, whether they are true ones or not.[43]

Hyper-vigilance is also a common reaction. The betrayed partner is constantly on high alert and may have feelings of paranoia. Any sign that the other partner might be cheating again, whether rational or irrational, seems to require an immediate investigation. The loyal partner might ask numerous questions about the cheating partner's daily activities and verify his or her responses, call the cheating partner repetitively and/or obsessively monitor the cheating partner's e-mail and phone calls.

The possibility for new crises to emerge is likely even if there are ideal recovery conditions. The new openness and honesty in the relationship allows room for previous lies to be uncovered, which might cause additional pain. Special occasions like holidays, birthdays and celebrations might invoke a crisis and cause contemplation of these occasions when the affair had not been discovered yet. Also, it might be difficult to appear to be a committed, strong couple when the relationship is unstable .

The culmination of lies, betrayal and secrets is enough to fragment any relationship. Once the cheating has been discovered, it is a long journey to rekindling what once was. Not only does it take forgiveness, but also it takes a tremendous effort on the part of both partners. Even with relentless work and communication, it is possible that the relationship will never fully recover.

If a positive relationship can't be restored, despite all willingness and sincere effort made, it is possible that getting a divorce might be the best option. Things might seem like they are going to get better, but living in an unsatisfying marriage is exhausting. To some people getting divorced might seem like they are losing, but really they are moving on with their lives.

As we've discussed, if a woman decides to leave her husband, she needs to prepare for it. She must try to set her emotions aside and think logically. If she has been a stay-at-home mom, she will probably have to enter the workforce. Even if she has a stable career, she should still plan her finances accordingly. Maintaining a household is more difficult without two incomes.

Telling her husband she wants a divorce might be very difficult for a woman to do, but chances are he has seen it coming. He probably hasn't been completely oblivious to her unhappiness. The wife must be prepared to spend a while talking things through. It is also important that neither partner is drunk or angry at the beginning of the conversation. This will most likely be a very emotional time for both partners.

Once the anger and sadness have subsided, it will be a relief to be out of the relationship that was brimming with cheating and lies. Women can concentrate on making new friends, decorating their new homes and taking up new hobbies. They do not need to recreate the lives they had with their mates. They can start new ones. It will take a while to establish new routines and adjust to all the changes, but being single will be liberating and eventually fulfilling.

Chapter 3

Unhappily Married Women

There are few statistical studies to tell us exactly how many unhappily married women there are in the world. However, I believe an unhappily married woman can be found on every street, in every city and in every town. Some are contemplating that next step toward divorce, yet divorce is such a big step. So many unhappy women will decide to stay in a stagnant or even destructive relationship, because it seems to be the easiest thing to do or because they do not know how to leave an unhealthy relationship. But staying in an unhealthy, unhappy relationship is never the best thing to do.

A woman may know that there is nothing left in her marriage relationship and she may want to leave, but the advice she has been given has her feeling guilty. It is time to look at all the implications and information on staying single once divorced. Many women feel that they should jump back into relationships; that is not so. The face of family is changing now. No longer is it a man, a woman and two or three children. Single parents are a fast-growing segment of the population in America and western European countries as well. According to a report released by the United States Census Bureau in November 2009, there were almost fourteen million single parents in the United States.[1] The trend is worldwide, as in Germany, where "the number of single parents has doubled in the past two decades" and in Britain, where "the proportion of families headed by a single parent has topped 25 percent."[2] This reflects a huge growth in the number of never-married mothers at a global level.

INADEQUATE REASONS TO REMAIN IN AN UNHAPPY MARRIAGE

What can you do when you know that your marriage will never get better? You feel sure that you cannot regain the happiness you once had in this particular relationship. Perhaps you have tried many avenues for help: friends, books and therapists. As difficult as it may sound, this is the time to ignore well-intentioned advice on how to save your marriage. You do not have to remain in this unhappy relationship. You can divorce and do not even have to marry again if you do not want to. It is perfectly acceptable and preferable to more women than ever to remain single after divorce.

Many of your friends and acquaintances will assume that you want to battle to save your marriage. Well-intentioned friends and others will give you many reasons to stay in a marriage that really stands no chance of improving. Although these people mean well and have your best interests at heart, they may not know or understand how hard you have tried to work things out. They have not seen the good fight you have fought. You know you have done everything that you can and they cannot comprehend the hopelessness that you feel. There comes a time when the fight for a relationship that is dead needs to end. When that time comes, you will need to consider divorce.

Indeed, it can be very difficult to dispute motives for staying married. They might even sound good or right at times. However, you need to move on and gain happiness for yourself. The truth is that some of the reasons experts, friends and family give for staying married just don't suffice in a stagnant relationship. Women need to make the choices that are best for them and gain empowerment.

Let's discuss some common reasons for staying in a marriage that professionals and laypeople give to those who are in severely troubled marriages and contemplating divorce. We'll also look at some facts that may help you to see that divorce does not have to wreck the rest of your life. Divorce may actually be the one thing that will bring you into the best life you could ever have imagined.

STAY MARRIED FOR THE CHILDREN

Many marriage counselors, ministers, family members and friends advise you to "stick it out" for the sake of the children. They warn that, should you divorce, your children will have serious self-esteem and emotional issues. Because you probably are seriously worried about the effect of your unhappy marriage and divorce on your children, their advice only makes you more unhappy but doesn't solve the issue that the marriage relationship has failed.

Your children probably know that you are not happy. They can sense that things are strained between their parents. The way to handle this difficult time and your children's mixed feelings is to assure your children that their parents love them and that they are not the reason for the tension in the marriage. All of those negative issues, disagreements and alienation of you and your husband in an unhappy marriage will do more damage to your children than getting a divorce and ending the strain. On the flipside, happiness is contagious. Children of happy single parents tend to be happier and more well-adjusted than those who have unhappily married parents.

One survey about divorce and children by the Pew Research Center (2007) asked a sample of Americans if children are better off when parents who are unhappy in their marriage get divorced. An overwhelming majority of respondents (67 percent) believe that divorce is better for the children.[3]

Nevertheless, you should still prepare yourself for emotions such as anger, frustration and sadness from your children. Change affects each of us in different ways. Most life changes are met with negativity at first. It does not have to stay negative. Talk to your children, discuss their issues and feelings and be patient with them as you prepare to transition from being unhappily married to being happily divorced.

Here are a few good suggestions when talking to your children about an upcoming divorce from M. Gary Neuman, founder and director of the Sandcastles Therapy Program and author of the book, *Helping Your Kids Cope with Divorce the Sandcastles Way*.[4]

Don't ask your children to choose sides. Remember that the divorce is not about them; it is between you and your spouse. You and your spouse can each show the children that you love them. You cannot resent the love the children receive from their other parent. Any loving parent knows that allowing his or her children to be loved by others is the best thing for them.

Don't criticize your spouse. Your children more than likely love their other parent just as much as they love you. They do not want to hear either of you putting the other down. That can hurt children deeply and they will end up not wanting to be around the parent who criticizes.

Talk to your children about their feelings and let them express their true feelings, whether they are positive or negative, without passing judgment. Keep communication lines open. Ask open-ended questions that will elicit more than one-word responses. You may say something like, "It sounds as if you are feeling angry (or sad or excited, etc.). Will you tell me more about this?" Let the child take the conversation from there. Sometimes children will open up to you and sometimes they will not. Let them know that you are there for them when they are ready to talk.

Staying married for your children is not the best policy. They can sense the unhappiness and the tension in their parents' relationship. Children would much rather see their parents happy, even if it means they no longer live together or are married.

The key to raising healthy, happy, well-adjusted children in the environment of divorce is to let them know they are loved and valued, which is the same as raising healthy, happy, well-adjusted children in the environment of marriage.

STAY MARRIED FOR THE FINANCIAL SECURITY

This is a serious consideration when contemplating divorce and not something to take lightly. You will need to be able to support yourself and your children, if you have any. Even if you are awarded child support and/or alimony, you still have to figure out your future finances, because in most divorces today women must plan on working themselves and contributing to their children's support.

However, financial security is not as big an issue for women contemplating divorce now as it used to be. Chances are you are currently employed; possibly you are the main breadwinner in your household. The Bureau for Labor Statistics (2008) reports that the labor force participation rates among mothers is significantly higher now than in the 1970s. This increase reflects a rate of 69.8 percent of married mothers and 75.8 percent of unmarried mothers working.[5] This is a global trend: throughout the industrialized Western world most women are now working and supporting their single-parent households.[6]

For those who have been stay-at-home mothers or wives, now is the time to expand your horizons. Financial dependence on a man no longer has to tether you to a relationship that is dead or unfulfilling. If you have a degree and have not used it, brush up on those long-forgotten skills. If you have not been able to get a higher degree, you can start now. Remember, it is never too late to start over.

Clarice's Story

Clarice, a woman who had just turned fifty, wanted very much to become a doctor. She felt she was too old to go to medical school though. Lamenting her sorrow over not working toward her dream to a friend, Clarice said, "I just can't go back to school now. At my age, I'll be fifty-eight before I finish medical school." Her wise friend asked, "So, how old will you be in eight years if you don't go back to school?"

At whatever your stage of life, whatever your age, whatever your level of education, this is where you start. Where you end up is up to you. While education does cost money, there are many financing options available for women. It should not be difficult for you to find a funding source should you decide to continue your education. There are many grants available to women, including ones specifically for single parents. There are also scholarship opportunities for specific areas of study. Try searching online to find new avenues for educational funding for today's women.

As well, women's financial security no longer depends solely on their husbands. Women can and do make ends meet on their own without their partners' input. Realistically, you will need to assess what cuts to make if your husband does currently provide added income. Cutting back could be well worth it if your marriage is irrevocably broken and you foresee personal happiness outside of the marriage.

Budgeting is necessary after a divorce. If you were the chief budgeter while married, you will find this natural. However, for those who depended on their husbands to take care of budgeting, this task can be daunting. But with some assistance and efficient resources (try your local library), you will be able to organize and get a handle on your finances. In the end, putting together a budget will pay off very well. With planning, you will be able to support your lifestyle and maybe even have a little money left over for a treat.

There is the added, usually self-imposed, burden of thinking that the children will suffer if you have less income. Again, the children will be fine. Talk with them openly about the financial situation and how you can work together to make your new financial circumstances work, even if they are tight. Children understand that life will be different. Sometimes, they understand better than the adults that things will not get worse; they will just be different.

If you have not previously been the principal breadwinner in your family, you will be amazed at the feeling of self-sufficiency once you begin to rely on your own finances. You will have the security of knowing that no matter who comes and goes in your life, your finances are your own. Your confidence will get a boost.

STAY MARRIED TO AVOID BEING ALONE

Many people are hesitant to leave relationships out of fear of being alone. There seems to be the widespread impression that if an adult is not married, then he or she must be lonely. This is not true for many women who divorce and have not remarried.

It is inevitable that feelings of loneliness will surface after being married to someone for years. But what you should know is that you do not have to stay lonely, even if you choose not to date for a while after divorce. Take a few moments to reflect on the time you have been able to spend with just you during your marriage. Just because you may seem to have more alone time when divorced than when married does not mean that you have to be lonely. This may be the perfect opportunity to rediscover yourself. Find out what you truly want for the rest of your life. In a *Psychology Today* article titled "Loneliness: Use It...And Lose It," Sheila Weinstein states that when she was "finally able to be alone and not lonely," she was "pleased to be in my own company" and felt "more connected to myself and the Universe."[7]

When you are single, you can focus on the dreams and goals that you may have forfeited while in a marriage relationship. Take some time to do some soul searching. More than likely, you will find that your needs and desires have changed over the years. Determine, at this juncture in life, to be your own happiness. Then, if you decide you still want to date, you still want to be with someone for an extended period of time, you will know that your happiness and contentment does not rely solely on that person. The choice is in your hands.

Once divorced, you have the freedom of choosing whether or not you want to date. Some women prefer to wait until their children have grown up; others want to date right away. This is a personal choice. You also have the freedom of not getting remarried. Many women today, divorced or single, are much happier just dating or cohabitating with someone. The idea that you have to be married is becoming less and less mainstream in today's world.

Should you find someone with whom you want to spend more time, you may later choose to live with that person rather than marry him. This may be beneficial to you and to your children who live with you. The main reason being that, though this may look like something long-term, it doesn't have to be. If it does not progress well, there is the option of breaking off the relationship without having to go through the cost and stress of divorce.

As an added bonus, the fact that you can live with someone if you want may actually help you in the financial realm. In one report titled "Living Together: The Economics of Cohabitation" by the Pew Research Center, those living with someone else, unmarried and with a college degree, have a higher level of household income than those with a college education who are married.[8]

STAY MARRIED TO AVOID LOSING SOCIAL STATUS

Although this is antiquated, there is still, for some, the thought that a woman may lose her social status if she gets a divorce. Don't be deceived by this idea or by those who try to use that claim to get you to stay in a dead-end marriage. Divorce is not limited to the poor, rich, famous or unknown. Divorce rates span the whole of the American and European populations. Because divorce is widely accepted at all levels of the social scale, fear of losing your social status should not be an issue.

Nevertheless, there is still a lingering stigma attached to being single in some circles or societies today. Some would try to make you believe that if you are single, then you are less than complete. Not so! You can be a whole, healthy, complete person without the added burden of having to fit yourself and your life with someone else. Staying single after divorce is nothing to be ashamed of, no matter if there are those who would have you feel otherwise. Remember, this is your right and your decision to make.

STAY MARRIED TO ADHERE TO RELIGIOUS BELIEFS

Religious beliefs are often handed down through generations and deeply ingrained into one's psyche. Women who were raised in religious homes seem to feel it is their "duty" to stay married. Oftentimes, even when husbands are abusive or neglectful, women are still expected to stick it out and remain married. The idea that "what God has joined, let no man put asunder" is prevalent in religion. Indeed, in most Protestant religions the only Biblically given reason for divorce is infidelity. Ask yourself, does God really want a woman to stay in a situation that makes her bitter, angry and very unhappy or in which she is abused physically, verbally or emotionally? Not if you believe in a loving God.

It is thought that those who practice religion are less likely to divorce. However, in a study of people across the United States, the Barna Research Group found that about one third of the people of each religion in the study had been divorced at least once. Those who called themselves atheists or agnostics had a lower divorce rate than the Christian denominations.[9] Religion is not a shield against divorce. If a marriage is not right, it just isn't. There is no reason for you to feel guilty or obligated to stay in an unhappy marriage because of religion.

It seems that religion can be a source of comfort and it can also be a source of unnecessary guilt. No matter what your religious persuasion is, you can achieve a balance between religion and reality without losing faith.

REASONS TO END YOUR UNHAPPY MARRIAGE

ABUSE

If your reason for wanting a divorce is abuse, be it physical, psychological or emotional, get out of this relationship as soon as possible! This type of relationship is detrimental to everyone involved. According to a domestic violence fact sheet published by the National Coalition Against Domestic Violence, each year 1.3 million women are victims of physical assault by an intimate partner.[10] If you feel that trying to get away from this situation may put you and your children in a more dangerous situation, there are national hotlines you can call that are manned by women who are empathetic to your situation and/or have been in similar circumstances. They can get you the help you need.

In the United States, the phone number for the National Domestic Violence Hotline is 1-800-799-SAFE (7233) or TTY 1-800-787-3224. In the United Kingdom, the National Domestic Violence Freephone Helpline can be reached at 0808-2000-247. Israel provides a Battered Women's Hotline at 02-651-4111. Australia offers its service at (02)-6280-0900 and TTY (02)-6247-0893. Call centers are available twenty-four hours a day, seven days a week. Advocates there can put you in touch with local and in some cases, immediate help. If abuse is the case, don't hesitate; act fast.

AFFAIR

According to Joan D. Atwood and Limor Schwartz, co-authors of the article "Cyber-Sex: The New Affair Treatment Considerations" in the *Journal of Couple and Relationship Therapy*, about 45 to 55 percent of married women have affairs and about 50 to 60 percent of married men have affairs.[11] Renowned psychiatrist and author Frank Pittman observes in his book *Grow Up! How Taking Responsibility Can Make You a Happy Adult* that 90 percent of all first divorces involve infidelity by either one or both partners and the cheating partner often attempts to hide the infidelity during the divorce process, further indication that the signing of a paper does nothing to diminish the desire to be involved with others.[12]

Maybe your husband cheated on you and you cannot forgive and forget. Maybe you cheated on him. More than likely, the reason you cheated in the first place is the only clue you need to tell you that the marriage is over.

A panel of fifty divorce lawyers in the United Kingdom were queried on the most common causes for divorce for the cases they handled in the prior year and found that "of those who cited extramarital affairs, 45 percent said it was the wives who cheated while 55 percent said it was the husbands."[13] Indeed, that is not a large margin between men and women cheaters. This same research study attributes much of the increase in the number of women having affairs in a faulty marriage to the fact that women are no longer dependent on their husbands for their livelihood. In many marriages, the women make as much or more money than their male counterparts. Thus, there is no longer the fear of being caught by the husband and getting thrown out, unable to support oneself.

If infidelity is the reason for your decision to divorce, you will want to weigh your options heavily before remarrying. You want to guard your heart if it was you who was cheated on. But if it was you who cheated, you will want to reevaluate your reasons for having an affair and work through those before becoming involved in another marriage.

LACK OF COMMUNICATION

Maybe it is not abuse or an affair but a general communication breakdown between you and your spouse. For some reason, you stopped conversing with each other. You may have begun the "grunt" phase of the deterioration of communication when coherent words do not pass between you. Though this phase may seem to be amusing from a distance, it can be a serious indication that the marital relationship has run its course. The grunt phase is an indication of a breakdown in communication between husband and wife. Another indication is constant bickering and the inability to have a civil conversation with each other. Unfortunately, this is common.

This inability to communicate can make it difficult to approach the subject of divorce when the time comes. If you have a propensity to bicker when trying to talk to your spouse, you will need to get that under control before you tell your partner that you want a divorce. Voicing your desire for divorce during a shouting match is not wise. Practice remaining calm during a few interchanges before you tackle the subject of divorce.

ABANDONMENT

Abandonment can take a physical and/or emotional form. Physical abandonment means that your husband has left your home and your life. In some cases, a husband will come back periodically for his belongings or perhaps to check on what's going on in the household to make sure that things are going according to his wishes. However, in some cases he may leave and not return at all. In most places, this is grounds for a divorce.

With emotional abandonment, your husband is probably still living in the home but does not appear interested in taking care of your emotional needs any longer. It is as though he wants to continue the relationship as if you are roommates who have no intimate connection whatsoever. This can be draining and debilitating to women. Most women are emotional creatures and they have the need to have their emotional needs nurtured. If their husbands are not willing to do that, then there really is no viable relationship.

SEXUAL INCOMPATIBILITY

You and your husband may have begun your relationship many years ago with a passion for each other that you thought could and would never wane. Now you realize you cannot remember the last time you and your husband made love. Or maybe you cannot remember the last time that you enjoyed sex with your husband. Sexual incompatibility in a marriage is an important aspect of marriage for both women and men.

However, sexual incompatibility can happen at any time and sex drive fluctuation can be influenced by many things. A decrease in libido can stem from certain medications, illnesses or elevated stress levels. This is normal in life. However, the problem arises when partners' sex drives are different and stay that way for an extended period of time. This can be an indication that something is amiss in the marriage.

GETTING YOUR FINANCES IN ORDER

When you think you might want a divorce, you will need to take care of ordering your finances. You want your divorce to go as smoothly as possible, but do not allow yourself to be taken advantage of when it comes to finances. Today, joint custody and fathers taking custody are possible, but chances are the wife will get custody of the children. Thus, you will have the largest part of the responsibility of raising your children, which also comes with a large financial obligation. Make sure that you and you legal counsel understand what you and the children, if any, will need and petition for reasonable funds.

Many believe that women are worse off financially after divorce than their male counterparts. This could be because women, in general, make less money than men do. Another factor that stands out is that some women are not aware of the couple's financial status before the divorce. You can guard against being in this category. Knowledge, especially financial knowledge, is power. Learn your finances intimately!

Remember, as discussed previously, preparing a budget is not as difficult as you may think it is. All that is necessary is listing your expenses and income and allotting certain amounts to the required expenses. You should begin your budget planning soon after you decide to divorce.

In order to begin this budget planning process, you will need to know where you are right now. Gather all the information you have on bank accounts, assets, debts, wills, powers of attorney, etc. Make or get copies of all financial records. Know what is in all checking and savings accounts. If you have any stocks, bonds, retirement accounts, etc., make sure you know where they are, what their values are and what will happen to these accounts at the time of divorce. It is essential to your financial future that you know how much money you have available. You will be doing yourself a great service if you know the status of your finances and what you would like to see as an end result of the divorce settlement.

One consideration that is often overlooked is the tax aspect of retirement accounts, stocks and bonds. It is a good idea to find out if, when and how much these accounts will be taxed. This way you can get a better idea of your after-tax finances. It is crucial for you to plan for the long term. Remember, you should not give up long-term financial security for an immediate, short lived settlement.

Also, it is a good idea to examine expenses for the children as well as for the household. This will give you an idea of how much you need in the way of financial support after divorce. Keep these expenses on paper so that you will have some proof of what is needed to help you make ends meet.

Sometimes divorce can ruin a person's credit score. Good credit is something you definitely want to keep intact after the divorce. Safeguard your credit standing by getting a copy of your credit report and knowing where you stand. If you have a lower credit score, start now, while you are still married, to pay down debt. Get rid of as much liability as possible before you file. If you have no credit background, you should spend time to build credit for yourself. Get a credit card in your name and use it, but do not build up any debt. Only charge what you know you can pay off as soon as the bill comes in.

With permanent alimony awards becoming rarer, it is a good idea to take care of any potentially large expenses before you divorce. If you plan to stay in the current house after the divorce, make sure that it is in top condition. Ensure there are no leaks in the roof and make any structural repairs and general maintenance that might be needed. Also, get your vehicle serviced and make sure that any repairs that are necessary are fixed. You do not want any big expenses when you have only your income.

Take necessary steps to reenter the workforce if you have taken time off to raise a family. Take a refresher class and buy new professional clothes. Also spend time updating your résumé and networking for employment. Today it is usually the case that educated women are expected to return to work and alimony, in many cases, is temporary or nonexistent. Be aware that usually after a divorce, a woman's standard of living drops an average of 27 percent while a man's increases 10 percent.[14]

You may want to consult a financial planner who has experience in dealing with this aspect of divorce. Make sure you know, as closely as possible, how much you will need to spend during the divorce proceedings. Ask as many questions as you can think of at this point. The financial planner will tell you how much it will cost to file and can give you a close estimate of what it will cost you personally.

Health insurance coverage is another consideration. If you are covered under your spouse's plan, this will likely change after the divorce. While you are still insured, get your wellness checkups and address any medical issues that you may have. If your employer does not offer health insurance coverage, you may have to shop around to find the best commercial health coverage for your budget. It is important that you do not spend any time without health insurance.

Plan to start a separate savings account to help with expenses the first few months after divorce. It is best to have at least three months of living expenses saved. This will give you extra security during and shortly after the divorce. With less stress over finances, you will be able to deal with other issues that arise during this difficult phase.

Make an inventory of all of your and your husband's possessions and all household items. This will help you decide what items you want to ask for in the divorce and what you can let go of. All of these things will have to be dealt with before the divorce is final. Familiarize yourself with the state laws concerning personal property during a divorce. Some states consider all property obtained during a marriage to be equally owned by both spouses no matter who purchased it. As such, this property is often divided fifty-fifty at the time of divorce. If you already know what you have and what you want, the less time and energy you will have to expend at this most critical time.

Once you have gathered all this information, find a secure place to keep it. You are not being underhanded; you are being safe. Sometimes divorce can make people spiteful. Since you will be prepared with financial information and with what you would like to see happen with the assets, you will have placed yourself in the position of empowerment. You can set the tone for how negotiations will proceed. This will give you confidence that you are making the best possible decisions for you and your children.

TELLING HIM YOU WANT A DIVORCE

Now it is time to break the news to your spouse. If you have talked about divorce before, this may be the next logical step for you and your spouse. If this is your husband's first clue you are unhappy, it can be a little tricky.

Do not begin this conversation by playing the blame game. You may feel the situation is entirely his fault, but now is not the time to voice that opinion. Listing his faults and the ways you feel he screwed up the marriage will probably start an argument. You do not want any extra heat at this point, so lay aside the blame. Just tell him plainly and calmly that you want a divorce. Now is the time to be open and honest about how you feel and how you came to this decision. If he asks what he has done wrong, don't engage in that conversation. Explain that you feel you both have grown in separate directions and it is time to move on. If there are reasons that you can voice that will not make him the "bad guy" or incite anger, use these reasons also. Do not bring up any specific incidents that have caused arguments in the past.

Let your husband know that this is a decision you have debated seriously and for some time. Tell your husband you have weighed all the options, what you have done to try to make the marriage work and how seriously you have thought this through. Although you do not want this conversation to become an argument, make sure he understands how unhappy you are in the relationship. Try to tell your husband this without making it sound like it is his fault, even if that is the case.

The best thing to do is to come up with a reason that your spouse can tell his parents, family and friends without being embarrassed. It could be that "you have both grown in separate directions" and that "both of you are ready to pursue your own independence." Give him the opportunity of being able to say that the decision to divorce was in part his choice. This will make it much easier for your soon-to-be ex-husband to accept that divorce is imminent.

Expect your spouse to be shocked. Even though your spouse may feel the tension and that the marriage is not what it should be, he may not have given much thought about getting a divorce. Keep in mind that you have had some time to think seriously and reflect on your decision to divorce. You already have determined the reasons why this is the best choice. Your spouse has not had this opportunity. This may be the first time your husband has thought about divorce. Give him the time he needs. Tomorrow, he will have different views on the situation; the next day, there will be different feelings again. Allow your spouse time to process this information.

You cannot predict how your husband will react, whether with tears, silent disbelief or outrage. No matter what your husband's reaction is, your response to his reaction means everything. It is important for you to remain calm and in control. You can be sympathetic to his emotions, but you must stay strong. Do not become angry or defensive. Above all, do not be apologetic! Stay calm and stand by your decision. If his reaction becomes violent, get to a safe place immediately. Give your spouse time to calm down before contacting him again. Consider meeting in a public place. Once you have come to a final decision to end the marriage, never waver in your resolve that the decision to divorce, for you, is final and irrevocable.

Sometimes a husband will resent your new independence and individuality. This could begin a very hostile divorce and should be avoided as much as you have control over it. Explain to him that you are not the enemy; you are just you. Divorces that start with conflict tend to continue in that vein. This can be devastating emotionally and financially as well as to any children involved. Try to keep this transition as peaceful as possible without giving up your decision to end the marriage bond.

Assure your spouse that you will not try to come between him and the children, unless their safety is threatened. It is important that you let him know that his relationship with them will be unimpeded by you. You can discuss specific visitation rights later on, but for now let your husband know you want him to nurture a close relationship with the children. If there is a record of abuse where the children are concerned, a different approach may be necessary.

Lastly, brace yourself. While you have thought about this, weighed the options and realized that divorce is the best and only solution for you, what may catch you off guard is your own feelings when you actually say those words to your spouse. Once the words are out there, you may very well feel a pang of regret, a flash of resentment or anger, even pity for your spouse. Remember, these are "in the moment" emotions. Do not let them discount the hours you have spent coming to this decision.

PREPARE YOURSELF FOR CHANGES

You are ready now to engage the attorney with whom you may have already consulted. You will want to discuss with him or her not only child custody, but also the business side of the divorce.

In his book, *Making Any Divorce Better!*, former divorce attorney Ed Sherman takes the position that the "real" divorce is not the legal battle, but rather the emotional, physical and spiritual changes that occur soon after the judge has declared you divorced. In order for you to move forward with your life in a healthy, happy fashion, you must prepare yourself for some of these changes related to divorce.[15]

No matter how resolute you are in your decision to get a divorce, there is still going to be an emotional bond to your spouse even though the relationship is severed during the process. If you are not prepared for it, it may cripple your chances of having that happiness you craved. As Ed Sherman states, "This is about breaking (or failing to break) the bonds, patterns, dependencies and habits that attach you to your ex-spouse—learning to let go and get beyond anger, fear, hurt, guilt, blame and resentment."[16] You will have to let go of that emotional attachment and begin to build your self-confidence and, in so doing, build a new life.

Do not ignore, deny or try to repress the emotions that you are feeling during this time. The mind, emotions and body are not separated; they are very much intertwined. If you do not deal with the often painful, raw, pre-divorce emotions, you could be putting your physical and mental health in jeopardy. Perhaps you have been seeing a therapist; if not, you may want to seriously consider getting counseling, even if it is just for a short while.

Getting divorced can sometimes feel like suffering the death of someone close. As with any death, grief is bound to be a part of the process. This feeling comes from the sense of loss. Essentially, you are losing a spouse. Many of the friendships that you had as a married person may not carry over to your new single life. This, too, can cause a sense of loss. Keep in mind that you will *not* be losing your family. Your family makeup will change, but it will not be gone. Do not stifle your feelings of grief, but rather work through them.

The grief that comes with divorce is a very complicated matter. For instance, when we grieve the death of a loved one, there are support mechanisms already in place: the ritual of funerals and last farewells as well as friends and family to grieve with you. But in divorce the support systems for grief are unstable. Often, friends and family have no idea what to say or how to comfort you. Some may even take sides against you, causing escalated stress. These feelings of loss are real and difficult, but remember they are temporary. This stage will pass, but in the meantime, cry if you feel you need to. However you deal with grief, allow yourself to move past it.

Guilt is another emotion that many women may experience during this phase. Guilt often drives women back to their spouses or causes them to renege on their divorce decision. This is a good time to do some soul searching. Remember, you already know that the marriage is beyond repair. You have tried everything to make it work. Nothing has helped or changed. You are not at fault. You are just in an unhappy marriage and you want to end it.

Another emotion you may feel is anxiety. Anxiety is not always a bad thing. It may have been feelings of anxiety that led you to the decision to divorce. That fight or flight feeling may have kicked in when you pictured yourself in your miserable marriage for the rest of your life. You have chosen to fly. Some anxiousness now may strike as you face the unknown future of your new life. That is why preparation is so important. If you prepare yourself, your finances, your children and your extended family, this will help to de-stress the situation on many levels and will, hopefully, lessen the tension.

MAKING IT OFFICIAL

Now that you have made the decision, notified your husband of your intentions and feel confident that this is the right thing for you, it is time for you and your attorney to take the legal steps to begin the actual divorce. Preparing yourself legally as well as emotionally will help de-stress this very strenuous time in your life.

Since, according to most reports and studies, women tend to fare worse financially and emotionally after divorce, you need to be prepared for the reality that you will face. Getting ready to live your new life of freedom will take some time. Do not scrimp on preparation. In this time of heated emotions, stress and tension, do not make the mistake of discounting money matters. Take the time you need to get your affairs in order, so that you will be able to negotiate the best possible financial settlement.

Child custody issues also may cause complications and disagreement during a divorce. It is best to forge an agreement on child custody and visitation. This is probably the worst issue for bickering in a divorce settlement. You will want to work hard at making your decision about your children as calm as possible, especially if the children are old enough to participate in any custody evaluations that may be required in your particular state or country.

Remember to reassure your child, especially the very young ones, that they are loved by both of you. When there are heavy arguments, young children might feel that it is their fault. Remind them that these issues are between the two adults. Try to keep arguments out of the hearing of the children. For the most part, this is for the children's benefit but it will also help you to diminish your worries about the toll the divorce might be taking on your children.

If at all possible, arrange the visitation dates and times. Work out holiday schedules. The court will look at both sides and decide what is best for the children. If there is an agreement already made and no sudden arguments occur in the courtroom, this phase should pass very smoothly.

Take a few moments to plan your divorce day. On the day your divorce is final you may receive notice in the mail or you may sit in the courtroom waiting for your case to be called. Afterwards you will be free to do something nice for yourself. Perhaps you'll want to go out with friends and enjoy yourself. Perhaps you would like to celebrate quietly, maybe have a spa afternoon to work out all the pre-divorce day stress. Later, you might want to spend time with your children to reassure them of their parents' love. If you are a planner, you may take some time this day to plan your life path from this day forward. Maybe you can reconsider old dreams and aspirations and let them shine a light on your new path.

If you cannot celebrate the remainder of the day when you finalize your divorce, perhaps you want to plan a divorce party. Invite your good friends who are as happy for you as you are. Some rules you may want to follow: 1) Tell your friends not to bring someone to set you up with. 2) Celebrate your freedom. 3) Propose a toast to the future. 4) Have fun.

If you decide on a party, there will be acquaintances and possibly some relatives who are going to give you looks and say things to let you know that in their opinions your party is in bad taste. Well, we commemorate all major life events, including holidays, marriages, births and deaths. Why not the day you regain your single life? Don't give in to those who want you to feel depressed and guilty for ending your unhappy marriage. Celebrate the finalizing of your divorce as the beginning of a whole new single life for yourself.

HELPING YOUR CHILDREN DEAL WITH DIVORCE

Your children will most likely be upset about the divorce. They may have trouble verbalizing the complex feelings and emotions they are experiencing. You might believe that they are doing very well, but they may be just putting on a front to please you. Children will undergo anxiety, fear of abandonment, loyalty issues and self-blame for the problems between you and their father. They probably want you and your ex-spouse to get back together and they have trouble accepting that it is not going to happen.

However, to help your children through this difficult period, reassure your children of your and their father's love for them. Watch for problems and keep your family routines consistent so as to provide a safe, reliable environment for your children. Be open to any questions your children might have and ask them questions about their opinions and feelings. They might feel a sense of failure after the divorce, so emphasize the importance of doing activities they enjoy, not just activities at which they are good. They might feel their father abandoned them and fear that you might leave them too. It's your role to assure them that you will always be there for them and that their father will still be a part of their lives (if this is in their best interest). In most cases, both parents continue to love and want close relationships with their children. Today, joint custody is a choice that many make and, in some cases, fathers have their children live with them.

According to Carl Pickhardt, author of *The Everything Parent's Guide to Children and Divorce*, divorce affects children differently, depending on their age group. During the childhood years, usually from birth to around the age of nine, children are dependent on their parents and focused on home life. Boys and girls still in childhood often have the most issues with insecurity and anxiety when their parents divorce. Older children might lose their sense of stability during the crucial time that they are searching for independence. You can prepare yourself by recognizing what your child is going through and working hard to make him or her feel secure.[17]

Young children often fear abandonment and creating new or keeping old rituals makes them feel more secure. When you drop your child off at school, she might be scared that you will not come back. She might say or think, "Will you be here to get me after school? Don't forget me." It is important that you assure her you or whoever will pick her up will be there and do what you promise so she can better handle her time away from you. Be sure you do not try to overdo your reassurances. It is normal for your child who is in the midst of your domestic change to be scared. If you try too hard to make your child feel safe, it may actually confirm her fears that the threat of being abandoned is real.[18]

During early adolescence, usually between the ages of ten and twelve, your child is trying to find independence. This is the time that she may begin to pull away from parents to find a sense of self, but a divorce causes a lack of stability from which to launch. Negative attitudes and rebellion may intensify at this point. She does not want to be treated like a child anymore and often she pushes your boundaries of authority. Keep her accountable for any acts of rebellion that are potentially harmful, such as shoplifting, lying or sneaking out past curfew. Do not criticize her for trying to find a new identity through new clothing styles, different kinds of music or countercultural beliefs. If you do, it might make her more resistant to open up to you.[19]

Mid-adolescence occurs between the ages of thirteen and fifteen. Most teens feel the need to spend a lot of time with friends and do things away from home. Conflict and lying sometimes coincide with mid-adolescence and often intensify with divorce. Divorce makes parents seem less dependable, so your teen becomes more dependent on her friends instead. Counter this by addressing problems directly. Come up with a punishment for each offense and, once the punishment is completed, reestablish your trust in your teen. If you do not give her any leeway at all, she will rebel even harder.[20]

Late adolescence includes the ages of sixteen through eighteen. This is the time when more adult behaviors begin, such as driving a car, getting a part-time job, significant dating and going to parties. If your divorce comes during this period, there can be serious issues. Independence seems scarier when there is not a strong, familiar foundation to step off from or return to. Encourage independence by assigning more adult responsibilities so your teen feels more prepared for the adult world, not frightened by it. One good way to moderate her adult behavior is by making her prove to be responsible at home and school before granting more grown-up freedoms.[21]

Between the ages of eighteen and twenty-three, your adult child goes through trial independence. In many cases, she is moving out on her own, starting college or working full-time. This can also be the time of maximum partying. With new freedom comes mistakes and financial problems when bills are due. Parents' divorce, during this time, complicates trial independence. She is past the age of custody agreements and her responsibility to divide time between parents. This is also a stage of life when she might be more inclined to start serious relationships, but her value of commitment and love has been shaken. You can ease the intensity by not competing with your ex-husband for your child's time and loyalty. As far as her commitment issues go, she is old enough that you can explain to her what went wrong in your relationship. This will help her see that her future relationships are not necessarily destined for failure.[22]

Following divorce, the routine of a single-parent household needs to be established. If you are the parent with primary custody, your ex-spouse may feel like he is being rejected from the family. While he might have the urge to come over every day to see the children, this is not a good idea, because your children need to get used to your establishing independence and new routines. You may have settled on joint custody, their father seeing them on weekends or other arrangements. In some cases, fathers will have primary custody. Whatever your divorce agreement calls for, there will be a needed period of adjustment.

If you have primary custody, do some family bonding with your children to show them that this new, single-parent household can be a safe, happy place. Enlist the children to do chores together. They need to understand that the whole family should participate in making this new phase of life a success. Make sure you do fun stuff together too. Let the children help you plan a trip, perhaps one that is inexpensive, like going camping for the weekend, or an expensive one, like skiing in the Alps. They will be proud to see their plans put into action and they will know that you value their input.

Also, set a good example for your children with your strong work ethic. If there is a decrease in money within the family, this might affect the children negatively, especially if your ex-husband was the primary wage earner. Demonstrate that if your family does not have a lot at the moment, you will be working hard to earn a good standard of living in the future. Tell them you must all pull together in this new family environment and that way you will all succeed. Show your children that it is always possible to start over and be successful.[23]

DIVORCE LATE IN LIFE

You might have been married for a few decades, but you have been incompatible for many years. Maybe you have heard continuous complaints and not heard a compliment in years. Maybe you bicker over small and large things and never seem to agree on what you want from life. You could be tired of him expecting you to handle every aspect of your life together, cook, clean, run errands and balance the bank account, without ever offering to help. You can be miserable about your sex life. No matter what the situation is, it has been going on for so long that hoping that he'll change at this point of his life is useless.

Couples can drift apart over the years. The focus is on the children in the early years, but then they grow up and move out. You and your spouse may have separate jobs and separate hobbies. For the first half of your life, you are just trying to establish yourself, handle your family duties and always on the go. But it is not until the nest is empty that you slow down to think about yourself for a change. That is when you realize that at some point you and your husband went in different directions. You now have completely different needs and wants and he does not know or is not interested in knowing what they are.

If you are the one who is dissatisfied with the marriage, your husband might not understand why you want to end it. While you have been desperate for communication, he might be blissfully unaware that there has ever been a problem. He may believe that he helps out around the house a lot, always remembers your anniversary and does nice things for you quite often. When you tell him you want a divorce, he might want to work things out, whereas you have been done with the relationship for years.

You are going to have to figure out your finances quickly. You want to be sure you get your fair share of the property and assets you jointly own. Women who divorce later in life have less time to recover financially and are usually eligible for alimony. If you were married for at least ten years, you are eligible for part of his retirement plan and can claim benefits on his social security. If you do not remarry, you will also be eligible for survivor benefits when he dies.[24]

You might be surprised to find that your adult children take the news hard. No one expects their parents to divorce after they have been together for many years. Adult children may blame the parent who initiated the divorce or, if cheating is the reason for divorce, they may be angry with the cheating parent. Your children might feel let down, but with time they will come to accept your decision and possibly even see things from your perspective. Conversely, if your marriage was full of constant fighting or abuse, your children might feel relief that it is over.

Now you are single again, perhaps after decades of marriage. You have taken care of everyone else for years, so do something for yourself now. Did you crave new experiences during your marriage when your husband just wanted to watch football? Then go to places you might enjoy, like museums, plays and symphonies. If you have extra money, you could even book a trip abroad. Spend some time reconnecting with old friends or with friends who are also divorced. If your social circle is small, join a social club that meets often. Start new hobbies. It does not matter how long you have been married. You can always start over and build a satisfying single life.

AFTER THE DIVORCE

The first thing you need to figure out after divorce is where you will live. You could stay where you are living now and ask your ex-husband to move out. This can be a good option especially when you've been renting, but if you own an apartment or home, make sure that the mortgage payments are not too high for you. You also might not want to live in the house that is full of memories of your marriage. In many cases, finances can be difficult for you at this time. There is no shame in asking a friend, parents or a family member if you can stay with them for a while. They will understand and most likely will want to support you through your difficult time.

If you stay in your current home, you may want to redecorate to make it look and feel like your own space. Ask your ex-husband to pick one day to move out all of his belongings. On that day, get out of the house and keep yourself occupied with something else. You don't want to get sentimental over old photos or help him move his stuff. Once he and his belongings are gone, enlist some friends to help you redecorate. Rearrange your furniture, paint a few rooms and buy new lamps or drapery. Do whatever you have to do in order to make the place your own special style.[25]

Instead of staying in your current home, you may want to move to a city or to a hipper part of your town. If you lived in suburbia before, you may no longer want to be surrounded by families and married couples. You probably want to live in a place where you can make new friends and try new and exciting things more easily. Living in a fun part of town will allow you to go out dancing, eat at trendy restaurants or take interesting classes. These are great ways to combat loneliness and fill your life with new adventures.

Even after a divorce there is more financial work to do. A good idea would be to change your will so your ex-husband is no longer a beneficiary. If you have ever given him power of attorney on financial or legal matters, find out if it is still valid; if so, act to change it. Also remove him as the decision maker for your health care choices in case of an accident. Cancel any joint credit cards, so you are not equally responsible for his purchases.[26] Remember, financial stability is the first step toward a happily divorced life.

After the divorce, you may run into your ex-husband on occasion. Even if your marriage ended on bad terms, try to be courteous and respectful. You want to be happier now and that can't happen if you get angry at the sight of him. Alternatively, your ex-husband might be extremely hurt about the divorce. He might telephone you or send you e-mails. Even if you two are on good terms, you need your space to heal. On the extreme side, he might lash out in revenge by maxing out joint credit cards, yelling at you during phone calls or even stalking you. If you fear for your safety, do not hesitate to get a restraining order and quickly inform your family and friends about his behavior.[27]

You might have to deal with questions about your divorce for quite a while after it is over. Those close to you will probably have the courtesy to respect your feelings, but your acquaintances may have mixed reactions. Some people will want to know exactly what went wrong. Have a few close friends to confide in, but for everyone else a simple, "It didn't work out" or "It was for the best" response will suffice. Some people might feel sympathy for you, but stay positive and let them know that you are happier than before. Other people might want to set you up on dates. Go for it if you want, but if you are not ready yet, don't feel guilty about declining.

Other people, especially those who are married, might find your new freedom intimidating. Unhappily-married women and couples who have doubts about their own relationships might envy the freedom you have. Some insecure married women might be under the delusion that you are after their husbands. Friends with whom you thought you had a solid relationship might be uneasy about your divorce. They might think that if you can't have a successful marriage, they are not going to be able to either. Try not to worry about how others view your new single status. These folks are most likely worried about their own relationships, not yours.[28]

Part II
Unmarried Women

Chapter 4

Marriage Deliberations

Many twenty-first century women are in enthusiastic pursuit of everlasting love. Undaunted by the discouraging facts and figures presented by statisticians and demographers alike, many women dream of finding their perfect partners, uniting in matrimony, giving birth to beautiful and talented children and living happily ever after. At first glance, these women and society appear infatuated with the idea of matrimonial bliss. Entire industries support the journey toward married life.

Women's hearts and minds may be set on romance and togetherness, but somehow reality offers a very different picture. Modern women feel pressured and confounded about the ideas of dating and marriage. Those who are already involved in meaningful relationships probably wonder how to proceed without risking the loss of their individualities, characters and hard-earned prosperity. While many women insist that getting married is the right thing to do, others are questioning whether the whole concept has become obsolete.

Single women today often find themselves in a dilemma. Though many choose marriage, some are realizing that companionship and/ or parenting can be accommodated in other ways. Although many are charmed by the old-fashioned picture of falling in love, marrying, having children and remaining together with the same partner through old age, the problems of making marriage fulfilling come to mind.

The expense of getting married can no longer be justified when divorce rates are at an all-time high, as we've discussed. Few women today would willingly contemplate a risky work partnership or business venture in which a large influx of cash is invested into a project based on the highly charged and sometimes illogical emotions of the participants. The consequences of these shaky unions often result in hiring expensive lawyers to divide the properties a few years later. Many women ask themselves if they are ready to invest their valuable time and money into a relationship which stands a very good chance of not surviving.

Emily's Story

Emily, one woman I know, struggled with a hostile split after several years of marriage. The previously well-off spouses went through a devastating period of financial austerity during a prolonged and difficult separation and divorce. The outcome reduced both parties to near financial ruin and, in Emily's case, resulted in monetary constraints that affected every aspect of her life.

Emily is not the type of person to remain bitter. However, she regrets her marriage and points out that it was her biggest mistake. "I should never have allowed myself to become so caught up in the whole ideal of marriage," she said to me. "I thought I had found everlasting love, but all I got was heartache and misery. We could have remained close friends, but now there is no affection between us whatsoever." Emily is still working to recover from the financial and emotional effects of this unfortunate incident, but she may never fully make up the economic ground she has lost.

Unfortunately, Emily's experience is not an uncommon result when marriages fail and the breakups are acrimonious. In many cases the matrimonial agreement or marriage contract fails to protect the parties involved. Even if women manage to survive divorce with most of their financial assets intact, they will be emotionally battered. Why, then, do so many women feel compelled to rush into marriage?

Consumer-based society is partially to blame. The costly and extravagant weddings that are presented on television and in popular magazines serve only to remind us of the supposed pinnacle of perfect relationship bliss. Ask yourself: Are you passionate about marriage only because you wish to experience your dream wedding? Is there some other way you can meet this need? After all, one day of extravagant ceremony is no excuse for a lifetime of regret.

Some women find themselves caught up in a wedding ceremony in order to appease their families. Perhaps your mother was unable to fulfill her own wedding aspirations and is hoping to experience the occasion vicariously through your "bliss." Ask yourself: Are you considering getting married because you feel that is what is expected? Remember, this is your valuable life, not anyone else's. Only your own decision that you want to marry should constitute a sufficient rationale for the possibly enormous cost, both financially and emotionally, if the marriage doesn't work out.

Marriage partnerships can be fulfilling or not. Furthermore, the institution of the family has been reworked many times over the years to include a number of options that would have been unimaginable even fifty years ago. Single mothers have proven themselves to be excellent parents and families today come in all formats, including single parents, same-sex couples and blended families.

Social change has influenced the roles of all family members, causing widespread upheaval and interpersonal challenges. Although there are more choices available to women in many countries of the world than ever before, for many women the traditional roles of wives remain more or less the same. The technological advances of the twentieth century combined with the acceptance of women in the workplace have created an uncomfortable balancing act for married women. While single women have the autonomy to control their schedule to include personal needs along with necessary activities of daily living, married women must constantly take the interests of their spouses into account.

Many wives admit that they feel enormously overworked and underappreciated. Although some marriages involve an equal division of housework and childrearing duties, the majority do not. It appears that many married women have gained the responsibility for working extra hard and have little time or energy to fulfill their own desires. Far from lessening the workload, the current social and financial climate demands that most married women earn paychecks out of economic necessity and then return home to complete household responsibilities. Many men, on the other hand, do not experience the same domestic workload or social expectations.

Thus societal change does not necessarily translate into better opportunities when it comes to the institution of marriage. Patriarchal systems of marriage, by their very nature, impede many of the gains made over the years by women in the feminist movement. Subtle shifts in power and authority may appear to benefit women, although many wives will admit that they acquiesce to their partners more often than not in order to keep the peace. While some may argue that women have come a long way since the days when females were considered to be the property of their spouses, others point to the high statistics of domestic violence.

The problem is that while strong, intelligent, empowered women are valued and respected in society, some married women in many countries must cope with strangely archaic systems that tie them to their spouses. It is especially ironic that the values that supposedly bind a couple together in marriage sometimes turn out to be the total opposite of those embraced by modern society. If you are presently contemplating marriage, consider how you and your partner can agree that you both will have the right to self-fulfillment. Remember, you do not have to settle for anything less.

In a shared relationship such as marriage, the needs of a partner must, at times, be placed before one's own. However, it is neither possible nor desirable to eradicate the distinct qualities that make each of the partners unique.

Many modern women privately disapprove of yielding to the priorities of their spouses while struggling with their own expectations and needs. Often these women spend many hours attempting to reconcile the values they perceive to be important in marriage with their own rights and ambitions as modern women.

Lynda's Story

When I met Lynda she was a young and successful thirty-two-year-old businesswoman who was engaged. "This should be the happiest time of my life," she confided, "but I'm actually really worried about getting married." Lynda went on to explain that her fiancé was an engineer who had been working on a local construction project for the past few years. When that job finished, he would need to move to a larger city in order to find more work in his field. "I love him, but I don't want to follow him all over the country," Lynda expressed to me. "I was born in this town and I want to stay here; this is where my friends and family live." Lynda's concerns highlight the challenges facing many married women. It is hard to resolve the needs of both parties equally and one person's requirements are set aside, if they are even considered at all. Lynda was contemplating the huge adjustments she would need to make if her fiancé insisted on following his career path. If she was unwilling or unable to adapt, the marriage would most likely fail.

THE SOCIAL CONSTRUCT OF COMMITMENT

Many women continue to seek romantic relationships that they hope will lead to long-term commitment and marriage. They truly want to believe that love will overcome all ills. While some scoff at the image of a knight on a white horse riding into town and sweeping a woman off her feet, many women still have the wishful concept of eternal love and marital harmony. However, I believe many women who are actively seeking a relationship only with the intent of marriage are actually missing the opportunity to experience a loving relationship with themselves first, which can ensure they remain true to their own needs and desires in future relationships. Love and commitment do not have to be synonymous with marriage and women need to apply these traits to themselves.

In her book, *Against Love: A Polemic*, professor and author Laura Kipnis points out that falling in love in our society is inexplicably linked to handing oneself over to commitment. She argues that women are so accustomed to the traditional progression of love and marriage, that they are unable to imagine any other options. Kipnis notes that marital commitment is merely a social construct. She sees matrimony as just one of many relationship alternatives and even notes other options such as a yearly renewable contract.[1]

Kipnis also discusses the perils of over-commitment, especially involving those women enmeshed in a destructive cycle of domestic violence. Women are usually abused by someone they know. An estimated 1.3 million women each year will likely suffer from physical abuse from their partners and one in every four women will be a victim of domestic violence in her lifetime.[2] Other equally destructive forms of mistreatment, such as sexual, financial and emotional abuse, also take their tolls, creating lifelong damage and personal heartaches. Sometimes leaving an abusive relationship can be so difficult for battered women who find themselves overinvested in the marriage that they can risk themselves to maintain the destructive unions with their abusers. But no woman should ever feel trapped in a relationship in which she fears for herself.

There has never been a better time to consider the option of remaining single in Western society. The demographics of America are changing rapidly and a larger number of women than ever before are choosing to remain single and at a later age. If you are contemplating the bold decision to stay away from marriage, you are in good company. The underlying social structure of America is changing faster than ever. The remarkable thing about this particular transformation is that these profound changes are taking place in an environment of economic turbulence, relationship instability and cultural tension. While uncertain times have been known to promote a return to the traditional values of the past, many women are welcoming the opportunity to enter a new era—one in which single women are rightfully proud of their status and their accomplishments.

Yet there is a deep divide between the values held by many and the reality within society today. It often appears that women are either unaware of this gap or choose to ignore it. In spite of all the advances women have made over the years, many still pursue the old-fashioned goals of love and marriage with grave and unwavering determination.

This volatile situation is complicated further by the very nature of many marital relationships. Demographics reveal that most women experience brief relationships with multiple partners in the course of their lifetimes, through circumstances such as divorce, death and extramarital affairs. Compared with other Western countries, Americans engage in numerous relationships much more frequently. While bonding with a single lifelong partner may be the goal, women instead are quick to marry, divorce and remarry.[3] This results in multiple short-term associations with different people, creating numerous and fragile connections instead of one distinct and long-lasting romantic partnership.

The question for single women in America today becomes one of priorities. If women are no longer confined to traditional choices regarding relationships and marriage and end up in multiple relationships anyway, why are women choosing to marry at all? Part of the answer may lie with the cultural expectations that persist throughout society. In the United States, marriage is seen as the culmination of the American dream and there is tremendous social pressure on young women to adhere to this. Although this view is unrealistic and outdated, women are still expected to marry.

However, it is not just the expectations of families and peers that influence this desire. Politics, too, have poor boundaries when it comes to the covenant of marriage. In his book, *The Marriage-Go-Round*, Dr. Andrew Cherlin, professor of sociology and public policy at Johns Hopkins, discusses the manner in which politicians have attempted to influence voters through the endorsement of heterosexual marriage. According to Cherlin, United States Government policy has been used to attract voters through the promotion of its own particular version of the cultural ideal of marriage.[4]

There are other societal changes that have contributed to the problems facing marital relationships. For instance, United States family law no longer focuses on the institution of marriage. Instead, the individual needs of each person are given precedence, which makes sense when you consider that individual rights and freedom are valued in America.[5] The legal needs and rights of children are foremost (although good intentions do not necessarily translate into positive action) and spousal obligations are more likely to be directed toward the children than each other. The institution of marriage is no longer supported by the same social values and legal rights as in the past.

What does all this mean for the average American and Western European woman today? Women owe it to themselves to stop and examine why they are so anxious to commit to marriage. They need to ask themselves: If there was a better option available, would I choose to get married at all?

A BRIEF LOOK AT THE PAST

Modern culture would have us believe that the practice of monogamy has occupied the hearts and minds of married couples for an eternity. But this lifestyle choice is a fairly recent event, the outcome of living in a society in which people aspire to more than just survival. Before the eighteenth century, marriages resulted from agreements between families out of economic necessity. The concept of marriage was based on the need for financial and household stability. Wives were regarded as the property of their husbands and the idea of marital romance was nonexistent. Passionate romance was something that took place outside of marriage and often was reserved for the privileged upper class. Women's rights were unheard of at that time and most complaints about adultery were based upon the idea that someone had infringed upon the personal belongings of the rejected husband.[6]

In the early and middle nineteenth century, the institution of marriage actually made a good deal of sense. In those days, many families farmed the land. This was hard labor and required lots of hands-on help. There was an endless supply of physically exhausting chores and the continued existence of people was dependent upon the successful completion of such daily tasks. There were crops to be planted, tended and harvested, farm animals to be cared for, food to be prepared, homes to be built and constant domestic jobs to ensure that the family was looked after. The old saying "many hands make light work" complemented the idea of joining together with someone in a lifelong partnership. A married woman not only provided her spouse with many children to help with the farmwork, but also contributed her own valuable skills, often supplying physical labor in situations where survival meant everyone pulled together. Pioneer women needed to be tough.[7]

In those days, life was generally difficult and short. The advances in health and medicine that we take for granted today didn't exist even a century ago. Infectious diseases were commonplace and usually fatal, with three leading causes of death being pneumonia, tuberculosis and diarrhea.[8] Sanitation and public hygiene were often sorely lacking, therefore many people became severely ill from waterborne diseases. A simple accident on the farm could have catastrophic consequences, as even limited medical assistance might be many miles away. The average lifespan for men and women in 1900 was 47.9 and 50.7 years respectively.[9] Therefore, the marriage union during that era was not usually a lengthy affair.

Things are much different in the twenty-first century. Because of science, health and medical discoveries, the average lifespan has lengthened greatly. Thanks to the much-needed achievements of the Women's Liberation Movement, women today have more opportunities to follow their educational aspirations and embark upon careers of their choosing. Women are more than capable of supporting themselves and their children, if necessary, while benefiting from the same freedom and independence that men have enjoyed throughout history. Strong, happy and financially capable women are thriving today. Traditional marriage is dying out.

The vast majority of women reside in urban centers nowadays; they experience a far different lifestyle from the one pioneer women faced. Women no longer need to commit large amounts of time to the rigors of outdoor survival, choosing instead to exercise when and how they want. As well, women's release from the bonds of producing and caring for offspring for the purpose of providing farm laborers has been facilitated by the availability of birth control. Women's life expectancy is now 81 years, providing them with a prolonged period of time in which they can nurture themselves and grow into mature, fully developed and happy individuals.[10] Most women yearn to reach beyond the day-to-day grind of mere existence and aim instead for higher goals in life, striving to attain their true potential.

FALLING IN AND OUT OF LOVE

The prevalence of the multiple partnerships that appear to constitute the relationship patterns of many Americans and Western Europeans today points to some dissatisfaction with the romantic concept of marriage. Falling in love when young is easy to do.

From a biological perspective, both men and women are well endowed with the physiological capabilities that enable them to make babies and maintain the population. While these reproductive qualities are beneficial to the survival of our species, they can be surprisingly misleading when it comes to selecting a lifelong partner. Many people have had the experience of a brief youthful infatuation, which years later seems inexplicable and somewhat repugnant. But people should not consider the possibility of entering into a lifelong partnership with someone while in their teens. Yet that is exactly what women are doing through the act of marriage.

As people's bodies change and mature, they may find themselves less attracted sexually to the partners to whom they are married. At the same time, everyday life stressors start to wear down their reserves for coping with the individual quirks and inevitable shortcomings of their partners. Personal compatibility becomes an issue.

At this time extramarital affairs can occur, causing enormous damage to the relationship, untold suffering to family members (especially the children) and permanently wounding the souls of everyone involved.

At this point, the marital relationship can go one of two different ways. In many cases, one or both spouses view divorce as the only solution—a definitive end to an uneasy alliance gone wrong. In other instances, the couple attempts to stay together, often for the sake of the children. They may seek therapists in order to "work" at their relationship. However, the problem still exists that the romance has gone. The original spark that attracted them to each other has dimmed or gone out. For many people, the love they experienced at the outset is not there anymore.

Gender differences can also wreak havoc on long-term relationships, illustrating another reason to reconsider the marriage bond in the first place. Although it is easy to fall into the trap of making sweeping generalizations and stereotyping, men and women are "wired differently." Attempting to form an emotionally based union with a male partner who may not prioritize emotional closeness to the same degree as a woman does is likely to lead to conflict and misunderstanding in an intimate relationship.

Complicating matters further, dissimilar communication styles cause frustration, as men are frequently less skilled in articulation and may come across as thoughtless or detached. These gender differences or even personality differences often result in men and women working toward different objectives.

Some women are anxious to prove that they can handle commitment and matrimony better than their mothers and fathers. They may remember intense arguments and childhoods split miserably between two different homes and they may be determined to manage things better themselves. One of the problems with this sort of pro-marriage reasoning is that it is based on an attempt to right the wrongs of the past, instead of a desire to make the right choice in the present.

The fighting and disruption produced by separation and divorce causes the most trauma for children. By focusing on the unresolved issues of their own childhoods, some women ignore the fact that what children need most is a loving and stable environment. However, this need can be satisfied in many different ways and through a number of diverse family combinations.

There are women who anticipate falling in love and getting married and who base their expectations on the fact that this was most likely the same vision embraced by their parents. Women may find themselves weighing the pros and cons of getting married in order to appease their relatives instead of prioritizing their own futures. These same family members may attempt to guide a woman with their misplaced worries over the woman's well-being should she choose to remain single. "Won't you be lonely?" frustrated parents demand of their daughters, despite the fact that these women are popular, altruistic and surround themselves with a circle of equally caring and generous friends. This sort of well-meaning but overblown concern emphasizes the undercurrent of disapproval that follows many women who choose to stay single. Indeed, there might be something unsettling about breaking tradition, a feeling of dread that women are somehow not measuring up to the hopes of their forebears. Contrast this with the exhilaration felt by the brave women who understand that they do not have to follow in the footsteps of their family members in order to live productive, fulfilling and contented lives.

Many American and Western European women and those in other countries around the world like China are becoming increasingly comfortable with the idea of staying single. Marriage today does not have to be the unequivocal choice for women. Because of advances in science, technology, career and educational opportunities, financial independence and even public opinion, women who choose a single lifestyle can experience all the benefits of a well-lived and authentic life while remaining genuine and true to themselves. The choice to remain single is theirs to make.

Chapter 5

Unmarried Women in Happy Relationships

Deciding that the antiquated institution of marriage is not for you does not mean that you cannot take full pleasure in long, committed, deep and authentic relationships. On the contrary, many women have found that not marrying actually makes their romantic relationships stronger. By not trying to fit a personal relationship into such a rigid structure as marriage, not only can you give both the relationship and yourself room to evolve and adapt naturally over time, but also you can avoid the costly, often ugly and probable outcome of divorce.

WHY MARRIAGE CREATES MORE PROBLEMS THAN IT SOLVES

Why do some women feel the need to drag either a legal system or a religious institution into a personal relationship? While it would seem downright absurd to demand that your best friend sign a document committing to being your friend until death do you part, many women do not hesitate or find it strange at all to ask that of their romantic partners. How does involving a judge or a church in your relationship make it a more valid commitment? With friends, you relax and trust that the love you share is something that will grow and evolve over time and that you will handle any issues that come up with respect and understanding to the best of your ability. You give friends space to grow, to explore and to enjoy the company of other friends.

By putting a title on a romantic relationship, especially one with such deeply-ingrained cultural and moral connotations such as *husband* and *wife*, I feel women engage in relationships with vast expectations as to how they should progress and automatically place restrictive rules, either consciously or subconsciously, on how both partners should act. Many couples who have stayed together happily for years without marrying state that one of the reasons for the success of their relationships is their willingness to adapt, to expect and allow room for change in both individuals and to take every day as an opportunity to assess and redefine the relationship, to address what both partners need at that moment. Both know that there is no written or formal guarantee that they will be together forever, so there is an urgency to live every moment to the fullest, never to take the other partner for granted and to address small problems as they arise.

Author Kahlil Gibran gave very wise advice when he wrote in his book, *The Prophet*, "Love one another, but make not a bond of love: Let it rather be a moving sea between the shores of your souls."[1] In a traditional marriage, many try so hard to put love into a rigid structure and guard it so strongly to make sure that the love does not leave that they end up suffocating each other. Another perspective is instead to take the opportunity to enjoy the unconditional love that is present and if things change in the future, to flow with that evolution. In a structured and rigid relationship, when a partner does not fit exactly into society's strict mold of what a good spouse should look like, it seems almost easier at times to say that the marriage is broken and move on to a divorce, instead of allowing for flexibility.

Reflect on the depressing reality: According to the United States Census Bureau, it is estimated that 40 percent of all marriages end in divorce. On average, first marriages that end in divorce last a mere eight years, a far cry from the expectations of most women on their wedding days, namely, that they will grow old with their cherished and beloved grooms. And it doesn't seem like the lessons are learned very well, because 49 percent of weddings involve a remarriage of one or both spouses, with the median time between divorce and a second marriage only at about three and a half years. The statistics become increasingly more depressing for each successive marriage, with 65 percent of second marriages ending in divorce and even higher rates for third marriages and beyond.[2]

Why continue to waste time, money and energy on an institution that is failing? I strongly believe empowered women with sharp critical thinking skills have the ability to see beyond the blinding fairy tale dream of the white dress and the golden anniversary to see the bleak reality that there is a huge chance that their future involves time in an expensive divorce court.

With the average divorce these days costing upwards of fifteen thousand dollars for a contested divorce and much more if there are children involved, it would seem to make more sense to avoid the possibility of finding oneself in the common divorce situation.[3] And what is the biggest cause of divorce? Marrying in the first place. With no wedding, there can never be an ugly and expensive divorce. Wouldn't it make more sense to invest that fifteen thousand dollars in your education or in your retirement fund to secure your future? If you had fifteen thousand dollars in a bank account and someone told you that you had a 40 percent chance of throwing it away, you would shake your head in disbelief at anyone who would accept the risk. Yet that is exactly how women are risking their hard-earned money the moment they decide to tie the knot.

Andrew Cherlin, author of the book *The Marriage-Go-Round: The State of Marriage and the Family in America*, explains how although the United States places more value on traditional marriage than any other Western nation, making it almost a hallmark of a successful life, it also has the highest divorce rate. This "merry-go-round," characterized by the great turbulence of frequent marriage, frequent divorce and more short-term cohabiting relationships than in other Western nations, creates great instability, not only for individuals, but also for society at large. In contrast, explains Cherlin, Sweden has much lower rates of marriage, but its couples stay together for much longer periods of time. Also, a child of an unmarried couple in Sweden has a much lower chance of seeing his parents separate than a child of married parents in the United States.[4]

While much of modern society, including governmental and religious institutions, preaches marriage as an important staple of stability and success in personal life, the raw facts and harsh reality of such a staggering divorce rate and quick remarriage rate show that buying into the concept of marriage leaves something to be desired in the quest for stability. There is a certain irony in the fact that most women walk down the aisle with high hopes and expectations that they have not only sanctified but also stabilized their lives through committing to this institution, when in reality the very probable subsequent divorce may be one of the most upheaving and difficult experiences they will go through in their lives.

Modern women have made great strides in the past decades and have proven that they can thrive financially on their own. For the first time in history, women are half of the nation's workers in America and high percentages in other countries like Finland and France. Many are the sole breadwinners in their households.[5] In more than eighty fields, women make equal or higher salaries than their male counterparts.[6] Whereas in the past a woman usually had to marry to ensure her financial security, the prospect of signing a marriage contract can now do much more harm than good when it comes to her finances and it can make much more sense financially for two partners not to marry.

While there are some tax benefits for married couples, overall, according the MSN Money article "7 tax reasons not to get married," filing singly is more beneficial. If two singles live together, each earning a yearly salary, they can both file singly in a lower tax bracket. If the partners were to marry, they would have to claim the total of their two salaries, likely pushing their taxable income up a bracket and forcing them to pay a higher percentage. Also, since more Social Security payments become subject to tax as a person's claimed total income increases, with a second income added "as much as 85 percent of your Social Security receipts are potentially taxable." The article also states that "depending on the numbers, in many cases two unmarried individuals receive more in Social Security benefits than they would if they were married."[7] So in the United States, for instance, it can be more profitable to stay legally single.

Further on a financial note, one of the leading causes for divorce is issues over money.[8] Many unmarried long-term couples sidestep this issue by keeping their finances separate. Not mingling pocketbooks means that it is much more difficult to fight over decisions made about money, which helps keep peace in the relationship. More than a third of all homes are now owned individually by women and most women would never jeopardize their hard-earned assets by legally sharing with men whom they may not be with ten years in the future.[9] A case could be made for making a prenuptial agreement to avoid future disagreements, but if one already has to imagine that divorce may be the outcome of the marriage, why bother?

HOW SINGLE WOMEN CAN BE HAPPY AND FULFILLED

Many of the notions that women have about the fairy tale of marriage are either spoon-fed to us by the sixty-billion-dollar-a-year wedding industry or have been reinforced in us since childhood by parents or grandparents.[10] It is important to take a step back and look at both of these powerful influences, to analyze if women really need a white dress to be fulfilled and satisfied with themselves and their partners.

Times have changed dramatically since women's grandmothers and mothers got married. While family may have only the best of intentions for women, older generations' situations are not like the unique experience of women living and dating in the twenty-first century. Whereas women in the past faced very difficult and intense societal repercussions for being sexually active or having children out of wedlock and were expected to be satisfied by marrying men who brought home paychecks so their wives could be free to stay at home, today's women have been granted much more flexibility to date whom they choose, to decide to have and raise children with or without a husband or partner and to be the sole breadwinner of a household—all outside the confines of marriage.

It could be argued that some of the main reasons to get married are to attempt to create stability, to ensure some form of sexual exclusivity with one person and to provide a framework and structure in which to raise children. However, as revealed, marriage can actually create a tumultuous instability as life unfolds for many couples, so let's look at some of the other issues.

Grandmothers may cringe at the idea, but one of the most striking variables that has changed over the last few decades is that fewer women in relationships are automatically buying into the idea of monogamy as the only morally acceptable option to express their sexuality. It is true that while there is still a large number of women who choose to sleep with only one partner and are honestly content with that choice, many others are exploring the idea that there may be more than one way to create personal fulfillment within the confines of a romantic relationship. Malcolm Potts, an expert on the biology of sex at the University of California, Berkeley, states that monogamy is a relatively recent intent in civilized history. Genetic evidence suggests that by nature we are not monogamous mammals, yet we try to be, due to strong cultural impositions.[11]

In the past, women often established monogamy as an ideal for themselves and their partners and insisted on it. Many of these are women who aimed to wear white wedding gowns, stubbornly wanting to stay virgins until their wedding nights. But now the lines have been blurred. At the World Congress of Sexology in Montreal, noted sociologist Pepper Schwarz, a professor at the University of Washington in Seattle, explained that around 25 percent of women ages eighteen to twenty-four are sleeping with more than one man at any given time. Almost 80 percent of women today are very sexually active by the time they are twenty.[12]

Modern women are more sexually liberated than ever before and are less likely to give up this freedom that they have become accustomed to by marrying. Outside of the constricting confines of a traditional marriage, a woman has an easier time maintaining her power and choice to spend time romantically with or to sleep with whom she chooses and when she chooses.

Many women who are in relationships but have not fallen into the marriage trap realize that, for some, it is unlikely that one partner could fulfill all their desires, which are not all sexual. A modern woman may enjoy fabulous sex with one man, yet adore how a different man listens to her after a hard day of work and may love how another man she spends time with knows how to cook all her favorite foods. Why should she have to choose? Why should she limit herself to one person for the rest of her life, naïvely buying into the fairy-tale notion that one person will provide everything that she wants and needs until the day she dies? That's a lot of pressure to put on one person; when one or both partners in a marriage realize that it is not likely that they can be everything for each other for life, it is no wonder so many marriages fail.

While one man may seem to fulfill your needs currently, it is natural that people evolve, grow and change. Thus the man who suits your needs today may do nothing for the woman you will be in ten years. So why lock both him and yourself in a marriage? By erasing the need for a white dress and marriage certificate, you are free to enjoy a man as he is currently. You will not be constantly examining every man as a potential husband. By taking that stress off both you and him, you allow the relationship to flow more freely, without any extraneous and unnecessary pressure. Actress Cameron Diaz put it well when she stated simply, "Who would want to be with the same person for eighty years? Why not break it up a bit? Have someone who suits you great for five years, then another person that fits you well for another five years."[13]

In my opinion, the decision to bear children and the decision to be in a romantic partnership with someone can very well be two completely separate issues to manage. If you plan to marry a guy for the sole reason that you want to have a father for your children, you can forget about romance and would be better off choosing a man who will be a good father and a good friend to you during the years when you will need the most help. But if you are going to focus on the children's best interests, a wedding resulting from imagined necessity does nothing for them. A husband who one day realizes that he has been fulfilling no other role than to be your baby daddy will most likely resent you and probably move to extramarital affairs, which is not the best environment for your children. Worst case scenario is a divorce and vicious custody battle, which is probably not what you had in mind when you married for the goal of becoming a mother.

Shotgun weddings are less and less common. In the *Time* article "Who Needs Marriage? A Changing Institution," author Belinda Luscombe states that "41% of babies were born to unmarried moms in 2008, an eightfold increase from 50 years ago." Additionally, Lucombe says 25 percent of children are now being raised in single-parent homes, which is "almost triple the number from 1960."[14] Having a child outside of wedlock has become, in many cases, a choice. In my opinion, society needs to adapt fairly quickly. Never before have women had such strong support for having a child, either with the involvement of the father or not. Many employers now offer more flexibility to single mothers and often allow them to work from home during the first few years. Other employers have implemented childcare centers in their office buildings to accommodate the special needs of today's families. A number of women who have not found their needs met by their employers have branched out on their own as entrepreneurs so that they can arrange for the needs of both their careers and their children. The days when having a child automatically meant staying at home are past.

Thus if you choose to have a child with your current stable romantic partner and forego marriage, you will not be alone. Belinda Luscombe goes on to relay research from the Fragile Families and Child Wellbeing Study that found "more than half of the unmarried parents were living together at the time their child was born and 30% of them were romantically involved (but living apart).[15] A child raised in a happy partnership, regardless if that partnership is an official marriage or not, fares much better than a child raised in a marriage that was instigated just because of a pregnancy.

I feel that consciously making the choice not to marry has, in my opinion, no impact on your ability to enjoy deep and profound relationships with men. Long gone are the days of the set formula of dating, marrying, having sex, having children and staying at home with them. Modern, empowered women know that healthy and fulfilling relationships come in many distinct forms and what works well for one woman or one family may not guarantee the same success for another woman. Likewise, what worked for one's mother or grandmother may be outdated and irrelevant in today's quickly changing world.

Little by little, many women have been acknowledging the fact that marriage is an artificial social and cultural phenomenon, a sixty-billion-dollar-a-year industry in the United States alone. With such profits at stake, messages come from all over, in magazines, television programs and commercials, movies and storefronts, selling the idea that women need this gadget or this ring or this dress to "know that he will be yours for life" or to "live the fairy tale that you have dreamed of since you were a little girl." But modern women can see through the slick advertising and realize that a more stable and realistic relationship focuses on the present day-to-day rather than decades in the future and that fairy tales come with many different adventures and endings and not all include a $27,800 (on average) walk down the aisle.[16]

Modern women should be aware that marriage is a moot point when it comes to their abilities to be financially secure and independent. Although they may choose to be monogamous, it will be because of what they think is the most positive decision for themselves and their partners. They will not blindly agree to monogamy just to comply with society's unforgiving moral code that originated in much different times. We're seeing today that many women who feel maternal longings carry the skills and strengths to raise happy and healthy children, with or without men. A happy and fulfilled woman can often provide stability outside of the bounds of marriage that some children of married parents will never have the good fortune of experiencing.

I feel modern-day women should conclude that marriage can be oppressive, archaic and holds the risk of a lot of hassle, expense and unnecessary social pressure to conform to a mold. Instead, women should put their time and energy into cultivating strong and healthy personal relationships that are built on love, mutual respect and support of individual growth, instead of on a stamped piece of paper authorized by the government.

Chapter 6

Unmarried Women
in Unhappy Relationships

Unfortunately, all of us know at least one woman in our lives who wants to be married at all costs yet is unhappy with either her partner or the level of commitment that her partner wants to give her. If this woman happens to be you, you are settling for mediocrity and you deserve better than that. Often, a woman who settles has been fed the fairy tale ideal since a young age: the notion that her gorgeous prince charming will appear one day to sweep her off her feet, wait for her with a kiss at the end of the church aisle, be by her side faithfully until the day she dies and make her feel beautiful, sexy, smart, funny and completely and profoundly fulfilled each day of their life together. What's wrong with this picture?

Women who search endlessly for princes are relying on many unrealistic details coming together flawlessly and expecting their personal happiness to come from an external event, as opposed to using their own time and energy to cultivate happiness and fulfillment from within. There is little chance of all of these details coming together and in the meantime women are frustrated that life does not go as planned in their dreams. They might spend precious time desperately trying to make whatever man comes along play the main character in their fantasies. In reality, men do not necessarily respond well to pressure of this sort and should not hold sole responsibility for making sure women feel good about themselves. A man who marries this type of fantasy-driven woman will probably end up disappointing her deeply, as no human could possibly live up to her unrealistic expectations and naïve dreams.

PROBLEMS IN AN UNHAPPY RELATIONSHIP

Many women are in unhappy relationships, yet for some reason seem to hold on to the idea that their boyfriends will someday marry them and all will magically come together for them and their partners. Many unmarried women are deeply frustrated by their partners' unwillingness to make an official commitment, but because of financial, physical or emotional dependence on their partners, they are reluctant to leave the relationships. Alternatively, pressures from society, family or themselves stress that it is better to have someone than to be alone. This keeps many women in relationships which do not fulfill them.

Courtney's Story

Courtney, a thirty-five-year-old sales manager, has two sisters who, in the last three years, both had large traditional weddings and seem to be the happiest they have ever been. Courtney has also seen how much joy the weddings gave her parents. The attention is now on Courtney, who has pressure from both herself and her family to marry. Courtney grew up with the belief that only very undesirable women with "something wrong" with them don't end up married by her age and she desperately does not want to visualize herself in this category. Though Courtney has been dating the same man for five years, when she is honest with herself, she knows that she is with him more for convenience and out of habit than anything else. She is not physically attracted to him, but he is kind and seems the best available candidate to fulfill her need for marriage. He seems to be her easiest, quickest and most logical ticket to a wedding. Also, she is frightened to separate and reenter the dating pool. She feels she would rather stay in a mediocre relationship that gives her some hope of marrying than open herself up to searching for a new relationship that genuinely fulfills her. She is filled with insecurities and because of this is willing to settle for a mediocre life that she knows does not fulfill her.

What is it about wanting to be married that entices some women to stay in relationships when they are not happy? Many times it is fear: fear of not keeping up with their girlfriends, who all seem to be getting married; fear that they will grow old alone if they let go of their current companions; fear that they will not be able to support themselves financially; fear that they will not be desirable enough to find another sexual partner; fear that society will label them defective if they are single, especially after a certain age. If this portrait sounds a little too close to your own, you need to take a good honest look at the pressures that you are allowing to control your life, from both exterior sources and yourself.

There comes a point when you need enough self-love and self-respect not to settle for any relationship where you are less than absolutely happy. You deserve much more than mediocrity. The worst thing that you can do is resolve to attain a dream that is more than likely not ever going to become realized. It is better to cut your losses as quickly as possible so that you can begin building and creating a life for yourself that is supportive and healthy from all angles.

Look at it from the other point of view also. How cruel is it to marry a guy when secretly you are more in love with the idea of being married than you are in love with him? When you walk down the aisle, he probably assumes that he is the man of your dreams. What good could come when one day he realizes that you just wanted to be married and it didn't really matter to whom? The only person who can give you a stable sense of happiness is yourself and the more time you spend waiting for it to come from someone else, the more years of your life you waste not living up to your true potential.

What is it about the idea of marriage that you feel you would gain in your relationship? Do you equate marriage with serious life-long commitment from your partner? Remember, 40 percent of marriages in America and many other countries end in divorce and in many other unhappy marriages one partner is unfaithful. A marriage certificate offers no guarantee that your partner will be committed or faithful to you. Additionally, of the many marriages that end in divorce, most end after an average of eight years, so the dreams of getting married and growing old with a partner are not very realistic either. Regarding the fear of dying alone, if a marriage happens to last a woman's whole life, which is unrealistic according to the statistics, there is a good chance the woman will outlive the man. Actor George

Clooney made a good point in *Singular Magazine*. He said, "People always go, 'Aren't you afraid of being alone or dying alone?' And I just go, 'I've also been in relationships where I've been shockingly alone.'"[1] We need to realize that *alone* does not necessarily mean *lonely*, just as we need to understand that being in a relationship does not necessarily equate to fulfillment.

If you fear that you cannot leave a relationship for financial reasons, you are underestimating your capabilities. There are millions of women in the world who support themselves, no matter what their education, age, race or previous work experience may be. You too can find a good job and a fulfilling career. Not only are you more than capable of providing for yourself, but also statistics show that single women can actually make more than their married counterparts. In a "RAND Labor and Population," cited in Leanne Coffman's article "Why Some Women Prefer to Be Single," researchers estimated that "women's hourly wages increased by 4 percent for each year they delayed marriage." That increase came to a halt if a woman married, as her career focus often lessened or was put aside.[2] Indeed, according to an article published by *The Economist*, married women's climbing to the top in careers was compromised by the issue of family and child caretaking affecting women's pay.[3]

By not obsessing over marriage and not waiting for financial support from someone else, a woman will have a lot of energy to invest in making money in her life's passion. The pride that she will gain and the respect that she will have for herself once she proves to herself that she can be financially independent and not just survive, but also thrive, will be worth more to her than a second income from a man she stays with even though she is unhappy.

Stacy's Story

Stacy, who was in a committed relationship for fourteen years, is a perfect example of creating profound happiness after detaching from a mediocre relationship. Stacey had three children with her partner. Her partner was a very successful real estate investor who was able to give her a luxurious lifestyle that many women desire. She had a large house in the suburbs, a new car, expensive clothes and a lot of free time. The income also made it possible for her to stay at home with her children when they were young, which was very important to her.

But as the years passed she started to become aware of the fact that, although she was superficially content and had all of her basic financial needs met, her life felt empty. She had always dreamed of a life of travel and adventure, learning something new every day, yet as the children grew older she found that her days had somehow become filled with manicures and drinking coffee, making idle chat with people who really did not inspire her.

All of her friends and family told her that she was foolish when she mentioned she was thinking of leaving her partner, who was a great father and businessman and who treated her well. But after fourteen years they hardly communicated and spent little time together. Stacy felt as though she had stopped developing as a person and she desperately wanted to feel inspired again. She realized that no one could do that for her; she alone was responsible for creating her own happiness and spark.

Outside of teaching some yoga classes and selling a few fine art photos in a gallery, Stacy had never had a job, nor had to support herself, so the idea of leaving her safety net was incredibly scary for her. She left their home with no money but with a lot of stubborn willpower and the conviction that she deserved more out of life. In the interim, she and her children were able to move in with a friend while she got her plans together. She found a job and rented a house in the next months. Within a year she started a business and established herself as a successful tour guide and started meeting people from all over the world. She was able to travel with her children, but most importantly, she had proven to herself that by letting go of mediocrity, one sets the intention and can make space for something even greater to come. Reflecting back, Stacy wonders how she had let herself live those years in her relationship feeling so reliant on someone else. While the new path was not always easy, it is clear to her now that her struggle for freedom and independence, even on its hardest day, has led to a more fulfilling and enjoyable life. Stacey's case shows us that you can have children, work and continue to go after your dreams without getting married.

A reason that some women automatically think they need to marry is because they always imagined themselves having children. In their preconceived notion of motherhood, they have always pictured the father by their side. But the reality is that women need to differentiate the notion of being a mother from the notion of being a wife. They are two different relationships that do not necessarily have to have to overlap or intertwine.

More than ever before in history, it is acceptable and normal for a single woman to have a baby. With adoption, in vitro fertilization and artificial insemination, any woman dedicated to the idea of raising a child can do so, with or without a husband. Being a single mom no longer carries a certain negative stigma in society. Among nations with the highest rates of children being raised by single mothers, the United Kingdom has 27.6 percent of children living with single mothers, Belgium 19.5 percent, Sweden 18 percent, Lithuania 21 percent, the Czech Republic 17.4 percent, France 17 percent and Germany 16.3 percent.[4] As stated by a report from the United States Census Bureau, there are approximately 13.7 million single parents in the United States alone, raising 21.8 million children, and 34.2 percent of single moms have never been married.[5] Tackling the challenges of being a single mom does not mean a woman must leave a job to raise a child or be dependent on food stamps or public housing assistance. According to the United States Census Bureau, 79.5 percent of single moms maintain their careers after children are born, only 23.5 percent receive food stamps and a mere 12 percent receive federal housing assistance.[6] It appears that the modern single mom can make her own way and knows with confidence that she does not need a husband to support either her or any children she wants to raise.

Evidently, the trends are changing from when the typical woman got married, stayed at home and had children. Nowadays, many parents and grandparents, who are experiencing spiteful and costly divorces themselves, will support and understand a woman's decision to stay single.

Being single is becoming mainstream and is not something of which to be ashamed. A Pew Research Center study found that most singles are not actively looking for a committed relationship: 55 percent of 3,200 adults eighteen and older surveyed reported no interest in a relationship, that they were not in a relationship and were not looking to be in a relationship. Specifically, in the age group of eighteen to twenty-nine, a cohort that, in the past, society thought should be at least partnered if not married, 38 percent said they weren't looking for a partner at all.[7]

Businesses have begun to take note of the fact that there are 92 million single people over the age of eighteen in the United States and that this market has more influence than ever before.[8] Major companies are now directing their services not just at brides, but also at the millions of other single women who have spending power. Companies have set up registry systems available to women to register for birthdays, housewarming events and other special occasions. Many travel companies now offer popular tours and cruises directed specifically at the single crowd, whereas in the past all the emphasis was on couple's vacations or honeymoon getaways.

Media publications written with the single lifestyle in mind are popping up all over the place, with names such as *Being Single Magazine*, *Single Edition*, *SoloMag* and *Singular Magazine*. These magazines showcase that making the choice to be single can be a change for the positive, not a negative. Articles address how to cook for one, how to select the perfect gift for other singles and how to manage juggling a household and career on one's own. If you are afraid to get out of a mediocre relationship to be single, you only have to peruse these publications to see many examples of single women leading healthy, happy, fulfilling lives.

Many women explain how branching out on their own after mediocre relationships pushed them to grow and develop. They had more free time, which forced them to find and discover new hobbies and passions. It also drove them to move outside their typical circles of friends. Many women in relationships spend free time with their partners. Without that obligation, women meet wonderful people who help them to grow and enjoy activities that they otherwise might not have.

Often, women are tentative about ending their relationships, no matter how unhappy they may be, because they cannot visualize themselves reentering the dating or singles scene. They do not look forward to going to clubs or bars or maneuvering through lame pick-up lines. But this is limited thinking. Who says that single women should be doing everything in their power to move quickly to the next relationship?

Open your mind to the possibility of spending your time working on your mind and body, doing things that make your soul wake up, that make you feel alive and that stretch your mind. If you like to travel, realize that you can get in your car or on a plane any time you like without having to ask permission from a partner and you will never have to compromise on the destination. If you always wanted to try gardening, plant a flower garden and fill your house with cut flowers as an expression of love to yourself. You deserve it! Women are often taught that to do such things for yourself is self-centered or egotistic. But modern single women know that a strong and happy woman who truly takes care of and nourishes herself in every moment has more energy and happiness to offer the people around her and society.

Single women may actually have an advantage over single men when it comes to not feeling lonely without a romantic partner. In general, men do not form deep bonds with others quickly. A woman, on the other hand, will fill that temporary feeling of void after a breakup with very close and profound relationships with other women or male friends. Analyses by sociologist Naomi Gerstel, Univeristy of Massachusetts, Amherst, and Natalia Sarkisian, Boston College, published by the American Sociological Association, show that marriage actually reduces social ties. Many married couples only spend their free time with each other, while single folks tend to spend their time among a wider and more diverse circle of friends. Sarkisian's study also found that married women have less contact with their parents than their single counterparts.[9]

There are endless benefits to breaking out of a mediocre relationship where you hope to fulfill yourself through a wedding. A woman doesn't need to wait for a man or a ring to begin to lead an intensely satisfying and full life, often much more satisfying than if in a relationship. It is understandable, though, that breaking out of the mindset that marriage is the ultimate goal for a woman could be unsettling and maybe a little scary for some. But it is important to realize that being single hardly means being half a person or living half a life. Women need to have confidence in themselves that they are strong, capable people who know that their personal happiness is their own responsibility and no one else's. Especially for women who have spent their lives with partners and have learned to rely on someone else for emotional or financial support, learning to deal effectively with problems alone can be a huge boost to self-esteem, self-confidence and sense of self-worth. Psychology professor Richard Lucas of Michigan State University analyzed twenty years of data and related that those individuals who never married actually reported the highest rate of well-being.[10]

In today's world, traditional marriage and its byproducts such as monogamy and the insistence on a nuclear family are no longer required for sharing a life with a loved one, if that is what women desire. We have seen that a marriage certificate has no bearing on the ability to share a deep love and offers no guarantee of commitment, faithfulness or lifetime happiness. A modern and empowered woman wisely chooses to spend her time in a partnership working on the issues that really matter to make a relationship work, not on picking out wedding napkin colors or inviting friends to a ceremony to demonstrate that she is in love with her partner. She would rather direct her energy at making sure that she is a strong and fulfilled woman who can stand on her own two feet, who just happens to have someone romantically in her life with whom she enjoys beautiful moments. She does not have any desire to risk putting herself through a complicated and costly divorce down the road. She knows that she chooses to be with a man only if she is truly happy being with him; but at the same time, she never needs to be with a partner to feel complete.

Women are capable of being financially secure, enjoying a satisfying sex life and raising happy and healthy children without a man. Societal norms have drastically changed in the last couple of decades and it is time that more women recognize not only that it is okay to be single, but that there are huge benefits to being single as well.

I strongly believe every woman deserves nothing less than complete happiness and that happiness must come from no other place than within. Spending time in a mediocre relationship just to avoid being single or expecting someone else to fill that responsibility of making you happy is a waste. A pretty white dress, a shiny ring and a signed certificate are no match, in my opinion, for the more stable and long-term happiness a woman exudes once she truly realizes that she is liberated and self-sufficient, with or without a man by her side.

Chapter 7

Divorced Women

With your divorce over, now you can pull yourself together and deal with all the major life changes that divorce brings with it. You need to face all the new problems, options and opportunities that will be coming your way.

You may view embarking on this new life as being a little scary, but you should view it as a completely new adventure. Will there be challenges? Yes. However, there will also be untold opportunities for you to live the life you want to live as a happily divorced woman. The options for women in today's world far outweigh the "security" of staying in an unhappy and unhealthy marriage.

CARING FOR YOURSELF

Taking care of yourself may sound like a very selfish way to begin a new life. However, if you take care of yourself and give yourself time to heal, it will benefit you and everyone around you. Lay aside feelings of guilt about devoting time for yourself. Now, more than ever, your family, especially your children, if you have any, need you to be calm, relaxed and focused.

Let's discuss some of the ways you can achieve this peaceful but optimistic state of mind and body. Meditation is a wonderful way to de-stress and let go of worries and concerns. Regular meditation also helps you to clear your mind of mental clutter and helps you to stay focused on the things that really matter to you. Think of this exercise as a washing of the mind. Choose a time when you can be alone and undisturbed, even if this is for five or ten minutes each day (setting a timer can help). If meditation is a new concept to you, you can find some excellent guided meditations online or you can purchase CD/DVDs. With guided meditation, you have someone coaching you through the process of relaxing, breathing, focusing and clearing your mind.

If you prefer total silence, you can do your own simple breathing meditation exercise. Sit comfortably cross-legged on the floor or in a chair with your feet flat on the floor. Relax your hands, allowing them to rest in your lap. Gently close your eyes and take a deep and cleansing breath, breathing in through your nostrils and out through your mouth. Now, focus on your breathing, continuing to breathe in through the nostrils and out through the mouth. Notice how the air feels as it enters your body, as it fills your lungs and the sensation around your mouth as it leaves your body on exhalation. Keep your mind focused on the breath. Thoughts will come into your mind; simply acknowledge them and allow them to fade as you take your awareness back to your breath. Never dwell on any single thought; just allow thoughts to pass through.

When you feel your meditation has come to a close or when your timer sounds, wiggle your fingers and toes, become aware of the sounds around you and then slowly open your eyes. You will be amazed at how much more relaxed you feel and how much more energized your coping mechanism is after a session of breathing meditation.

Physical exercise is yet another way to de-stress and it also keeps your body fit and energized to be able to do all the things you need to get accomplished during any given day. Taking a walk after dinner is an excellent way to keep fit and spend some quality time with the people who are dear to you: family, friends and children. If you have children, walking benefits their health as well as yours, by helping them to de-stress after a day at school. Taking along the family pet, if there is one, will also help it to keep trim and have family time.

Take the time you need to grieve your marriage, even if you were unhappily married or if you were the one who initiated divorce proceedings. There is an emotional bond between two people who have lived together as husband and wife. For most women, there will be a period of grief with which they must deal. It comes from all of the changes that flood your life after a divorce. Don't hold back. If you want to grieve alone, find a quiet place and some time and cry. If you need to talk to a friend or therapist, make arrangements to do so. Express and release your feelings and then you can truly let the past go.

Do not waste your time being vengeful; make the best use of your time by going after your own new happiness. Think about what you love to do. Maybe you could try new hobbies or even pursue a new career that you have always dreamed of. The opportunities are endless for you now.

Take care of your appearance. It is easy and comfortable to relax and not worry about fixing yourself up. However, it will make you feel better about yourself and build your confidence if you put on some makeup, do your hair and get out of the house, even if you don't have somewhere specific to be. Meet a friend for lunch, go to the library or stroll leisurely around the park. And *smile*, especially when you really don't feel like smiling. Thich Nhat Hanh, a Vietnamese monk, activist and writer, wisely said, "Sometimes your joy is the source of your smile, but sometimes your smile can be the source of your joy."

Set goals for yourself. If all of your goals and dreams for the future of yourself and your family ended with the divorce, it is time to set new ones. Don't fret about what could have been, but give yourself and your family some things to which you and they can look forward. By setting new goals, you create a destination. If money is tight, you can still plan a vacation for you and your family. Arrange a mini-vacation. It does not have to be elaborate and expensive, but bring your family together to choose a place on which everyone can agree. For those who want to go somewhere else, that is another mini-vacation to look forward to at another time.

DEALING WITH LONELINESS

You are a human being with the human need to have a special someone close. However, be cautious in forming new romantic relationships until you have given yourself time to heal. Make sure your heart is ready and remember, even if you do choose to love again, you do not necessarily have to marry again. You should seriously consider whether remarriage is the route for you. According to the article "Is Marriage Outdated?" between 60 and 67 percent of second marriages end in divorce.[1] So it may be best for everyone involved to look at other options when it comes to finding another love.

Before you jump into another relationship, take the time to find your new, single sense of self. Become emotionally independent. During your marriage, your husband was one of your primary social outlets. Spend some time reconnecting with friends and family whom you didn't have time for during your separation. They can form your support network when things get tough. In turn, you can be there when they need someone in whom to confide.

Do something fun just for you, like taking a painting class or learning yoga. Maybe take a day off from work and go to a spa. Did your ex-husband always want to go to the same Italian restaurant? Well, try a Thai restaurant next time you don't feel like cooking. You have probably changed a lot over the years, but the usual marriage routine has prevented you from embracing those changes. Now is your time to figure out what you like, without it being about what you and your husband both liked. Trying new things will fuel your confidence and wash away self-doubt.

Do not try to fill the void with a new love interest. Learn to love yourself. A new relationship can add to your happiness, but you should learn to be happy with yourself first.

When and if you form a new, serious relationship, instead of remarrying, you may wish to have your significant other move in with you or you may move in with him. Cohabitation of this sort depends on many factors. You will have to take into consideration your thoughts and feelings on the matter and those of your children, if you have any, or if they are still living with you. Once, cohabitation outside the bonds of matrimony was frowned upon, but trends are shifting. Having discarded such tags as "shacking up" and "living in sin," many modern couples choose to cohabit. In an article for *USA Today*, Sharon Jayson explores the trend of cohabitation becoming the new dating scene, especially among partners who are very compatible. Most couples reason that it makes more sense financially to live together, instead of paying bills for two households.[2]

FACING FINANCES AFTER DIVORCE

Discussing finances may leave you feeling depressed or frustrated; however, this is one area that you will need to address, if you haven't already. Getting a handle on your new financial situation will make all of the other transitions of divorce go a little more smoothly.

Being a divorced woman no longer means that you cannot live as well or nearly as well, financially, as you did when you were in an unhappy marriage. Financial security is one of the main reasons that women may stay in miserable relationships. Although many women do not have the same level of income after a divorce, if you plan well, re-equip yourself through education or training for a new career and utilize all of the many new opportunities and options for single women, you will not be plunged into poverty and, perhaps, through being happier, you will find a better lifestyle.

Nowadays, women have nearly the same opportunities as men as far as financial resources are concerned. You can make the shift from being a two-income family to being a one-income family without too much of a jolt. Gone are the days when the men were the sole breadwinners and women stayed at home to keep house and raise the children. Heather Boushey, in "The New Breadwinners," part of a study done by Maria Shriver and the Center for American Progress, notes that "Nearly 4 in 10 mothers (39.3 percent) are primary breadwinners." The report also states that "nearly two-thirds (62.8 percent) [of mothers] are breadwinners or co-breadwinners."[3] Around the world, in prosperous countries women's employment is on the rise, up from 48 percent to 64 percent since 1970.[4]

There are likely some changes needed in your financial situation after divorce. These changes need not be depressing. Try to look at your new state as a time to make positive changes and don't be overwhelmed by the financial issues facing you. You can succeed by meeting the challenges head on.

Get your finances in order and create a budget. For most women, taking care of the day-to-day income and expenses is the smartest and easiest place to start. Then you can move on to making sure your other assets are in order and solely in your name. If budgeting or bill paying is new to you, there are a few simple things that you can do that will help you.

One good step is to set up a central location for all of your financial functions. Having one location for this purpose helps keep you focused when bill paying time comes. Usually, bill paying comes after you get paid. Divide your bills up according to when you get paid. If you are paid weekly, divide the bills up by due date and pay those that will come due between one pay period and the next. If you are paid twice a month or biweekly, divide your bills into two piles. If you have too many bills due for one paycheck, you may be able to speak to the companies to change the due dates so that your bills are more evenly spaced. Your priority is to get your regular monthly bills paid. Pay those first, then use the rest of your income for gas, groceries and other necessities.

If you have been awarded custody of your children, then child support is an important issue. Hopefully, you or your attorney have negotiated a good settlement to help you with the expense of raising children. You should not have to support your children financially on your own.

Another move forward is in your career. According to the *Economist* article "Here's the next half-century," there are a few key reasons why women tend to earn less than men do. While women are excelling further than men when it comes to education, they are not holding the highest paid positions in the workforce. The crucial part of a woman's career often coincides with the time that she considers starting a family. A woman can choose not to have children and climb the corporate ladder instead or she can choose to start a family and gain a different kind of fulfillment. If a woman wants both, she can choose a career in a field which supports or accommodates motherhood. Another reason women are not getting ahead as quickly is that they are not as confident in their abilities as men are. While a man is self-assured and he feels he deserves a promotion or a raise, a woman is not likely to ask for one if she has any hint of doubt.[5]

Luckily, these issues are not detrimental. If you have children and need or want to work, go after the career you want now. You will be setting a great example for your children by showing them that events in life, such as divorce, do not have to hold one back from achieving one's goals. As far as getting what you want out of your career, be more assertive. Tell your boss that you plan to go after that higher paid position that just opened up. If you think you did a great job this year, ask for a raise. You can be one of the women who adds cracks to the soon-to-shatter glass ceiling.

FIGURE OUT WHERE THINGS WENT WRONG

Getting past your divorce requires figuring out what the relationship problems were so you don't repeat them. One answer might be that you and your partner fought too much, another may be that there was no communication. You have to find and examine the root causes to these actions. What pushed you to divorce? What happened that led to the decision? There are, in my opinion, very legitimate reasons to pursue a divorce at any stage in life. After all, why should you settle for a marriage that is only bringing you grief and frustration?

One reason for divorce is infidelity. It comes in many forms and it is not always obvious when it is happening. Let's look at male cheaters first. Some wealthy men seem to think that having a large income grants them permission to have access to more than one woman. He could go through multiple mistresses quickly or he could keep the same one for years. Women are attracted to powerful men, so in a common scenario, a cheating husband will begin an affair with a woman who works in his office. Often, after the betrayed wife finds out about the mistress, she will ask for a divorce or make her husband choose, and he may well choose his mistress.[6]

Habitual male cheaters do not form strong emotional connections with their extramarital partners. They enjoy the satisfaction of seducing women. These men are often trying to compensate for shortcomings in their careers or lives. Some will not acknowledge any shortcomings, however, and insist that women cannot resist them and they are just taking advantage of opportunities. If you find out that your husband is a chronic cheater, you may decide that the marriage isn't salvageable, as Tiger Woods' wife Elin Nordegren and Mark Sanford's wife Jenny Sanford did.

Women cheat for different reasons than men do, but those often lead to divorce also. In many cases women believe that they are falling in love with another man. Even if their marriages are not awful, they feel their relationships might be lacking something important, such as communication and attention. Conversations turn bland, no one says "I love you" or makes an effort to show that he or she cares. Women need emotional support and many may find it hard to resist when it unexpectedly appears in the form of a love affair. If you had a lover and left your marriage as a result—even if that love affair did not last afterwards—perhaps that decision turned out for the best. It might have taken this kind of wake-up call for you to realize that your marriage was not what you needed it to be.[7]

Another common cause for divorce is the serious issue of physical, verbal or emotional abuse. Husbands who are abusive do not usually

see themselves that way. They may think that their wives are unreasonable. These men display a wide variety of abusive characteristics. They
might try to seclude their wives from friends and family, be overly critical of their wives, refuse to share any financial information or money,
act extremely possessive or belittle their wives' feelings with cruel comments. If you endured this sort of abuse, you might have had trouble
seeing a possible escape from the relationship. You might have feared
the financial ruin of a divorce, because you were unsure of the family's
assets or afraid of the consequences of telling your husband that you
were leaving him. There is no reason to put up with persistent abuse,
pain and stress that might harm you and your children. Divorce is usually the best decision in cases of abuse. You have nothing to regret and
should now feel satisfaction that you and your children, if you have
any, can move on.

Some women leave their marriages in order to pursue happiness.
If you had no two-way communication with your husband and he
never listened to what you had to say, the frustration was not worth
it. Lack of communication and affection can be too emotionally damaging for some women. But some men do not feel the need to communicate as much as women do and some might even be surprised when
their wives leave.[8]

Financial independence is another reason why women choose
to divorce. Perhaps your husband took care of the finances, kept you
ignorant of your financial status and excluded you from important
financial decisions. If you wanted to buy something, you had to ask
him for money. Even if he always said yes and gave you the money, it
was still annoying and demeaning that you had to ask. Sometimes this
controlling behavior continues even after a woman has a frank and
serious conversation regarding the matter with her husband. In such
cases, divorce may be the best solution.

On the other side of the financial spectrum, maybe you were the
one who made more money. Maybe your husband drifted between jobs
and went months at a time without work. Perhaps he incurred debt
that you were responsible for paying. In such an irreparable situation,
divorce, again, may be your best choice.[9]

Sometimes the decision to divorce comes after the death of a parent. In families that are particularly religious, women often do not want
to deal with the criticisms of their parents if they choose to divorce,
so they stay in their dysfunctional marriages. This is true especially if

their siblings have happy and successful marriages or marriages that are purported to be so. Often, women with such old-fashioned parents do not want to be labeled as "the bad one." When the parent dies, a woman may be free to divorce without her parent's criticism.

Another motivation for divorce is partners playing parent-child roles. Perhaps you felt like you had to mother your husband, picking his dirty socks up off the floor, doing all the cooking and cleaning, having to take responsibility for the children and running his errands for him. He expected you to care for him completely, despite your responsibilities in the household and at work. He did not want any responsibility and acted as though he was your child, not your partner.

Even today women do at least twice as much household work as men, according to an *Economist* article titled "The cashier and the carpenter." Women contribute an average of thirty-three unpaid hours a week, while men hover somewhere around sixteen hours. Most of these women hold jobs as well. If you were doing it all, you may have made the decision that to do it alone was better.[10]

REENTERING THE DATING SCENE

Within the first month or even six months after your divorce, dating is not likely to be at the top of your to-do list. You are probably more concerned with getting your life back in order and moving ahead or beginning a new career as well as building a new family life. But once you have a system that is working for you, you might have the urge to gain companionship. If you are wondering where to meet potential partners, there are many places to begin, including your church or synagogue, Internet dating sites, your local YMCA or YMHA and many other avenues.

You may fall into one of three temporary categories that Kay Moffett and Sarah Touborg, authors of *Not Your Mother's Divorce*, classify as ice queen, boy crazy and pretend married.[11] If you are an ice queen, you probably got hurt or were betrayed during your marriage. The idea of getting involved with another man might be a little repulsive to you. It seems like you need extra time to figure yourself out. During this time, however, do not stay at home and feel sorry for yourself. Go out with your friends, try some fun activities, do some sports or go on vacation. Enjoy everything that is out there. Seize all the opportunities you missed while you were married.

The next category is boy crazy. You feel you cannot get enough of all the men who are available now. You go out to bars often and always find someone with whom to flirt. You are full of energy and you always have a smile on your face. You feel liberated from your ex-spouse and you want to explore more of your sexual and romantic sides. This period won't last forever, but be aware that many of the flings you have during this time will be short-lived but also intense. It is a good idea to have a group of single girlfriends with you, so you can support one another and have fun together.

The third category is pretend marriage and it is probably the most emotionally damaging category. You might be looking frantically for someone to replace the relationship you lost. You feel the need to have someone to cuddle up to at night or talk about your feelings with. Unfortunately, progressing too fast in a new relationship means you are putting off dealing with your feelings from your divorce and sorting out the relationship problems you encountered in your former marriage. You might find yourself acting very demanding or needy in this new relationship. The pretend marriage route is a temporary fix and not a solution for long-term problems. It is better to avoid such rebound relationships until you figure out what went wrong in your last one.

After being married, you still might wrongly correlate dating someone with finding a new husband. You might overstress yourself with worries and thoughts about your chances to remarry. Now it is time to look at dating and marriage as two separate things. You should not go on a first date expecting to spend the rest of your life with that person. Seize the opportunity to meet someone new and expect nothing. After ending an unsatisfying marriage, you need to be relaxed and figure out your personal goals. You might feel the need to love somebody, but your feelings needn't necessarily translate into marriage!

One good place to start is online dating sites. You can be as active with it as you choose. If work gets busy, put your online dating pursuits on hold for a few weeks. Finding a match means chatting with many nice and also some not-so-nice men.

The first steps are to sign up and create a profile. Be sure to create a profile that is reflective of who you really are. You may be tempted to highlight only your exciting qualities, but that will only lead to dates with men with whom you may not be compatible. Be honest and it will work out well for you. Consider recruiting a friend to help you make your profile the best representation of you. You may see yourself differently from how you actually are. You might even downplay your greatest qualities. Input from a friend will help make an accurate but awesome profile for you, a profile that may bring you that lover or friend for whom you've been longing.[12]

When you start receiving messages from guys who think you are interesting, don't feel you have to respond to all of them. There will be some who do not seem like men you want to meet. Save your time and energy for those who embody the qualities you admire. You will probably exchange a few e-mails before you actually meet in person. Do not reveal too much information or get too intimate over e-mail or chat sessions. You are not really sure whom you are talking to on the Internet. Be careful and take precautions.

Once you have corresponded with a man who seems nice and intriguing with mutual interests, it is time for a date. Pick a public place where you will have an opportunity to chat quietly. Coffee shops, parks, restaurants and museums are great options. Avoid certain places, such as bars, movie theaters and locales that remind you of your ex-husband. These locations may encourage inappropriate behavior (e.g., excessive drinking), may not allow the two of you to get to know each other or evoke negative feelings in you.[13]

When you are confirming plans for your date, keep in mind that it is best to keep the date short. If you hit it off and have a good time, he will be excited to ask you out on a second date. You will still have plenty of exciting stories and interesting personal details to share on future dates. Short dates are also useful if the two of you do not hit it off.

If you go to a restaurant, you will also have to consider who will pay. You might feel compelled to pay for your half, while he might think that he should cover the bill on the first date. A good strategy is to offer to split the bill and let him decide if he wants to split it or pay for everything himself.

Online social networks are not the only way to find companionship. Use your friends and family to network. You are probably already familiar with networking to find jobs. It is the same concept, just a different scenario. A friend or family member may be able to set you up on a good date. Keep in mind that if your date goes badly, you might have to explain to your coworker, relative or friend why.

Another good way to meet men is to try new activities. How about signing up for that scuba diving certification class you have been too nervous to try? You could also join the local writer's club. Go to a church social or an adventure outing. Host get-togethers with friends. Take a bartending class to brush up on your skills if you like. Train for a marathon if you are capable. Take your dog for walks in the park. Good guys turn up in unexpected places. Be open to new experiences and people.

Now that you are divorced, it is time to start living life the way you want it. You will be spending your time and money as you choose, focusing on having a career that works for you, establishing a new family unit and getting in touch with your new interests. You deserve that change!

While you will probably hit a few rough patches along the way, keep your head up high. You have come this far, gotten through troubled waters and now you can make it through anything. You are getting a second chance at a happy and fulfilling life.

Chapter 8

Single by Choice

One of the greatest challenges facing women who remain single by choice is that they are often made to feel that they are somehow missing something. I believe nothing could be further from the truth. Staying single is a clear and simple reality for women today; a reality in which women no longer need to feel dependent upon another person and are free to focus their attention on their own goals, whatever they may be. Women should not be held back by the conflicting needs of a significant other, nor should they be. Women do not need a partner to make them happy. Every woman deserves the opportunity to be joyfully happy and self-fulfilled, just because of who she is.

Think for a moment of the female role models introduced to women when they are young. In almost every case, these women are capable, talented, self-determined women. Modern women have had the good fortune of being introduced to groundbreaking discoveries and innovative breakthroughs thanks to the hard work of these talented women. The enormous impact of these courageous human beings has served to open up a new vision for women around the world. The dream of true self-actualization has never been so close.

Each day we are presented with amazing women we can admire. The media shows us wonderfully accomplished, compassionate, intelligent and self-reliant women, women who occupy all ranks in the workplace and often do this while successfully balancing the needs of their children and other family members. Many modern women are accomplished managers of their personal lives, their children, their communities and their workplaces. Some women are also taking charge on an international level, positively influencing the world in which we live. Never before have women been in a better position to leave their mark on society, break new ground and challenge themselves.

In this regard, women who are single by choice put themselves in the most advantageous place to continue this tradition of discovery and excellence. Far from setting themselves up to miss something in life, they are actually taking steps to ensure that they are in a position to create the life they really want for themselves. Thanks to modern advances in fertility medicine, a woman can choose to have a baby much later in life if she chooses, putting time and energy into her education and career while young. Single women can choose to travel if they wish or devote themselves to a special cause that touches their hearts. The possibilities are abundant.

Think of some women you admire and ask yourself why. You can learn a lot from other strong, empowered women who may inspire you to open yourself up to new possibilities and challenges. Remember, don't sell yourself short. Always keep in mind that you deserve to nurture your special gifts and talents and that by choosing to remain single, you have ensured that no one is going to come between you and your life achievements.

One of the most difficult things for many women today is to embrace total honesty and self-awareness, both with themselves and with others. The hectic pace of modern society has made it very easy to get caught up in the daily rush of obligations and responsibilities. Few women take the time to examine their lives closely, choosing instead to carry on with grit and determination. While hard work and persistence are both admirable traits, they can also create a distraction from the messages and signals that something is not working quite right in a woman's life. Many women have experienced the need to put on a "mask," a public face that suggests all is perfectly well, while in reality, things are not progressing perfectly at all.

Deep unhappiness has a way of catching up with anyone. There are so many times women wear the "mask" but eventually it starts causing additional problems in their lives. Some women may experience symptoms such as high anxiety or depression, while others attempt to cope with their unease through the use of drugs or alcohol. While some are better than others at self-assessment, there is no one who can continue living a lie for very long without serious repercussions to her health and psyche.

The beauty of being single is that a woman does not have to pretend that she is happy when she is actually not. I feel single women are truly free to be who they are. They do not have to "put on a brave face" to create the illusion of blissful togetherness. Single women can present their authentic selves to the world without pretense, comfortable in the knowledge that they are happy just the way they are.

Those who choose to remain single never have to convince themselves that they want to give up important career goals of their own in order to promote their husbands' career agendas. They have no reason to cover up their precious individuality by presenting themselves as something or someone they are not. They are unlikely to submit to the demands of another person unless they wish to and they have no difficulty expressing their own hopes and aspirations. Single women do not have to choose between two families during holiday celebrations and they don't have to act as if they're having a good time during sex if they're not.

I have come to believe that remaining single is one of the greatest gifts women can bestow upon themselves. Take a moment and ask yourself whether you are able to be completely honest with yourself. Sometimes, women may feel that they are being frank and open, but upon a closer look, they discover that deep down they are hiding little secrets in order to protect their partners. You owe it to yourself to reconnect with your real self. You cannot find true happiness while covering up your feelings.

This is not to say that single women are always open and truthful with those around them. There are occasions when everyone needs to use a little discretion and may choose to make light of the facts in order to avoid hurting someone's feelings. But the difference for women who are single by choice is that they have control over when and how they decide to share their innermost feelings and thoughts. There are no hidden obligations to a marriage partner and they can look within themselves for the answers, rather than simply saying what they think their spouses would want to hear.

There is a certain sense of comfort and safety that comes from dependence upon another human being. Infants and children need that sort of nurturing in order to develop properly, secure in the knowledge that their needs will be met. But as people grow older, that same reliance on another person may become terribly limiting and lead regressively to dependency and stagnation. Freedom from the bonds of marriage can release a woman to experience her own personal challenges and growth fully. A way that a woman can be truly responsible for her own destiny is if she resolutely sticks to her own personal plans in life in order to work on accomplishments that are meaningful for her. Women who choose to be single are often perceived by society as infinitely bold and courageous, even if they do not necessarily see themselves that way.

Janet's Story

Janet, a self-employed artist, works out of her home. She got married right after she graduated from college and she endured a tumultuous relationship for several years before she decided that she needed to restore peace and serenity in her life. Realizing that she no longer had anything in common with her husband, Janet ended her ill-fated marriage. "It was actually a huge relief to both of us," she commented. "We were no longer the same people who had met in art school. My husband wanted to go back to college to study acting, whereas I was trying to build a reputation offering art classes to local children. We were really struggling to keep it together."

Janet had always been the main breadwinner in her unhappy marriage and was fortunate to avoid suffering any serious financial difficulties following her divorce. She continued to work out of her home, which she owned, and proved herself to be an astute businesswoman. Her art business flourished and she never lacked for new clients.

Then Janet found herself attracted to Robert, a successful lawyer. One night he asked her to marry him.

Though Janet was determined not to repeat the mistakes of the past, she enjoyed the company of her new companion and was anxious not to end the relationship. After thinking seriously about Robert's proposal, Janet explained to him that although she loved him very much, she did not wish to live with him or get married. They decided they would continue to see each other but would do so as separate and individual people, each with his or her own home, business and private life. Janet pointed out to me that she does not consider this to be a compromise: "I vowed I would never allow myself to become dependent upon anybody. I respect myself too much for that to happen." Janet's decision to get involved in an ongoing and committed relationship while staying unmarried is not an unusual choice in our era.

Janet's Living Apart Together (LAT) relationship is an example of the opportunity available for women like her; women who are looking for a committed relationship, without losing their independence and self-reliance in life. There are more possibilities for women than ever before to engage in creative relationship options. No one should feel that she is forced into marriage because she is afraid of losing a relationship. A world of possibilities opens up for those who have allowed themselves the privilege of remaining single.

NEW POLICIES FOR CHANGING TIMES

One of the concerns expressed by women who remain single by choice centers on the challenges of living in a society which appears to reward partnerships and married couples. Discrimination does exist, for example, in double occupancy requirements at hotels or on cruise ships. But it is often the case that policy takes a while to catch up to popular trends. After all, a firm commitment from government in the form of policy and legislation is a clear endorsement of changing social values. But the single trend is advancing and is surely here to stay.

Single women and, to a lesser extent, single men must sometimes navigate through a minefield of ridiculous bureaucracy and senseless regulations in a society where public policy is commonly geared to couples. Single people frequently tolerate biased legislation in order to attain their most basic needs. Everything from health insurance premiums to financing a mortgage is oriented toward couples.[1] Single women may experience housing discrimination in locations which encourage traditional families and discourage singles living together. No wonder women are urged to challenge these outmoded policies with "vigor and also humor."[2]

Despite the effort necessary to cope with day-to-day reality, women who choose to be single should not regret their choice. Most single women are absolutely happy with their decision and merely regard the trials of living in a world oriented toward couples as an inconvenience to be resolved as the issue comes up. Many single women regard these petty irritations as perfect opportunities to right a wrong and instigate change. Under no account should single women wish to consider marriage in order to "fit in."

Women are not about to relinquish their hard-earned freedom of choice. Modern women have more options than ever and are accepting of many different family alternatives. Many contemporary women are aware of the varied family alternatives found in society. Single parents, gay and lesbian couples, cohabiting individuals and partners who don't live together are all examples of family combinations that would have been thought implausible even fifty years ago.

According to statistics, women today constitute more than half of the workforce and yet they often still struggle to find sufficient childcare, flexible, family-oriented work schedules and adequate pay.[3] Single women, by the very nature of their status in society, are in a position to promote women's rights and pave the way for generations to come. They do not have to accept someone else's vision for their lives and they must not allow themselves to be silenced or discouraged.

Women who are single by choice are, by necessity, a resilient and courageous group in society. Although the agonizingly slow pace of change is frustrating, single women should remind themselves that placing their needs first is truly essential in today's world. Women are working to right the wrongs of a male-oriented society which has resisted change, whether that means promoting their rights from a financial and employment parity perspective or asserting their desire for different relationship formats. Women all over the world are working to amend public policy in order to better represent modern reality. And slowly but surely, policy makers are recognizing that they are not going to back down.

TRUST YOURSELF

As a woman who chooses not to marry, I am often struck by the way in which some single women sell themselves short. Very few would admit to longing for the past in which a woman felt that she needed to ask permission before acting. More importantly, I believe no self-respecting woman today would acknowledge that she is waiting for someone else to manage her life. However, women sometimes fall into the trap of believing that they are less worthy or capable of taking charge. They appear to lack the confidence to control the very elements that contribute to a life well lived.

The truth is that single women can control their destinies! To settle for anything less is tantamount to handing over one's power to someone else, exactly the situation women are attempting to avoid by embracing the concept of staying single. Even though a woman may believe herself to be completely in favor of the idea of women's rights and empowerment, a lack of action and resolve can hamper her ability to realize fully her potential and dreams. It is not enough to declare oneself independent if the reality is otherwise. The only way for single women to transform into the powerful and capable women they can be is to accept total responsibility for the decisions they make in all areas of their lives, including their relationships and marital status. Single women must trust themselves!

Mona's Story

Mona is an attractive, intelligent woman who knows exactly what she wants out of life and has no problem ensuring that she gets it. She is an extraordinarily high achiever, a trait she credits to her mother, a woman who made sure that her daughter never lacked confidence or the means to achieve her goals.

Mona has been involved in a number of relationships over the course of several years but always makes it very clear that she does not want to settle down or consider marriage. "I just don't think I'm ready for that sort of commitment," she said to me, "and I'm not even sure that I ever will be." Mona has been careful to address any issues that might mislead her boyfriends into thinking that she could be convinced otherwise and maintains excellent boundaries. She is articulate, assertive and fun.

Therefore, I was taken aback when one day Mona explained that she felt that something was missing in her life and that she was anxious to correct it. She had chosen to undergo in vitro fertilization, using sperm from an anonymous donor, and was five months pregnant.

Even more surprising was the angry reaction of her current boyfriend. "I never did this to hurt anyone," stated Mona. "I really want to experience motherhood and I'm fortunate that I'm in a financial position to be able to do this. I have lots of resources and hands-on support and I know I'll be a good mother." Mona wanted the freedom of choosing the father of her baby without involving her boyfriend, as she believed that he would consider parenthood to be a step closer to a shared and committed relationship. She was, however, unprepared for the vitriolic attack on her character from someone she counted as a close friend. "He called me inconsiderate and selfish," she added. "It's really quite hurtful, especially from someone who supposedly cared about me."

Mona's situation underscores the challenges women face today as they attempt to balance their own individual needs with the antiquated values of society. Although Mona's encounter with her resentful boyfriend is unfortunately not an uncommon occurrence, there is actually an increasing trend toward acceptance of women who choose single parenthood. This is amazing progress, based on the realization that marriage does not turn women into good and caring mothers and debunking the myth that having a child without a partner constitutes failure on the part of the woman. Nearly 35 percent of single mothers today have never been married, indicating that attitudes and opinions are slowly changing.[4]

These statistics reveal that, for many people, marriage is no longer a requirement for having children and that being a single mother by choice is common in the Western world. Many women who enter motherhood without partners feel they are under no obligation to involve the fathers of their children and are free to raise the children according to their own standards and preferences. The freedom to decide unilaterally how to raise a child is enormously valued as a harmonious and child-centered parenting practice; it is free from the conflicting opinions on childrearing that typically arise among married couples.

Women who are single by choice embody many positive characteristics. They are not afraid to challenge old models and pave the way for new and exciting relationship options. Single women are frequently motivated by intrinsic values. They are less concerned with how others view them and more interested in using their gifts to benefit society at large. Single women possess the time and the energy to devote themselves to a much wider audience.

Most importantly, single women do not define themselves by how others perceive them. They are comfortable in their own skins and are at the forefront of social change, working in order to improve their own lives as well as the circumstances of those around them. Women who are single by choice know themselves better than anyone else and they are in a position to smooth the progress of women's rights for generations to come.

Independent women around the world continue to make impressive headway in their quest for self-determination and autonomy. As women progress and move forward, it will be interesting to see the positive impact on alternative relationship options for women. Modern women are encouraged to realize their personal goals and aspirations. Chances are they will see even more opportunities for independent and alternative lifestyle choices in the future.

Currently women who are single by choice are in a position to drive social change as well as promote themselves. Most of all, single women owe themselves the same love and consideration as they surely impart to those around them. Women who are single by choice place themselves in the powerful position of never having to lean on a man physically, emotionally or financially. I believe strongly that it's a good place to be.

BENEFITS OF BEING A SINGLE WOMAN

Despite the fact that some people in a variety of countries believe that marriage has become obsolete, there are those single and unmarried women who are scrutinized and criticized for their decision to stay single. I feel strongly that it's time to update the attitudes and perceptions about the old-fashioned family structure as well as about being single or a "spinster." I believe the benefits of being a single woman outnumber the benefits of being married.

FREEDOM

Single and unmarried women have a lot more freedom under their control than married women do. They don't have to worry about reporting to a partner every time they make, do or decide something. They don't have to account for themselves or their whereabouts; this alone is a liberating feeling.

This fantastic freedom can manifest itself in many different ways from the big to the small. One of the big ways is deciding who to talk to in any kind of situation. For instance, if a man approaches a married woman, she constantly has to think about what the situation looks like to an outsider and what it appears to look like to her husband. Even if the conversation is completely innocent, there is a certain amount of guilt that is involved, because that man is not her husband.[5] But single women do not have to think in this same fashion, because there is no one holding them back. They can choose, if they want, to continue the conversation or to end it. The power is in their hands.

Single women have the luxury of being able to have a sexual relationship with anyone they want. They can have sex with someone once, twice or as many times as they please and still do whatever they want to do afterward. They can opt to date a man for short or long-term relationships. Single women can pursue any man they want. There is no one telling them that they can't or shouldn't and there's no reason to feel guilty. In the same situation, no one thinks twice if a single woman approaches a man in a bar, but if a married woman tried it, there would be a societal and marital backlash.[6]

This freedom plays into not just the big decisions women make, but also the little ones that shape regular daily life. For example, single women can choose to watch whatever they want on television, without having to check first to see what a partner wants to watch. This is also true when making decisions about food. Single women do not need to compromise on their food choices or on the timing of their meals. They can eat anything they want without checking what their husbands might be in the mood for. They can also decide how to keep their households and what kind of music they would like to listen to. Again, all such things are minor decisions, but each of them helps to shape your personality and there is no reason to give any of that up, especially not for a man.[7]

TIME

Time is precious and most people can never get enough of it. They are always rushing from one activity and place to the next. People who are married have to keep track of not one, but two schedules. Partners have to find ways to make their free time sync up with each other just to keep the relationship going. At times, they might even find themselves having to schedule time just to see each other. Does this work-around look so great to you?

Single women are free and they don't have to worry about synchronizing their lives with their husbands'. They have more time in their days—hours they can choose to spend on themselves or others. Aside from eating, sleeping and working, there are no immediate obligations (such as husbands' lives to integrate) that eat up their time. Still, there are those obligations that single women can choose to have. There are also experiences and pleasurable activities single women have more time for, such as reading books, watching movies, going out on the town, exercising, volunteering or other activities that married women just don't get to do. Without anyone taking up your extra time, as a single woman you have the time to make your life into exactly what you want it to be.[8]

MONEY

Single women have to accommodate only themselves in their financial calculations. They have their own budgets to cover their own expenses. Considering the bare necessities to support themselves, single women may need less money than married ones. That means that single women, depending on their profession and qualifications, can choose the desired industry and workplace and figure out their price in the market in order to live what they would consider to be a comfortable life.[9] Aside from work, in housing, too, single women have the luxury of deciding where they want to live and how. For instance, they can opt to live in a small apartment, rather than a larger, more expensive one and in this way save money and spend it on other things they prefer.

Unlike married women, unmarried ones do not have to worry about choosing the more "responsible thing" over the "fun thing" to

do at any given time. Of course, single women have their own responsibilities, duties and destinations in life to live up to, but without husbands by their sides telling them what to do, they have more freedom.
No one is going to argue with them or look down on them for choosing
to treat themselves to a gourmet meal in a restaurant every so often
while they are trying to save for a new house or a new car.

When it comes to how and when to spend money, single women
have the upper hand again. They don't have to check with anyone but
themselves whether they spend money on something for themselves
or others. Since the money is all theirs and they are the only ones
controlling the budget, they don't need to ask anyone before making
financial decisions for themselves. They can have a shopping day whenever they want, eat out every day if they like or get a pet. The possibilities are endless and the choice is theirs.

A single woman should be financially stable nowadays. She must
have a job that she enjoys and should be able to support herself fully,
without leaning on external help, family or friends. Being financially
stable brings freedom for the woman and opens for her a whole world
of possibilities. She can choose to support someone if she wants to or
choose someone who is successful in his own right. If you are a single,
independent woman, be aware that there are people who are looking
for a free ride and they will not hesitate to use any methods necessary
to get exactly what they want from you. As a single woman, you have to
be strong and not waver just because someone is trying to charm you.

EASY TO KEEP UP WITH FRIENDSHIPS

You probably have heard of or know a woman who gets a new boyfriend or partner and from that moment onward, all she can think of
is her relationship with him. She suddenly disappears from her circle
of friends, since all her spare time is caught up in this new relationship. But when the freshness of the relationship with him wears off
and problems surface, the women tries to reconnect with her long-time
friends. But things are never the same, as she now has to juggle her
relationship with her boyfriend and the relationships with her friends.

Single women usually maintain their friendships as integral
parts of their lives. They can drop everything at the last minute to
comfort a friend in need and they can meet up and head out to a club
on Friday nights without a problem. Unmarried women can also dress

to impress and not worry about who's looking at them and what others are thinking.

In this regard, one of the emotional issues that single women might face is the feeling of loneliness if their friends start dating long-term or eventually marry. These friends may suddenly change location or move to a new circle of married friends. While spending less time with old friends is always sad, finding time to meet might be challenging, especially if friends relocate and make new friends. The benefit of this situation is that while your friends might be changing their life-styles due to marriage, your lifestyle, the single and free one by choice, remains the same.

Single women can also be beneficial to their married friends. For instance, if a married friend has a problem, whenever she needs help she can always go to her single friend, surely a safe place to go. Unmarried women are also in the unique position of being able to offer some outside perspective to their married friends. They can give married friends ideas to think about outside the framework of marriage. If you have such a married friend in trouble, be careful to be honest and supportive without bashing her husband. Let your friend vent if she needs to, but refrain from trashing the man she picked to marry. Remember, when an old friend has marital troubles, she might be envious of your happy single lifestyle choice.

NEVER HAVING TO SETTLE

People, especially those who are introspective, grow and change. With each new experience and passing day, such people learn more and more about themselves. As they mature, they learn what works for them and what does not. They are learning about who they are and which people they want to avoid.

Ask yourself: What are the odds that two people, complete strangers at first, who enter into a lifelong commitment such as marriage, will grow and change in ways that will complement each other? Pretty slim, in my opinion, looking at recent divorce statistics. This is especially true for women who marry young. By the time most women reach the age of thirty, their hopes and dreams for themselves are vastly different from the time they were twenty or even twenty-five. Have the men they married developed the same dreams as they have? Are their husbands willing to help them achieve their goals? Such questions cannot be answered until the critical time comes, because no one knows how women and men evolve and change over time within their roles, obligations, interests and the constraints of the bond.

This is yet another benefit of being a single woman. A single woman can pick exactly whom she wants to end up with, but she also has the privilege of changing her mind if the relationship isn't working out. Married women can change their minds too, but divorce is more complicated. For single women, there is absolutely no reason to rush into a relationship with the wrong person. There's no reason to get into a relationship at all unless you choose to do it.

Part III

Today's Women

Chapter 9

Women's Education and Careers

Modern women are more powerful, more successful and more independent than ever before. They are maneuvering through the changing world and creating lives for themselves that fit what they really want. These women have more options than ever when it comes to their careers, relationships and families. They are also free to pursue their goals in the workplace and in their education. They no longer feel the pressure to get married, have children and stay at home.

The high school girl with the top grades, the career woman who is climbing toward major successes and the stay-at-home mom who is returning to work all have one thing in common: they share the same modern woman attitude. They know what they want and they are going for it. They are going to be the ones who push boundaries and break glass ceilings. They are excelling in school and in their careers. When it comes to relationships and children, women are making the choices that are best for them, compromising less and less with partners. Modern females demonstrate day after day that if one wants, one really can have it all.

TAKING THE LEAD IN EDUCATION AND THE WORKPLACE

Currently, women are excelling in education, while in many countries men are falling behind. In many prosperous countries around the world, such as Sweden, the United States, Russia, the United Arab Emirates, Brazil and Finland, according to *The Economist*, 33 percent of women who are over twenty-five have some higher education while the percentage of men in the same age group is only 28. The article states that "In rich countries they account for over 70% of degrees in humanities and health" and more post-graduate degrees. Girls' reading scores are higher in all countries, according to the OECD annual study of education performance.[1] More women are going to college than men, doing better in their classes and putting more effort into their education. In America, men are "less likely than women to get bachelor's degrees" and those who do get degrees take more time to finish.[2]

Women make up 58 percent of the student body at two- and four-year colleges in the United States. They are also the majority enrolling in graduate and professional schools. Most students would agree that the class slackers are mostly male, while the students who are excelling are mostly female. It is possible that women are ahead because while they have been breaking out of their domestic roles and stepping up in education, men have remained the same in their work ethic.[3] Generally, women are more eager to prove that they are capable, smart and employable. The majority of men feel more of a sense of entitlement. They have always been the breadwinners and they do not yet see any reason to change their attitudes or behavior.

Many women feel the need to move quickly to get the most out of life. They want a high-powered career that they love, but most also want a family someday. Having a family means that they will probably have to put their careers on hold for a while, so they want to be well-established in their fields beforehand. Men, on the other hand, have a more leisurely attitude toward their college years. They believe that when they are ready to graduate, there will be a job waiting for them. Having children will cost more money, but generally, their day-to-day lives will still be the same. Their careers will still be there for them, unlike for most women.

As well, men are more likely to admit to spending at least eleven hours a week relaxing and socializing, while women say they spend that much time preparing for class. An annual study from the University of California, Los Angeles found that "men were more likely than women to skip classes, not complete their homework and not turn it in on time."[4] It is possible that women are just better with organization and time management, but it is also possible that men are not as motivated.

I believe today's generation of women is unstoppable. From an early age they strive to do well in school and in extracurricular activities. Many high school girls have high test scores, excellent grades, impressive recommendations and are applying to colleges. They are going after scholarships and pursuing their dreams. They are not intimidated by the guys and most of them believe that they are smarter than their male peers.

Thus modern women are becoming fierce competitors in the workforce as well. While men still make about 20 percent more money per week than their female counterparts, that gap is closing. Women now constitute 51 percent of all workers in high-paying management and professional positions. Women are also breaking into many fields that used to be male-dominated.[5]

More women are moving into the business field. In 2007, women received 44 percent of all master's of business administration degrees awarded.[6] Chief executive positions are the top-paying jobs for women. Currently only one fourth of chief executives are women, but that is expected to change in the near future.

Among emerging careers, the field of pharmacy is expanding and women are filling many of those vacant positions, currently holding almost half of all pharmacy jobs. Now women dominate the field of occupational therapy also, a field which is expected to grow 26 percent by 2018. They hold 82 percent of all positions and are paid the same salary as men. Computer programming is a high-paying field for women as well. Although women currently hold only 21 percent of computer programming positions, with the current globalization trend, many women around the world, especially in Israel, China, India, Russia and Ukraine, are filling these jobs quite successfully and getting paid equally to men.[7]

The lowest-paid jobs for women are still in the service industry. Launderers, dry-cleaners, waitresses, maids and childcare workers are the lowest-paid positions. These are also positions that are predominantly filled by women.[8]

Nevertheless, during the recession from 2008 to 2011, women have been coming out on top. Of the total jobs lost since late 2007, only 26 percent of those jobs belonged to women. Women hold 49.83 percent of jobs in the United States and that number is expected to

rise. The fields of healthcare, education and government are traditionally dominated by females and continue to grow in opportunities for
women.[9] Working in the public sector allows for a smoother climb to
the top than in the private sector. However, much work is still needed
in order for women to rise in the private sector in regards to advancement to the top and equal pay.[10]

Despite all their advancements in education and careers, when it
comes to political representation, women lag behind men. For example, the United States is number 90 out of 186 nations in regards to
female representation in government. Female political leadership has
hovered around 18 percent for the last several decades and congres-
sional representation is expected to drop. One reason is that men
make up 83 percent of Congress and incumbents are reelected 90 percent of the time.[11]

Twenty-five nations across the world have at least 30 percent
female representation. In the Nordic countries, women have surged
ahead in the political arena. For instance, women in Finland, a country that gave women the right to vote in 1906, have, at different times,
been appointed or voted into 50 percent of ministerial positions
including prime minister (Tarja Haloren). Other countries have also
elected women leaders: Angela Merkel (Germany), Dilma Rousseff
(Brazil), Julia Gillard (Australia) and Ellen Johnson Sirleaf (Liberia).
Of those nations, 90 percent had to give the process a "jump-start
to secure permanent gains." Half of all nations have legally required
minimums for the percent of female representation.[12]

The current changes in women's positions in education and
careers as well as new family choices appear to be a sweeping global
phenomenon. It is an international trend adopted by most industrialized Western countries and many civilized nations that are non-
Western by definition, such as China, Japan, India and Israel.

Israel has experienced a rise in the number of employed women.
Upon finishing their army service at the age of twenty, most Israeli
women either join the workforce for low paying service jobs (before
commonly traveling abroad on lengthy trips, oftentimes to East Asia)
or go directly to colleges or universities for higher education. After
graduating, women can compete against men for the same jobs. The
attitude toward work is serious, with most households depending on
two incomes, as the cost of living is high compared with Europe and
the United States.

The attitude of employers is usually respectful of women's rights for equal opportunity and equal pay. The "equal opportunity at work" law works for women's benefit. As in most industrialized Western countries and the United States, by law Israeli employers cannot discriminate against their employees or job applicants for reasons such as gender, age, sexual preference, parenthood, race, ethnicity, religion or nationality. This antidiscrimination legislature covers women getting jobs as well as securing their working terms, promotion, compensation and retirement. Female senior employees can be found in many companies, especially in the academic, scientific, technological, financial and healthcare areas. However, as in the United States and Europe, most top management positions are secured by men.[13]

One of the reasons of the relative progress in female employment compared to two decades ago is the Israeli high-tech industry, which is known as one of the world-leading business arenas. With various start-ups and large-scale international companies locating their headquarters offices and research and development (R&D) centers in both Israel and the United States, many Israeli women take advantage of the global capabilities of such firms to advance their careers in management, finance, marketing, sales and technological professions.

In most Israeli high-tech firms there is no significant difference between men's and women's pay for the same job title. However, as in Europe and the United States, there are more men in the industry in pure technological, engineering and scientific fields than women.

In developing regions, women make up the majority of those in higher education. Women hold more first degrees, but men still earn more doctorates, with America being the exception. Despite excellence in academia, women do not progress as quickly as men in the workforce. Women in prosperous countries hold 70 percent of all degrees in humanities and health.

Another explanation for women not getting the highest paying or powerful jobs is that they often put their careers on hold when they start families. If a woman spends a few years out of the workforce, her skills can become outdated, she can become less confident in her abilities and potential employers worry about the gap in her work history. Often, when women return to the workforce, they work for less than they are worth and are just thankful that an employer is giving them an opportunity.[14]

A career break that lasts years also has a big impact on lifetime earnings. This is not because of the loss of pay, but because of the loss of promotions, lost seniority within the company and lack of gaining new skills during that time off.[15] For most, it is as if they went backwards in their careers instead of staying stationary. Often, women work for lower pay rates while their children are young, because it means they have less work responsibilities. This allows them to have more time to take care of the children and be more available if a family emergency should occur.

A special report in *The Economist* points out that while many women choose to have children, most are waiting until they are older. The average age of women in prosperous countries who have their first child is twenty-eight, a four-year increase from 1970. Additionally, some women opt out of motherhood, a decision that is correlated to how highly educated and successful a woman is. Reports *The Economist*, "Of those born in 1965 (who will by and large have completed their families), 18% [in the United States] are childless, with large variations from country to country. In Portugal the figure is only 4%, in Italy around 20%."[16]

GETTING TO THE TOP

In the realm of high-paying careers, more and more women are now entering the six-figure earning bracket. In two years, from 1996 to 1998, the number of high earning women went up by 68 percent, while men's earnings only increased by 36 percent.[17] How are these women fulfilling their financial goals? What does the modern woman know and do that makes her so successful?

Ask yourself: What are your goals? Do you want to make more money, get a promotion, make a career change? Once you admit to yourself what you want, the goal becomes easier to attain. It is no longer a distant idea in your mind. You do not have to have a full plan in place but just enough to take the first step. Often women do not achieve their goals because stepping outside of their comfort zones can be frightening.[18]

Remaining in their comfort zones is what keeps many women from achieving their potential. But holding on to what is familiar, such as a bad relationship or a dead-end job, makes it impossible for goals to manifest into reality. What feels like a safety blanket sometimes equates to dissatisfaction, boredom and low income. After you set a goal for yourself, you also have to let go of all the restraints that are keeping you from reaching that goal.[19]

Successful women know that once they take the right steps to achieve their goals, they have to keep going. It is easy to revert back to what one was doing before, what was comfortable. If a person meets with failure it can be difficult to continue to be turned down by potential employers, have ideas rejected or not get the promotion. But the crucial step is learning from failures, not letting them deter you and continuing after your goals. If you persist, it will pay off the most.[20]

Another important part of women achieving success is learning how to speak up. Normally women make less money than men who are working in the same positions. You are not going to start making more money until you ask for it. If you know that your work results are just as good as or better than that of your male coworkers, then you should not be silent. It might feel intimidating to tell your boss that you are worth more money than you are making. But since you are being underpaid for your efforts and achievements, you should become an activist in voicing your desired monetary goals. In the worst case scenario, you will just continue to make the same amount of money. In the best case scenario, your paycheck will rise appreciably.

Career women learn the importance of appearing confident and self-assured. If you do not think highly of yourself, no one else is going to either. Even on days that you are filled with self-doubt, act like you are not. Do not be afraid to get no for an answer. If someone tells you no, do not accept it. Successful women continue to push themselves upward and onward. Dive into projects you know nothing about, do your homework and develop new skills and knowledge. That is the best way to learn. Stretch beyond your abilities daily, because that is the best way to continue improving yourself. There will be times when you fail, but that just means you have to continue working hard to succeed.[21]

To make your dreams come true in the current circumstances, you need to have a group of people who are on your side. You need a group of friends and family members who believe that you will be successful. They will give you encouragement when you doubt yourself and they will cheer you on when you do well. You also have to recognize that you are not perfect and it is okay to ask occasionally for help from others. You do not always have to do everything by yourself. It is also important to appreciate those people who are offering moral support. At the same time, it is just as important to weed out those people who belittle your achievements and bring you down.[22]

One key tool that can really make the difference in workplace success is the help of a mentor. Mentors can guide you toward good decisions and show you how to get ahead in your industry. Find a person for whom you have a lot of respect and ask that individual if you can brainstorm ideas with him or her and request suggestions on how to move ahead. The absence of a mentor has been shown to significantly reduce a woman's chances of advancement.[23]

When you do have the fabulous job you have been dreaming about, do not waste the current opportunity. Live by this strategy: spend less, save more and invest wisely. You do not want to spend your paychecks only on buying new things. You want to have money saved for different potential plans, such as buying a home or condominium, sending the children to college and funding your retirement. Seven out of ten women never retire because they can't afford to. Another one in three women owes more in credit card debt than she has in her retirement fund. It is easy to get caught up in spending paychecks and thinking that you are just going to get paid more later on. That kind of thinking leaves you unprepared when emergencies happen.[24]

It is also important to invest your money wisely. Money that you will not need for at least ten years should go into stocks, bonds and certificates of deposit. Have a set amount of money automatically transferred from your bank account every month. Often, the reason people do not invest their money is because they are too busy. But make it a routine process that you do not have to think about. Sometimes you might need a financial advisor to get you on track with investing your money. Stay up-to-date on what is happening in the financial world by reading informative magazines and newspapers. Having a regular stream of information will make you more confident about your financial decisions.[25]

One famous business initiative led by a woman is Oprah Winfrey's Harpo Productions. She is now trying to make her Oprah Winfrey Network succeed. She is one of the richest women in America and a self-made success. Another high-profile example of a woman who followed her passion to success is J.K. Rowling, author of the Harry Potter series. Her first Harry Potter book was rejected repeatedly by publishers until one finally said yes. Now she is a highly successful writer. Mary-Kate and Ashley Olsen, who were child television and film stars, are two examples of women who are maximizing new opportunities. They have used their fame to create a fashion empire.

There are several key reasons why women do not make it to the very top in their fields of work. Much of the workplace is still structured in the same way it was many decades ago when men were the primary breadwinners. Women and men do not work the same way. Women with children need more flexibility to juggle their maternal and employee roles. But many employers often think that it is the women who need to change, not the system.[26]

Another reason women have problems in reaching their goals is that women are often too critical of themselves. They do not voice their suggestions for solutions to business problems unless they are completely sure they are right. Although they are often very good at negotiating for other people, they do not negotiate for themselves very well. They also seem to be less self-confident than their male peers.[27]

Despite the strides in careers that women have made, workplace discrimination still exists in subtle ways. The article "Here's to the next half-century" in *The Economist* notes that "men are promoted on their potential but women are promoted on their performance, so they advance more slowly." This is unfortunate, because female leadership makes for "more diverse and probably more innovative workplaces." The article also points out that with the aging population, "women's talents will be needed even more in the future."[28]

An important question that should be considered: Do most women even want the top positions in their companies? Society puts a lot of pressure on men to be successful and make a lot of money. Some women do not feel that same pressure. They see how much work has to be put into one of the top jobs and they might decide, "No, not for me."[29] They may want rewarding careers instead.

Catherine Hakim, in *The Economist* article "Too many suits," separates people into three categories: those who are home-centered focus mainly on family life and children, those who are work-centered put the largest emphasis on their careers, and those who are considered adaptive want to combine both. Women who are at either extreme only make up 20 percent, with the other 80 percent trying to find balance in the middle ground. On the other hand, men make up 50 to 75 percent of the work-centered group. The remainders are mostly adaptive, while just a small percent are home-centered.[30]

CAREER WOMEN IN CHINA

Around the world the work situation for women is changing and improving. For instance, women with careers in China are on the rise, despite the difficulties they face in a society where they must compete fiercely with men. Businesswoman Pully Chau, in *The Economist* article "The sky's the limit," believes that "There are lots of opportunities for women in China...but in business life it is still easier for men." In China, women make up 49 percent of the population and 46 percent of the workforce. This ratio is higher than in many Western countries.[31]

Among state-owned companies, few Chinese women are in the top ranks, because highly conservative views remain in effect there. Jobs in such companies are still popular with women, because at the lower levels the hours are predictable and the work environment is comfortable. Many Chinese women find more satisfying careers in multinational corporations, because there is less sex discrimination. Women are beating the odds, though. On Forbes' worldwide list of self-made billionaires, seven of the fourteen women were Chinese.[32]

These busy women still manage to have children. They have one benefit that Western cultures do not have abundantly: grandparents who are very involved. After a child is born in China, he or she normally lives with grandparents for the first few years or the grandparents will come live with their children to help care for the grandchild. Most women only have one child. Caring for children becomes very expensive. State-run kindergartens might ask for a sponsorship of up to the equivalent of thirty-two thousand US dollars just for acceptance. Also, children are expected to excel and education gets more expensive as they get older. Despite the phenomenal progress of Chinese women, most Chinese men still expect their wives, whether working or not, to be responsible for all household and family duties.[33]

THE CURRENT SITUATION FOR ISRAELI WOMEN

Israelis are currently facing a major issue that has been neglected for some time: the divide between the natural rise of feminism along with full acceptance of women's rights to study, work and contribute to society in every aspect and the radical suppression of women in the ultra-Orthodox Jewish sector.

The beliefs of the ultra-Orthodox Jews are evident in their multi-child families, restricted neighborhoods and synagogues. Their male chauvinism manifests in what is called hadarat nashim, translated to "exclusion of women," which has infiltrated Israeli public life and moved to center stage.

In an extremely modern country where women serve in the army (five of whom have recently successfully completed the air force's pilot course), hold prestigious positions in the Supreme Court, work while raising children and take leading roles in academia, science, technology, banking, politics and business and where 74 percent of secular women take part in the workforce (12 percent above the average in most developed countries), this ultra-Orthodox chauvinism throws society back in time.

While there has been some progress, secular women in the public sector still have a battle to gain respect from the ultra-Orthodox community. Additionally, the children of the ultra-Orthodox are growing up to believe that these unjust actions toward women are normal.

Luckily, approximately 87 percent of the Israeli population is secular today and does not accept the ultra-Orthodox rules and lifestyles. Many Israelis accept women and women in Israel have equal rights, serve in the military, pursue education and work hard to contribute to society. The ultra-Orthodox issue is not new; it is unclear how much longer secular Jews, especially the secular women among them, can bear this religious coercion that manifests itself in a negative way, especially in the attitude toward women.[34]

SINGLE WOMEN AND WORK

New roles for women in the workplace open new possibilities for the single and the unmarried. There are many advantages over married women at work, advantages that are not normally articulated publicly, due to legal constraints. Oftentimes, companies are notorious for keeping their hiring practices a secret, because they are worried about what might happen if word gets out. Even if everything is above-board, the companies do not want to have to deal with scrutiny from outsiders.

In reality, the advantages to single women in the workplace start even before hiring. Companies love to hire single women over married ones, because the assumption is that single women will not have to take many days off to deal with family matters.[35] Additionally, some companies still hold to the outdated notion that married women's careers come after their husband's careers; therefore, if the husband has to move for work, the wife will follow, leaving her job. Currently, in many countries the hiring company is not allowed to ask about marital status. If a single woman is interested in emphasizing her availability for work, her added value that she is single by choice and won't relocate anywhere, she should somehow weave it into the conversation with the recruiter. She could even just mention it as a throwaway line. It is something the hiring manager will keep in mind when looking over the applicants.

When it comes to maintaining a job, unmarried women have a clear advantage over the married ones. A study conducted by Moen and Smith found that unmarried women were more committed to the workplace than married women. The study theorized that this could be so because married women have other commitments to accommodate, including spouses and children, if they have any.[36]

Additionally, single women are often paid more than married women. There are several reasons why this is the case.[37] The first is the idea that married women can rely on their husbands' incomes and single women don't have anyone to rely on but themselves. It's an old idea, but in this case, it tends to work to single women's benefit. The other reason why single women are paid more is the commitment level I spoke of previously. When people are more committed to their work, productivity rises, employers take notice and often increase salaries.

Single women do not have to worry about being tied down to one location when a new career option comes up. This gives them the freedom to move up in their careers. On the contrary, if a married woman is offered a job in some other region or country with a significant pay raise and promotion, she needs to check with her husband first and work with him to see if it would benefit both of them. She may or may not be able to take the job opportunity based on what her husband does for his work and the arrangements for the children (if there are any). Time is taken up in the decision-making process. Single women, on the other hand, think about themselves and their careers first. They can make the big career moves and take promotions without worry. Single women enjoy the freedom of taking more risks within their careers. They can choose to change companies and see how it turns out without having to worry about anyone else's jobs, preferences and interests.

HAPPILY UNMARRIED, HAPPILY DIVORCED

Marriage is on the decline today. In 1960, 72 percent of adults were married. By 2000, that number had dropped to 57 percent. In 2010, only 54 percent of adults were married.[38] Adults who do decide to marry are waiting longer than ever before to do so. The median ages at marriage in the United States rose to twenty-eight for men and twenty-six for women in 2009.[39] In the United Kingdom, for the same year, the median ages were 32.1 for men and 30 for women.[40]

Why are these numbers rising so drastically? I believe there are some important reasons. Women are making more money today. They can be more selective when dating, because they don't actually need men to support them financially anymore. They are also focusing on their careers more and gaining more success. That means that they have less time to date and more money to support their financial independence.

Additionally, cohabitation is becoming more common today. The number of people cohabiting has doubled since 1990 and 44 percent of adults have cohabited for some period of time.[41] With the difficult economy, people are skipping big, expensive weddings and moving in together to save on bills and other expenses.

People are also taking marriage more seriously and being more hesitant to make the commitment. This often results in couples not getting married, because they are not absolutely sure that it is for them. In a survey, 39 percent of people said that marriage is becoming obsolete today.[42]

Another issue is that heavy divorce rates contribute to wary attitudes toward marriage. Almost half of all marriages end in divorce today and many adults have witnessed divorce firsthand in their own childhoods. They do not want to relive the pain divorce causes. They are also less willing to commit to something permanent. Men and women generally think about marriage a lot more carefully. They look at all the reasons they should and should not marry their significant others, not just at love.

Many women are remaining happily unmarried or choosing not to remarry after a divorce today. Independent women are finding the appeal in being able to travel as they please, handle their finances as they prefer and forego making decisions with a partner.[43]

When it comes to how much extra work married women do, it is no wonder that many women are choosing the single life. Married women do 70 to 80 percent of the housework, whether they are employed or not. They are usually responsible for doing laundry, cooking meals, cleaning, driving carpool and staying home with sick children. Also, most wives maintain family relationships for their husbands by mailing birthday cards, doing the holiday shopping and hosting gatherings. Wives are also the ones who monitor the well-being of children and husbands by making healthy meals, encouraging exercise and scheduling doctor appointments.[44]

Many women play multiple roles throughout the day: employee, mother and wife. While men are also employees, their roles as fathers and husbands are not as demanding as that of mothers and wives. Women do about 80 percent of the childcare, which is as much as they did in the 1960s. The birth of a first child normally adds thirty-five hours to a wife's domestic workload. When fathers do help out, they are normally in charge of playtime activities rather than cooking, cleaning and laundry. Dads get to read stories and make up games, while moms are in charge of discipline, play dates, homework and caring for children when ill. No matter how much a couple declares their partnership equal, it normally becomes unfairly balanced when the first child comes along.[45]

Even if a woman didn't sign a prenuptial agreement, postnuptial agreements are becoming more acceptable today. The reason a postnuptial agreement might become necessary is if one spouse gets a significant raise or inherits a large amount of money. It can also be necessary if one partner suddenly starts making risky financial decisions. When one spouse, usually the wife, gives up a career to raise the children, a postnuptial agreement might reimburse her for the loss of income.[46]

Women in wealthy countries outside of the United States may have an easier time balancing work with children. Many countries provide paid maternity leave that averages twenty weeks in length. Finland is a leader in paid paternal leave, with 20 percent of new fathers taking about a month off work. While this is expensive for employers, they accept it because children are seen as the responsibility of society as a whole. In Nordic countries, affordable day-care with an excellent staff is provided. Low income families can send their children for free. America is the only rich country that does not require paid maternity leave. Until the Pregnancy Discrimination Act of 1978, American women could be fired for getting pregnant. It was not until the Family and Medical Act of 1993 that women had the right to take time off from work to have their children.[47]

In Israel, the system supports pregnant women by providing maternity leave of 3.5 months, fully covered by social security and an allowance payment for each newborn child as well as tax benefits. Kindergarten is free from the ages of four to five and, largely speaking, babies are encouraged on a national level. It is not surprising, then, that the birthrate is relatively high for the industrialized country with 2.97 children per Jewish mother for the year 2010. However, the women who reproduce most are still the religious ones, with four or more children.[48]

Although for most career women in the United States childcare is expensive and maternity leave is short, American women still have more children on average than European women. European countries average 1.7 children per woman, whereas American women have about 2.1 children.[49]

RETURNING TO YOUR CAREER
AFTER HAVING CHILDREN

While an equal number of women and men are part of the workforce, some women today choose to step out of the workforce to start families. Many are only content at home for a period of time. After a few years of packing lunches, seeing the children off to the school bus and classroom volunteering, they might decide to reestablish a career woman identity. Though it seems an intimidating prospect, it becomes easier when you take one step at a time.

There are several main motivators in wanting to return to work. The first is money. Maybe your partner's income is no longer sufficient to support the family. Maybe you are concerned about the financial future, mortgage payments, school tuition and retirement. Other possibilities are that you are ambitious or want or need the validation. While you chose to stay at home after proving that you were capable of having a career, you may once again want to prove that you are able to earn a substantial income. Another reason to go back to work is that you want to feel equal to your partner.[50]

Those women who do not feel intellectually stimulated at home may want to re-launch their careers. They may feel they will get a sense of achievement from doing difficult work tasks and assignments. There are also many mothers who love staying at home but want to avoid empty-nest syndrome. They need something to do and feel ambitious about when their children do not need them as much anymore. At that point a woman might want to return to work to serve as a good role model for her children, especially daughters. Some women may feel the need to fulfill unachieved career ambitions.[51]

As a modern woman who enters into the job search, there are a few things that you will require from a job. It is important to keep in mind that you will need control of your schedule. If your spouse is unable to get flexibility in his work hours to accommodate caring for the children, you will have to find a job that gives you flexibility. Some women don't want or can't have a set work schedule and prefer one that lets them do their work when and where they need to. Most likely, you will want the content of your job to be fulfilling. Find a position in which you are truly interested. You will also need adequate compensation for the work involved. Do your research to see what the rates are for the positions for which you are applying. It is likely that you will have to make some trade-offs in your schedule control, job content and compensation when you first return to the workplace. You may want or need to trade high compensation for a very flexible work schedule. It is all about finding what best fits your life.[52]

Take some classes to refresh your skills and get your confidence back. If you are contemplating a big career change, you might want to go back to school for an additional or new degree. Writing a new résumé is also important. Outline your past achievements and employment history. Keep the résumé concise. Cover letters are key. Explain why you are a good fit for a specific job. Spend time preparing for any potential interviews. Do a mental review of why you would excel with the company and what your strengths are.[53]

Getting the job takes a lot of work. Many open positions are not advertised. One way to get them is by being recommended by someone who already works at the company. For this you need to network. Start rekindling friendships with former coworkers. Let the other people in your volunteer groups know that you are on the job hunt.

Talk to neighbors who work in your target field. Networking is not about using people to get ahead. It is about showing a genuine interest in other people, so they in turn want to help you as well.[54]

You may want to prepare for your family's reaction to your going back to work. If your partner is highly dependent on you, it may be difficult for him to adjust to less attention from you. However, he might still be appreciative if the family could use more income. Talk to your children so they can adjust to not having you around as much. They are used to consistency and it will take some time before they accept and can adjust to a new routine in their lives.[55]

Many independent women feel they do not have to rely on a man to provide security in their lives. If a woman chooses to have a relationship, she is in it because she wants to be. At school or in the workplace, the modern woman does not let anything hold her back.

Women are good role models in their environments as well. They demonstrate daily that whether young or old, single or divorced, childless or a mother, they are intelligent, capable and caring. You can have a career and a family if you want; you can choose to stay unmarried and single and be very happy and caring as well as respected in your decisions about your life. So step ahead; make your choice. There are really no limits on what you can achieve.

Chapter 10

The Sexual Revolution:
Stage for New Options

Looking back briefly at the history of the first half of the twentieth century shows that women in the United States and many other counties around the world could vote and study, but a conservative aura prevailed with regard to work and matters of sexuality. It was made clear to women that after they studied at a university, the most logical and privileged option was to marry and begin a traditional, monogamous nuclear family. Rather than deal with the negative social stigma of being a single woman in a married woman's world, most young women found prospective husbands and became wives soon after college and quickly started to produce children in an effort to insure their "success." Between 1940 and 1960, the amount of women with three or more children reached a new high. Until the very liberal free love counterculture of the 1960s, which proposed freedom for all, the cultural opinion of the majority of people was still deeply ingrained toward pushing traditional marriage upon women.

Some affluent wives concentrated on dressing and living well. The image that was presented was that the institution of marriage afforded "princess-like" luxuries: being elegantly outfitted, living in lavish homes and bringing up successful children with the help of maids and nannies. This propaganda was put out at the same time that many women in the middle and lower classes were stay-at-home mothers or laboring at low-end jobs, but also working hard to provide their families adequate food and clothing. The media broadcasted the dreary lives, for instance, of Soviet women, many of whom had to raise their children alone in poverty under a communist system, with no other choice.

Before the sexual revolution, what many women failed to consider was the fact that they were capable of providing material comforts for themselves and security for their children if needed. Had they given half the energy that they gave to their husbands to furthering their own careers, there would be zero necessity to marry for financial reasons. Providing for themselves could have given these women both financial and emotional security, knowing that no matter what happened, they were capable of taking care of themselves.

One of the worst parts of earlier marriages is that many of these women became totally dependent on their partners financially and, after a while, could no longer conceive an exit plan if they ever wanted or needed to leave. Many believed that if they left their husbands they would become destitute and they and their children could become homeless and starve. Thankfully, nowadays many women have started accepting the idea that they can take care of themselves just fine if the necessity or desire arises.

With money being such a strong fear-based tie to a man, financial freedom is a crucial part of a woman's path to becoming liberated. Without financial freedom, a woman will never be able to feel sufficiently emotionally and physically free. Men know this and, until a few decades ago, many sadly controlled their women through financial dominance.

A STEP AHEAD WITH THE CONDOM

It was bad enough that, in earlier times, women were financially and emotionally dependent on their husbands, but also the majority of families were composed of at least three children and perhaps more. The dependence on their husbands of women who had no careers became even stronger with the birth of children. They became even more persuaded, no matter how valid their reasons to leave, that they had to remain tethered.

There were always some women who desired to break free of this lifestyle, but unfortunately, there was not an effective contraceptive available to the majority of people. This lack of easily accessible contraceptives meant that many women, whether they wanted to or not, entered a couple of decades of their lives where they faced child-bearing years in an almost mechanical reproductive mode, bearing child after child.[1]

This is not to say that childbearing cannot be a positive option in a woman's life. On the contrary! If a woman has created a solid foundation for herself—for example if she is educated, financially sound and independent and has had the chance to develop herself through following her passions and interests—that provides a good start for both her and her child. Unfortunately, this was not the case for the typical woman in earlier times.

Another issue facing women was not just the quantity of children that they bore, but also the short amount of time they had to recoup between births. This rapid childbearing put undue physical, emotional and financial pressure on women and their family structures.

The condom, an early form of birth control, had been recognized by 1666. At its inception, condoms were made from the linings of animal intestines or from cloths that had been treated with certain chemicals to kill sperm. The problem with these first condoms were that they were incredibly expensive, inaccessible to most people, uncomfortable and unreliable.[2] The situation improved a little when the first condom made of rubber appeared on the market in 1855 and then made leaps and bounds with the invention of Latex, which made for thinner, cheaper, disposable condoms that could be mass produced. Once the Food and Drug Administration approved these condoms as a legitimate source of birth control and regulated their quality, the condom became more popular.

However, although condom use became more widespread after the 1950s, even among married partnerships, there was increasingly heavy pressure from the Catholic Church against their use.

One negative of condoms for women is that although they are cheap and easily accessible, it puts the power of safe sex in the control of the man. If a man does not choose to use a condom or uses it incorrectly, a woman unfortunately isn't left with too many options for safe sex.

Another negative of condoms is that although they are relatively reliable with proper use, they still do not guarantee perfect safety. Condoms break, slip off or can even be intentionally used improperly by a man who wishes to get his partner pregnant.

During earlier periods, unmarried women who got pregnant were often sent away by their families and were shunned by society. They were thought of as a disgrace and were often pressured to give up their children to other, more responsible adoptive families. This type of harsh treatment toward young women impressed upon other women that marriage was the first step. This way they could avoid shame from society and their families.

The problem with this rigid and oppressive attitude toward sex is that it does not address the issue as a whole. Most believe today that sex is not just about procreation. Sex can and should be enjoyed on many different levels to deepen intimacy in a relationship, enjoy the company of another, diminish stress or have a good time. Many feel none of these things should necessarily be bound to marriage. Procreation can happen, especially with irresponsible sex, but it should only have to happen if both partners are fully committed to the idea of raising a child together. If neither wants to be a parent, that does not, in most opinions, negate the other benefits of a sexual relationship.

One of the problems with the strict and unforgiving moral codes of the mid-twentieth century is that sex for pleasure was completely denied. This type of sex was propagated as being sinful. But many, myself included, believe that sex for pleasure is a simple act, given to the human race to enjoy. Denying this right, this blessing, only leads to an intensification of sexual desire, which can be expressed through masturbation, cheating on your partner or enjoying the company of prostitutes who live outside this moral code. As we should have learned from the Victorian Era, trying to restrain sexuality only seems to deepen attraction to it in all of its shapes and forms.

Nevertheless, by the end of the 1950s, many women were still having a number of children.[3] Despite use of condoms and the more complex, lesser use of the diaphragm, women were pressured to have large families as a measure of success and single women were expected to abstain from sex altogether.

REVOLUTION WITH THE PILL

As the civil rights movement was gaining support, women began to take note of their own sense of being discriminated against. They had received the right to vote, which should never be underestimated, yet they still lacked the ability to control their bodies or their procreation and they were not sexually liberated. Most decisions regarding sex still resided heavily in the male partner's control.

One of the effects of women having so many children was that it directly impeded their abilities to achieve higher work positions or professions or to explore their own passions and desires so that they could grow as individuals. Women could study and also do some work outside the home (as many of them did during wartime) but husbands and the culture often reiterated the fact, overtly and covertly, that a woman's natural place was in the house with the family and that any other personal desires of hers, such as a career or further education, were silly dreams that needed to be forgotten. As for trying to better plan her pregnancies so as not to overburden her financial, emotional or physical capabilities, that seemed out of the question.

For most single women, societal and religious reproaches did not mean that they stopped being sexually active. But a freer lifestyle, which I strongly believe should be the undeniable right of any single woman, came with a steep price to pay. Social pressures were harsh and sexually active single women were met with intolerance. Without good contraceptive options, these women were forced to live in constant fear of becoming pregnant, which meant that society and their families would shun them and they would be at high risk of losing their jobs. Both married and single women were searching for answers to their birth control issues. It was high time that sexual choice and power was given back to women.

In the 1960s in the United States, the birth control pill was approved by the Food and Drug Administration. Although some parts of the United States restricted sales of the pill to married women and some women had some slight medical complications, nonetheless it was finally a viable option for women to take charge of their own reproductive choices without having to rely on the cooperation of a man.[4] The pill started out as a popular and well-received method of birth control and grew in popularity by huge leaps every year that followed for the next ten years.

The fact that many pharmacists were able to provide pills not only for medical reasons, but also for supporting social choices, was a huge step toward cementing women's independence. Once women had this choice, there was no going back. Women's lives changed rapidly as their birth control dependence on men diminished. A mere two years after the pill's release to the public, over a million women had taken their sexual choices into their own hands by choosing to use the pill.

The pill was the most effective contraceptive that had been released so far and this power was given to females. For the first time in history, women could enjoy sexually active lives while being released from the fear of unwanted pregnancies. They could avoid pregnancy altogether or give their bodies time to rest between wanted pregnancies. With the risk of conception diminished, women could finally enjoy sex for all of its benefits besides procreation. This empowered women in a way that should not be underestimated.

SEXUAL LIBERATION

As the 1960s continued, there were more women working than ever before, even more than during World War II, which had seen an employment boom.[5] Women had become used to earning their own incomes and were starting to express themselves not only as mothers and wives, but also as individuals who were just as capable, just as competent and just as filled with sexual desire as their male counterparts.

Having access to the birth control pill opened up women's ideas about sexual freedom. Women started to question the rigid roles that society had pinned them into and they began to break out of these narrow roles. In addition, social norms gradually became much more relaxed and women began formulating less conservative decisions in regards to the traditional sense of relationships, marriage and childbearing. When the risk of pregnancy was diminished, sexually active single women became much more relaxed about enjoying their newfound sexual freedom, knowing that they weren't facing the social stigma of becoming unwed mothers.

Not everyone took so well to the idea of sexually liberated and empowered females with the control of childbearing fully in their hands. Some religious groups, including the Catholic Church, felt the pill represented a breakdown of morality and would cause the destruction of the family unit. Huge rifts erupted between parts of society: those that thought of the pill as one of the best things to happen to women and those that thought it was the worst thing. Some even went so far as to say that this new form of contraception was the push that started the "free love" sexual revolution of the 1960s.

Even though some forces tried to create a backlash against the pill, the breakthrough in women's mindsets had already been made and there was no going back to the confines of the past. The appearance of the pill made possible a dramatic shift from sex as procreation to the possibility of sex as recreation. Women, both single and married, were able to enjoy sex for pleasure, without the worry of an unwanted pregnancy, which would likely tie them in marriages to partners with whom they might not want to raise a child.

With the risk of pregnancy reduced, both women and men began to explore this new sexual world. Sex was more casual and laid back and sex before marriage became almost a norm. Married couples had more freedom to think about cheating without the risk of bringing an extramarital baby into the equation. Women who had been, in the past, so weighed down with the natural association of sex with unwanted pregnancy had not been able to enjoy sex for pleasure with all of these other thoughts running through their minds. But with this risk gone, they could enjoy sex for the sake of having sex, for no other reason but the fact that they are sexual beings and can derive vast amounts of pleasure from the sexual act. The empowerment of this realization of sex as recreation, which men had enjoyed for a long time, was now in the hands of the females.

Historically, men had always had the easy end of the bargain. They could enjoy sex and, if a pregnancy occurred, it was not their bodies that had to bear the consequences. A man could also leave a partnership with minimum stigma from society, whereas a woman could not turn her back on the pregnancy or family without serious results. Now the person who dealt most with the effect of a sexual relationship held the power in her hands to control its outcome.

So, with a new world to explore, many women decided to postpone marriage to allow themselves the time and the freedom to enjoy themselves and their singlehood. The 1960s was a decade of experimentation with relationships and the idea of family and monogamy. Women, in one short decade, went from stifled, meek beings consumed by household chores and in charge of large families, with their husbands having almost no childrearing duties while the husbands enjoyed furthering their careers, to being fully empowered, self-assured, equal partners.

Whereas in the past a woman was expected to be a virgin until her wedding night, these social norms were forced to come under scrutiny and evolve. Many women were attending co-ed college campuses and saw sexual experimentation as just as much a part of their education as what they learned in the classroom. Some women even engaged in premarital sex to rebel against the rigid social structure that had been set up in earlier times.

THE SEXUAL TURNS POLITICAL

This newfound sexual freedom's scope was wide. In many societies in past eras, the integral foundation of a healthy society was the idea of a nuclear family. Now in the Western world, values such as freedom of choice, equal rights and social expression became valued just as highly.[6] Many of these younger generations, who saw their parents grow up in the rigid 1930s to the 1950s, decided that the next generations should never have to deal with those same unjust ways. The young generations, especially in America, started to rebel.

The women's liberation movement could not have come at a better time in history, because of the other events that were taking place around the world. With the Vietnam War overseas, which sparked ferocious anti-war protests, and the Civil Rights movement in the United States, all of these endeavors were basically going toward the same end: peace and freedom from oppression, no matter which form that oppression came in.

Many people, especially within the younger generations, awakened and began to fight back against oppression in many forms. They fought against war, poverty, racism, environmental destruction, technocracy and oppression both in society and in the family structure.[7] These fights, I believe, were all tied together by an attempt to liberate people.

Although in the past open discussion of sex, especially among women, was considered taboo, these new generations pushed the limits in ways that their forefathers never would have imagined. The 1960s brought the onset of the "free love" hippie generation, filled with flower children who talked openly and unapologetically about sex, masturbation and erotic fantasies and experimented with psychedelics and open relationships with multiple lovers.

This created a large shift in the psyche of many people, especially Americans, and caused upheavals that forced people to question both the old ways and the new. Boundaries were pushed further and people had to find their own comfort zones, which could not be dependent on traditional structures anymore. The old ways were crumbling fast.

People no longer held on to past conventions, which was good. This liberated them to find their own freedom without the coercion of institutions or establishments such as government or religion. Much was being done in regards to freedom of speech and expression, but on the home front many women were fighting specifically for freedom from patriarchal oppression.

Many women at this time were beginning to question the Church's and State's involvements in their sexual choices.[8] Women were strongly taking back control on the concepts of marriage, sexuality and birth control. It was a new world for these women, one that their mothers and grandmothers would not recognize.

THE BREAKDOWN OF PATRIARCHAL MARRIAGE

With new generations breaking boundaries and experimenting, authority, especially patriarchal authority with puritanical undertones, had officially been lost. Free-loving women who had had an authentic taste of freedom were not enticed by the idea of marrying and settling down in a house where they could raise children while their husbands furthered their careers. After college, many of these women set out to better themselves by whichever form of expression worked for them. For some it was travel, for others their careers, while still others found personal happiness though cohabitation without marriage.

Without the focus of the rigid and streamlined education-marriage-children route, many women took advantage of the access they had to condoms and the pill, which together diminished risk for both pregnancy and sexually transmitted diseases, and they began to experiment with sex as a way to know themselves more fully. Also during this time, many girls engaged in promiscuous sex and got pregnant, so there was a rise in unwed teen mothers too.[9]

Perhaps because of all of the changes that had come so quickly as industries tried to sell happiness to society, these generations that fought for women's liberation also fought for liberation on the happiness front. They were smart enough to see that happiness needed to come on a personal level, that it was not something that could be created by heavy industry nor bought with a credit card. While these people were enjoying more material success than their forebears, at the same time they were aware that the future should encompass much more than the ability to buy goods.

This new generation challenged norms and fought for what they believed in. Where they saw injustice or exploitation, especially when it came to women, children or minorities, they fought vigorously.

There were many ties between the fight against capitalism and the fight for women's liberation. Women were having a hard time finding where they stood in their power. Either they served on the home front as dutiful wives or mothers and supported a patriarchal institution or they entered the workforce and served the needs fueling capitalistic powers. Either one of these roles repressed the sexual liberties that women had just recently been afforded.

Because the patriarchal system meant that women were oppressed and employment meant that women were oppressed, a new method had to come about to further the liberation of women. The fight became more revolutionary and political, with issues such as abortion, birth control, homosexuality and relationship status becoming politically charged.

This shift from personal freedoms and sexual expression to political issues divided society, especially in America. The liberals saw the work for women's liberation as essential to any country that was looking to base itself on human rights and equality. Conservatives believed that this fight for women's equality could destroy everything that they had come to know and love about traditional family structure and saw empowered women as a threat. The conservatives argued against what they saw as moral evils, such as pornography, single moms, abortion and anything that defied traditional marriage and raising children within a patriarchal system, a system they saw as crumbling.

As much as conservatives would have liked to blame the collapse of marriage as an institution on promiscuity and the sexual liberation of women, it is a contemporary issue that must be studied in depth. Marriage was not declining because women were having sex. On the contrary, I feel women were having enjoyable, pleasurable and healthy sex because marriage as an institution was not enough to fulfill them as human beings.

Once women became aware that they deserved more than what they could receive within the confines of an oppressive marriage, some no longer accepted marriage as a viable option. I feel deeply that not only in the 1960s but also today, patriarchal control is no match for a liberated, empowered modern woman who knows exactly who she is, what she wants and what she deserves—a woman who trusts fully in her belief in herself and in her ability to create everything she wants in life, with or without a man.

HOW SEX IS CHANGING

The sex lives of single people have changed dramatically in the past decade. One-night stands and multiple sex partners are less taboo for women today, who used to be called "sluts" if they had sex with someone who wasn't their boyfriend. Now many single women have purely sexual relationships. "Friends with benefits" relationships are becoming more common.

Many late-night hookups are facilitated by texting today. While in the past women would not call a man while in a crowded bar late at night, now it is easy to send a quick text to someone. Guys especially will text multiple women to improve their odds of going home with someone. Texting makes communication easier sometimes and keeps people in touch more quickly and effectively. Many women have busy day-to-day lives and can't call someone while in a class or meeting. It also makes initiating dates less nerve-wracking for both sides. One only has to send a casual text, so rejection does not hurt as much.

Social networking sites make it easy to find out who is single. If a woman is interested in someone who isn't part of her regular social circle, she can contact him online instead of just hoping to bump into him somewhere. Guys, in particular, will use social networking to find women they met at parties and then invite them out. For many men, the more women they are friends with online, the cooler they appear, and the odds of finding a hookup increase accordingly. In addition to the college party scene that is common for younger women, dating sites can be used to cultivate potential romances at any age. There are sites tailored to finding true love, finding hookups, senior citizens, Jews, Christians and homosexuals. Currently there are also dating sites exclusively for beautiful people, for people who are geeks, for gay men who like younger men, for those who are seeking affairs, for women looking for rich men and for people who want to have their DNA analyzed to test compatibility.

The expectations of men have also changed. Women used to expect to be taken to dinner and lavished with attention before they had sex with a man. While some men still might do these things, many today will not. Often, women are too preoccupied with their own schedules to have much free time for dating, so some women want to get right to the point.

Sex is no longer a topic that people shy away from discussing. Popular magazines print covers with features such as "Improve Your Sex Life," "Be a Bad Girl in Bed," and "21 Naughty Sex Tips." On top of this, people are overwhelmed with information about sex and for many it starts to seem like a casual act. Sex is frequent on television programs, in advertisements and in movies today. Sex scandals among celebrities and politicians are considered ratings boosters and almost always make headlines. Friends discuss their hookups openly with one another. And women worry less about pleasing men in bed and more about mutual giving and receiving of pleasure. Sex is no longer a dirty word. Sex is empowering and liberating today.

MODERN AND POSTMODERN RELATIONSHIPS

The dating rules have changed and now a woman does not have to commit to one man. There are many different ways that women today can maintain relationships, short-term or long-term. There are also many women choosing to live the single life.

Living together is becoming a popular option for couples who are not sure whether they want to get married. According to a *Time Magazine* article, "There are currently 5 million heterosexual couples cohabiting in the United States, a number that has tripled since 1980."[10] Cohabiting can provide an abundance of benefits to both parties involved and no longer requires wedding rings and a joint bank account. Both partners can save money, because there are two people contributing to rent, utilities and groceries. Partners can both reduce stress, because there are two people to do the cleaning and household chores. Many young couples are choosing to cohabit and have children together. The advantage is that both partners can still be a part of their children's daily lives.

Couples that cohabit can keep their finances separate or handle them together. Women still have security, but they also have the option to walk away if something goes terribly wrong in a relationship. When a cohabiting relationship ends, the partners will not spend thousands of dollars in legal fees and settlements as married couples do in a divorce.

Many long-term couples are now trying the Living Apart Together (LAT) dwelling option. Such partners may cook together, go to family events, spend time with mutual friends, go on vacations and are part of each other's lives. The difference is that the partners do not live together under the same roof. Each has his or her own home paid for by that partner and finances are kept separate.[11]

This arrangement works especially well if one partner has children who have already experienced a divorce. Often a woman chooses this arrangement because she does not want to expose her children to potential pain by moving in with a new boyfriend, having the children accept him as a reliable figure and then not having the relationship work out. This way, children can see their mother's long-term partner as a role model. But if there is a breakup, their day-to-day lives will not be disturbed very much.

However, LAT is not just for people who have children. It can work well in other relationships. Not being with each other constantly makes partners appreciate the time they do have together. They may find that they also are more attracted to each other when they spend time apart. Partners might even find that they are more productive and successful in their careers or education. Extra alone time in the evenings allows partners to brainstorm and focus on work when they would normally be spending this time together. In the United States today, 7 percent of women and 6 percent of men classify themselves as Living Apart Together. Additionally, 3 percent of married couples are trying this option today.[12]

Many modern women refuse to commit to one man. They believe that they have everything they need on their own: a home, a career and the option to have children without a husband. These independent women are single by choice, but still enjoy dating. They go on fun dates and maybe have a few flings, but their sense of self is still intact. Since they are the boss, they can have as much time to themselves as they desire.

THE CHANGING MODERN FAMILY

The definition of *family* is changing today. Only 25 percent of American households live as a traditional nuclear family.[13] Some parents remain unmarried, some single women raise children alone and some gay and lesbian couples adopt or choose to parent with a surrogate. Modern women and men seem to be acknowledging that the conventional family route is not well-suited for their lives. Fortunately, today's society gives more acceptance to nontraditional parenting and living arrangements.

Most people would agree that a family does not have to exist in the traditional sense in order to serve as a family. For many people, families are constructed more like a set of relationships. According to the *USA Today* article "What does a 'family' look like nowadays?", results from a survey indicate that "86% say a single parent and child are a family, 80% say an unmarried couple living together with a child is a family, 63% say a gay or lesbian couple raising a child is a family."[14] Families still care for and support family members, but the big change is that families no longer require marriage.

The number of unmarried women having children has risen significantly. Today, 40 percent of babies are born to single or unmarried women compared to 1960, when only 5 percent of babies were born to unmarried mothers.[15] In the age group of twenty-five to twenty-nine years, 30 percent more unmarried women have had babies since 1991. Amongst the thirty- to forty-four-year-olds, there has been a 17 percent rise in births out of wedlock.[16]

Some people worry that children growing up in nontraditional family settings might not get the necessary emotional support or attention. In reality, children living in nonnuclear families receive about the same amount of parental involvement as children who have traditional family lives. This is good news, because some behavioral problems in children have been linked to low levels of parental involvement.[17] Many children get the same amount of time with their mothers regardless of the type of male figure that is in their lives. Children often receive the same amount of attention from a male who lives in the household and who is unmarried to their mother as they would from a biological father who is married to their mother.[18] According to research, a happy childhood appears to be more about the type of attention and care a child receives and not about whether they live within the "ideal" family model.

Many people have the belief that men and women should contribute equally to raising the children and taking care of household chores. While many progressive, unmarried couples do live by these standards, other people get married and fall out of this pattern shortly after saying "I do." In rich countries, women contribute an average of thirty-three unpaid hours a week doing household chores, while men only contribute sixteen hours. Because women are often responsible for maintaining home life, they generally put in fewer work hours than men. However, among European countries, only 16 to 18 percent of women reported being dissatisfied with their work-home balance, while 20 to 27 percent of men were dissatisfied.[19]

A large number of women are now choosing not to have children at all. Nearly 20 percent of American women and more in Japan, Germany, China and Spain as well as other countries end their reproductive years without having children. In the United States, this statistic is up from only 10 percent in the 1970s. Worried about their biological clocks, many women struggle with the idea of having children, because they don't want a baby at the moment, but they fear that later they will regret not having children.[20]

Not wanting to have children often stems from not wanting to give up freedom or success. Many women now view their careers as more than just a means to pay the bills. They want to do work that they are passionate about and good at. They want to fulfill their potential and make their dreams a reality. So if, in the case of having a child, the focus shifts from career to family, women worry that they will ruin their success. Additionally, independent women are not used to changing their daily lives to fit someone else's needs.[21]

Some women just do not have a domestic motivation. The idea of getting married and caring for a husband and children doesn't sound appealing to them and may instead seem intimidating and boring. Changing diapers, doing loads of laundry, cooking dinner every night and driving carpool puts a damper on careers and personal time. In some relationships, both parties share the household responsibilities. But it appears to be harder work than happily living the single life.

SINGLE MOTHERHOOD BY CHOICE

More and more women are putting their relationship pursuits on hold to achieve career and personal goals. Some women are also getting the urge to have children before they find "Mr. Right." Among the reasons a woman may choose to have a baby alone are: she doesn't want to compromise with someone else on the way the child is raised, she feels her biological clock ticking but she is not in a long-term relationship, she decides the best thing about marriage is children, so marriage is not necessary.

Whatever the reason, women are not alone if they choose to have children as single parents. According to an article in *The New York Times*, "the birthrate for unmarried college-educated women has climbed 145 percent since 1980." For unmarried women without a college education, the birthrate has risen only 60 percent. About 40 percent of unmarried college-educated women "give birth for the first time after age 30."[22] Many of these women decide that they don't need to wait for a man before they have a family. They decide to have the family and life that they want.

After having a first child, women are not necessarily looking for a man to fill the father role. In some cases, they even decide to give their child a sibling.[23] Most women who choose to be single moms plan ahead financially. Since a great many have college educations, they don't necessarily need the second income that a spouse would provide.

It is a common belief that children in single-parent homes end up emotionally damaged. High school dropout rates are high, boys become criminals and girls become promiscuous. These scenarios, however, tend to happen with children who witnessed their parents' emotional divorce and have experienced a substantial decline in household income. A child born to a single mother by choice does not experience a parental divorce. In my opinion, that's a big plus. Most single-by-choice mothers are financially stable and their children do not have to go through an economic decline as well.[24]

Some single mothers choose to find sperm donors. The two types of donors are known donors and unknown donors. Known donors can be friends or relatives. The benefit of having a known donor is that a woman can observe the man's physical traits and what his personality is like. He is available to share his medical history, which better prepares mothers for the future. The downside of having a known donor is that emotional conflicts can arise. It is important to sign an insemination agreement before committing to a known donor.[25]

Unknown donors are usually found through sperm banks. For a small fee, women can browse the profiles of thousands of men in sperm bank databases. One can search for a man based on physical traits, educational background and medical history. The sperm bank will ensure that donors are disease-free, healthy and have quality sperm. For additional money, a sperm seeker can see baby photos of the donor, hear voice recordings or read an extended profile. Doctors charge between two hundred and four hundred dollars for donors' sperm and there is an additional cost for the insemination procedure. Donors are not notified when their sperm is used and the sperm bank provides the donor agreement.[26]

There are no government regulations for sperm banks, so women choosing this route should do research. There are several standards a good facility should meet: perform personal interviews of all donors, obtain complete medical histories of donors going back four generations whenever possible, freeze sperm for at least six months to allow complete testing for diseases, track and limit the number of pregnancies per donor, perform physical exams and blood tests on all donors, rule out genetic mental health issues from donors, perform genetic and chromosomal analysis on donors, set a minimum number of sperm per sample.[27]

Another option for women who want to raise children is adoption. Adoption provides nurturing, loving, safe environments for parentless children. Single women who adopt are usually older, more mature and in a stable financial situation to raise a child. Since single women who adopt have to provide all of the income, that means they generally have to go to work every day and are often happy to adopt a child who is old enough to go to school, while most couples want to adopt babies. Disabled children may also benefit greatly from being adopted by single mothers. Women can devote more time to their children when they do not have to commit time to husbands as well.

While single parent adoption is permitted in all states, there is some bias against it amongst social workers and agencies. The main concern is usually the support system for the child and potential parent. Women pursing this path should have a plan for all potential scenarios, because it may be difficult for them to get approval from a social worker. These women should demonstrate that they have planned to support a child financially and have friends and/or family willing to help.[28]

For international adoptions, a local agency can coordinate with the international agency. Each country has its own requirements. A woman must consider how she feels about raising a child who is not the same ethnicity as she. Some countries will assign a child while other countries will have a prospective parent go to the orphanage to select one. In either case, once at home with the child, the new mother needs to help him or her become a citizen in her country. She may have to readopt her child in a state court, since the government is not required to recognize an adoption that took place in a foreign country.[29]

Another method for women who can't have their own children or who don't want to adopt is to find surrogates to carry their children. There are two types of surrogacy: traditional and gestational. In the traditional method, the surrogate mother's own eggs are used with donor sperm. In gestational surrogacy, eggs that don't belong to the surrogate mother, but to another woman, are used. The potential parent pays the surrogate's medical expenses along with a possible fee for carrying the child. The cost of surrogacy can be anywhere from twenty-five thousand to over fifty thousand dollars, depending on the contract, unexpected medical issues with the pregnancy and the difficulty of conception. In some states today it is illegal to pay for surrogacy, while in some other states surrogacy contracts are not enforced.[30]

There are programs that match surrogates with potential parents. Most programs try to find surrogates who are married and already have children. The intention is that these women will be aware of what pregnancy and birth are like before taking on surrogacy. If a surrogate is fulfilled in her own family life, she will be less likely to change her mind and want to keep the baby. Another option is to find a surrogate on your own. A close friend or relative might be willing. California has the clearest and most definite laws and legal procedures in place regarding surrogacy, so some people go there to avoid potential conflicts.

NON-SEXIST MINDS THAT LEAD THE WAY

As a self-determined and informed woman living in today's world, you are probably aware of the many advantages available to you in society. Women today have incredible educational and career opportunities that seemed unimaginable fifty years ago. There are many choices for women in this era to follow their dreams and make their unique marks in life. Women have come a long way in just a very short period of time. Some women might think that they have it all and the battle has been won. But the system requires more adjustments in order to ensure continuation of the progress made.

Maintaining the status quo will not suffice for modern and ambitious women who occasionally face discrimination, sexism and stereotyping that commonly categorizes them as less intelligent, less capable or less serious than men. Unfortunately, even today some men still consider women the "weaker sex," "dumb blondes," "bitches," "just mothers" or "whores."

Sexism and stereotypical thinking about women and their roles in society and family, which characterizes men's attitude toward women in some radical Muslim countries, is still present in some cases in the industrialized world despite the egalitarianism and women's rights that have been won. It might be more subtle than the blatant stereotyping of the past, but it still exists. As a woman, perhaps you have no problem speaking up to defend yourself if you are told that you can't handle a man's job; yet you may let slide the very circumstances that discourage fairness and equality.

One way in which this stereotypical thinking affects women lies in the misguided concept that women need "fixing" and not the system itself. For instance, many organizations today still structure their work using methods that were effective in past decades. Although many women work full-time today and serve as breadwinners in addition to their roles as mothers, in dual-income families many companies and organizations fail to acknowledge that women's circumstances are fundamentally different.[31] The issue of childbearing and childrearing still prevents many women from succeeding in their careers.

Women do not demand special favors in this realm. They are simply asking for society to consider their needs from a female perspective instead of offering "equality" within a patriarchal structure which does little to instill pride and promote effective change.

It is not just in the workplace that women at times find themselves at a disadvantage. The cultural expectation that women are supposed to fall in love, get married and live happily ever after places enormous pressure on those who choose instead to engage in new relationship options, family structures and lifestyles as well as on those women who believe that marriage is not the ultimate means to fulfillment in life. The pressure to conform to old-fashioned values in a world that is changing its rules by adopting new and legitimate modes of behavior creates unnecessary anxiety and stress for some women who embrace the new relationship options and family structures that are non-traditional.

This stereotypical social pressure to marry is inconsistent with modern times. In our postmodern world, I strongly believe there is no reason for an independent woman to say, "I do." Today's women should absolutely have the unequivocal right to be self-sufficient in all aspects of their lives, including their sexual, relationship and family choices. It is clear that in order for women to fulfill their true potential in society, a non-sexist mindset is necessary.

Chapter 11

New Roles Women Can Play in Relationships

Sixty years ago, the dominant goal that women had for themselves was to get married and raise a family. It was an idea that was emphasized repeatedly with little consideration about what women might actually want for themselves. Women became convinced that without husbands, they were doomed to live as spinsters and never find the happiness that all the married couples around them seemed to have. Some of the more popular television shows of the 1960s furthered this view: *Leave it to Beaver*, *I Love Lucy*, *The Dick Van Dyke Show*, *Family Affairs*. These shows depicted mostly happy families or marriages. They attempted to model for people how to live everyday life and they illustrated for women how to be good wives and mothers and take care of their husbands.

Times have changed and now being a single woman is no longer a curse or a detriment. It's something to be celebrated and enjoyed, because single women have made leaps and bounds in the past few decades to diminish the stigma attached to them. During the past twenty years the media has showcased single women in such shows as *Murphy Brown*, *Friends*, *Ally McBeal* and *Sex and the City*. These shows went against traditional views of women's roles and allowed single women to rejoice in their singlehood.

With every year that passes, more women are choosing to remain unmarried or to escape unhappy marriages. Divorce is no longer taboo, because almost half of the people who get married end up getting divorced. Also, most people today are more understanding of divorce and feel that it is better to be single and happy than to be married and miserable.

There are numerous benefits to remaining single and unmarried. Single women have more freedom to make the choices that benefit them. They have more control over where their money and their time goes and, as a result, more time for their friends and family. Being single in today's world can be fantastic as long as the single woman is active and spends energy pursuing family, friends, education and career.

It used to be the case that no one would hire a woman when there was a man available to fill the same role. The prevalent idea was that men have to provide for their families; therefore, it made sense in the mind of the employer to hire the person who needed the job the most. Today women are slowly receiving the jobs for which they are qualified. Employers' state of mind is different. As we discussed, some employers now see single women as assets.

This sweeping change in the perception of single women also applies to single mothers across the Western world and more recently has even spread to China, where more women remain single. Unlike in the past, they are embraced and helped on their journeys. They don't have to feel disgraced, ashamed or overwhelmed by motherhood. If necessary, resources, support and aid are available. In some countries such as France and the Nordic countries, there are government programs, support groups, daycares and many other options that single mothers make use of in order to give their children the best lives possible.

In light of the new roles that women play in today's world, there are many options available to single women. Singlehood is something to be reveled in, not something to shy away from or be embarrassed about. With the new alternatives to traditional marriage, more single women carve their own paths and create the lives they desire for themselves.

MARRIAGE AND DIVORCE IN THE UNITED STATES

The United States is one of the last of the Western countries to hold marriage in such high regard. When questioned, people in the United

States tend to respond that they believe that marriage still works and that it is important for two people to remain together to raise a child; however, Americans' actions tell a different story. In the 1960s, 72 percent of people married and remained married. Over the years the number has diminished and by 2008, only 52 percent of adults married and stayed married.[1] It looks like people's actions betray their spoken ideals about marriage.

In the United States, about 40 percent of marriages end in divorce. Why is that? Part of the reason is fact that singles, especially in the US, tend to feel "incomplete" without a relationship of some kind.[2] Couples are also quick to marry without deep contemplation. The problem is that the notion of marriage is so deeply ingrained in people's minds that they believe women need husbands to make them happy, to give them babies, to make them whole. Because of this, many US and Western European women come to believe that an unhappy relationship is better than none at all. With such stereotypical perceptions about relationships and marriage, it is no wonder women end up in unhappy marriages and divorce. But since divorce no longer imparts the same negative stigma that it had in the past, it's no longer a shameful experience for the couples. The end result: some couples who stayed together in the past out of concerns about social status no longer feel a need to do so.[3]

Similarly, more people in the US are reporting that their divorces ultimately made them happier. They were no longer stuck living with or pretending to love someone whom they no longer loved. They realized that their individual freedom and happiness were more important than the false compromises they had to make. Women realize that there are many options available after divorce, options that would have never materialized while still married, such as work opportunities, financial freedom or not having to account for their activities, time and money to anyone.

Also, many people feel that love is more important than marriage and this idea is even more meaningful to those who have been married and divorced. Men and women can still be in relationships, if they choose, without ever getting married. They can share finances or not, live together or not, have children or not, raise the children together or not. Through not being married, women are left with so many options available to make their own choices. And if they make the wrong choice, it is also easier for them to correct.[4]

SINGLE WOMEN AROUND THE WORLD

In some places around the world, marriage isn't critical. In England, for instance, interest centers on a couple's child and how he or she will be raised, rather than on saving the marriage from ending. It is more important for the child to be in a happy and stable environment than it is for the couple involved to stay married.[5] The English system is more focused on ensuring a happy childhood for the children, whether their parents are married or not. Unlike in the US, couples are not pushed into remaining married "for the kids."

In France, more people than in the United States think that marriage is an "outdated institution."[6] Such people recognize that marriages in the Western world are failing at rapid rates and marriage may not be the best solution for two people. This perception is currently spreading to other parts of Europe and the US, a phenomenon that is paving the way toward full acceptance of remaining single or unmarried as a valid choice for women to make.

This also holds true in other parts of Europe and Scandinavia. For example, unmarried couples in Sweden who raise children are more apt to stay together than married couples with children in the United States.[7] This further strengthens the idea that marriage is not necessarily the key to having healthy relationships and raising happy and healthy children. It could also mean that relationships may work better outside of marriage due to less pressure on the partners. Without marriage as part of the equation, happy and successful relationships can still be attained but with much less stress.

Such a conception about marriage is also prevalent outside the US, Europe and Scandinavia. One Australian study analyzed women between the ages of seventy-two and seventy-five who never had married and never had children. Women in this group were generally happier, because they had more time to take care of themselves, their households and their hobbies. Unmarried women in their seventies were more likely to make home improvements, volunteer and socialize.[8] This demonstrates that many women who opt to stay unmarried or single by choice without children are likely to have active retirements full of happiness and joy, without feeling remorse or regret about their decision to remain unmarried and childless.

NEW RELATIONSHIP OPTIONS

Many women around the world are still conditioned culturally to enter into marriage whether it is right for them or not. No one should be in a relationship just for the sake of saying she is in one. Some women are not accustomed to the idea that they actually have a choice in this extremely important matter. Other relationship options or possibilities might look strange or inappropriate at first. Today, many people are entering or bypassing relationships solely based on what a relationship can do for their own benefits, whether sexual, emotional or financial. More people are entering alternative relationships and enjoying mutual satisfaction, both physical and emotional, rather than marriage as the end goal.

SINGLE BY CHOICE

You do not have to feel compelled to follow in the footsteps of those women who opt for traditional marriage, unless that is your choice. On the contrary, many contemporary women are coming to the realization that remaining single by choice is the perfect option for them. These strong, confident and successful women are not afraid to place their own needs first. They do not waste their precious time and energy searching for husbands in order to feel fulfilled. Instead, they set their sights on their own personal goals and accomplishments. These women do not need husbands just so they can measure up to others' relationship expectations and they certainly don't see themselves as missing anything.

I strongly believe a woman should never have to justify her decision to remain single by choice. While there are those who believe that marriage is the ultimate goal for all women, this is just another example of the stereotypical thinking that persists. By choosing to remain single, a woman has the freedom to follow her personal dreams and devote herself wholeheartedly to her life goals and meaningful aspirations. She is in a perfect position to nurture herself and celebrate all the wonders that this amazing world has to offer.

Remember, choosing to remain single does not limit your options in life. Many independent women are relieved to discover that marriage is an unnecessary milestone which does not fit the way many of them want to live their lives.

UNMARRIED IN RELATIONSHIPS

Just because a woman chooses to remain single does not mean she can't have a healthy relationship. There is no reason why a single woman cannot enjoy the love and companionship of a man, should she desire, or experience the benefits of caring for children. The difference is that these essential values and experiences do not have to be constricted by the outdated institution of marriage. There are many different possibilities available today for women who wish to enjoy the benefits of relationships with partners without marrying.

The beauty of choosing to share yourself with another person (whether that means a partner or child) outside of marriage is that you alone control your priorities and have the right to make independent decisions about important issues in your life. You avoid dependency on a man while opening yourself up to the benefits of a meaningful relationship with another person but on your terms.

You have enough self-respect to distinguish between a healthy, loving and supportive relationship which encourages your growth as an individual and an enmeshed bond with another based upon obligations to others, dependency and neediness that, more often than not, characterizes marriage.

You do not need a contract detailing the rules of your love and relationships nor your obligations and rights within them. Such contracts are ridiculous, because matters of the heart cannot be confined or regulated. You should be free to live your life exactly as you like, as long as you're acting morally and without compromising others' interests. You should be free to create your own set of rules that benefit you as an individual.

LONG-TERM COHABITATION

There used to be a stigma of "living in sin" for those who were unmarried, but today partners are choosing to cohabit without marrying.[9]

One of the most famous examples of unmarried partners cohabitating is Oprah Winfrey and her long-term boyfriend/fiancé, Stedman Graham. Oprah has been with Stedman for almost thirty years and they are not married, nor do they appear to want to do so. Oprah and

Stedman have their own lives and they each do their own activities. Yet they still support each other in their endeavors and proclaim their love for each other. If someone like Oprah, a successful and independent businesswoman, does not need a marriage contract, do you?

Indeed, cohabitating with a partner has many merits. Women can still be with the person they choose without the obligations and limitations of marriage. Women who cohabit without getting married also save some money, because they do not have to arrange a wedding celebration, which can include expenses such as a caterer, a dress, a tuxedo and a reception hall. This means that partners may have extra money to invest in a house or in vacations.[10]

Many relationships break down over financial conflicts, which can be avoidable if each person retains control over his or her own money. Some women choose to live with their partners while maintaining separate budgets and retaining financial autonomy. These women recognize the pitfalls of financial dependency and are reluctant to complicate an otherwise good relationship with money issues. Additionally, there is tremendous pride and satisfaction in remaining financially self-sufficient and, frankly, many successful women are unwilling to sacrifice their hard-earned prosperity.

Needless to say, cohabitating with a partner also makes it easier to break up in the event that things do not work out. Single women who cohabit do not have to go to court, have lawyers split the assets or sign papers to end their commitments. Surely there might be some aspects that have to be decided by a mediator, especially if children are involved, but it is far easier for unmarried partners than for married ones.

LIVING APART TOGETHER

For some women, as we've begun to explore in this book, the best relationships involve more than just financial freedom. Some women are content to be in a relationship with someone without having to see that person every day. In Living Apart Together relationships, both parties sustain their independence through maintaining separate financial affairs as well as residences. Women who opt for this lifestyle choice are confident in themselves and in their abilities to determine how they wish to live. They don't need or want to share all aspects of their lives with their partners, but they do enjoy the fruits of a close relationship with them. In my opinion, it is the best of both worlds.

Such women still get to maintain most of their single habits and lifestyles. For instance, they can have their own homes and decorate their tastes. Partners can plan visits to each other during the week and still have time for family, friends or a night out with the girls. Women can move forward in their careers the way they want to.

Typically, women choose this type of relationship when they like the life and the space that they have created for themselves. They don't have to worry about deciding whose furniture to use or which decorating style to put on the walls, because each partner has his or her own space. However, should the couple choose to have a sleepover, the option is still available.

Also, living in separate households makes it easy to decide what to do in the case of an argument between partners. No one has to sleep on the couch and the partners can choose to stay in their own spaces for as long as they want before they face each other again, if at all. It gives them a chance to cool off and come back to each other with calmness and control over their emotions. In most cases, living separately also means that the finances are individual and separated. It means that both partners are responsible for themselves and their spending habits and they do not need to worry about someone else spending their money frivolously.

LONG-DISTANCE RELATIONSHIPS

Maintaining a long-distance relationship is another popular option, especially in the United States and in Europe, where people travel freely by cars, trains and planes. Some modern women are unwilling to forfeit career advancement in order to stay in one location because of their partners. Many high level positions today require flexibility regarding travel and an enormous dedication of time and energy.

The economic recession from 2008 to 2011 impacted many women, who then expanded their searches for job alternatives outside of their usual geographic areas in order to find suitable work and maintain their standards of living. While at first men were hit disproportionately hard early in this recession, there were also cuts within the public sector due to the debt crisis, affecting a large number of women around the world.[11]

Women in long-distance relationships are willing to adapt and remain open to different work environments and locales in order to promote their careers, both in the public sector (where advancement for women is smoother, especially in the Nordic countries) and outside of it.

Additionally, women in long-distance relationships have the benefits of a relationship on their terms. Every time the couple gets together, the time is more special and precious to them, because they do not see each other all the time. They can choose to spend as little or as much time together as they like—a weekend here or there or longer vacations together. This type of relationship is ideal for people who love each other but know they would never be able to live together in one place.

OPEN RELATIONSHIPS/POLYAMORY

Some women choose open relationships or polyamory to fulfill their needs. Polyamory refers to the concept of romantic love with more than one person. In this situation, those involved believe that human beings have a great capacity for romantic love that can be satisfied best by romantic relationships with more than one person at a time. Unlike monogamous relationships, polyamorous ones encompass a belief in the idea of sharing abundant romantic love with other people.

Women in this type of relationship recognize that, although they may care deeply for another person, they do not wish to feel obligated to that individual. An open relationship gives a couple the opportunity and the freedom to love each other honestly, without the usual burdens that can cause tension and discontent between partners who are together "too much." This option allows a woman to remain committed to another person without the exclusivity that is expected in other types of relationships.

In an open relationship, you never have to explain or justify your decisions or actions to anyone. You are even free to move on should you desire or to have more than one relationship. For example, you may discover that one companion is a wonderful emotional support during difficult times, whereas another may be a fantastic companion for happier occasions, such as dining and dancing. A third can be a perfect intellectual mate.

In a truly open relationship, your loved one will know about your other relationships and support your autonomy and independence and vice versa. Women who opt for open relationships generally value commitment to their partners at the same time as remaining faithful to their own needs and desires.

Open relationships require a certain amount of trust among partners and open and honest communication throughout the entire connection. Each partner has to say what is okay with him or her and what is not. For instance, is sex with an outside partner okay or just emotional bonds? Is sleeping in the same bed with another fine? Is bringing a partner home okay? All such issues should be addressed and agreed upon beforehand. Another topic to discuss together is the issue of jealousy. The couple needs to be able to sit and talk openly about their emotions and feelings without feeling judged. Questions such as what happens if one partner doesn't like the person that her significant other is involved with should be addressed.

If you decide to enter into an open relationship, you should exercise caution and use your best judgment. Remember that you don't always know whom your partners are sleeping with or whom their other partners are sleeping with, so be sure to practice safe sex. Also, regular tests for sexually transmitted diseases must be done in order to keep yourself disease free, for your own benefit and the benefit of your lovers.

While not yet accepted by mainstream Western society, polyamory does offer some individuals the opportunity to experience deeply loving relationships with more than one consensual adult. This type of connection is still controversial in a monogamous world with rules by which most people live today. But some people are opting for this type of relationship. Being in an open relationship means that you and your partner are able to seek other outside sexual mates. Each of the partners should be fully aware of what is happening outside the relationship and must give their consent to it.

FRIENDS WITH BENEFITS, ONE-NIGHT STANDS AND FLINGS

Sexually-based liaisons such as friends with benefits, one-night stands and flings differ from open relationships. In a friends with benefits arrangement, there is no implied commitment to the other person. Two people get together for sex without the expectation of the encounter progressing into anything else, such as a date or a relationship. Friends with benefits are physically attracted to each other on a sexual basis but nothing more. They do not engage in romantic behavior common to couples who intend to get to know each other better on a number of levels, such as emotionally or intellectually.

Hollywood has taken this idea mainstream with movies such as *No Strings Attached* and *Friends with Benefits*. Both of these movies show the good and bad aspects of this type of relationship; however, both of the movies end with the friends forming a relationship beyond sex. That "happy ending" should not necessarily be the goal for all single women engaging in friends with benefits, but the option to evolve into more of a commitment is always there.

As long as the woman and man can keep their emotions and jealousy in check, this type of sexually-based relationship can work well. The couple dictates the schedule, whether they meet once a week, once a month or whenever they have the opportunity to get together. Being friends with benefits can be the perfect relationship for someone who wants to experience the intimacy of a sexual relationship but avoid dealing with all the feelings and emotions attached.

For the purpose of having sex, friends with benefits is safer than one-night stands or flings. One does not need to "prowl" for sex. And also one knows the background and probably the basic sexual history of the friend. This is not the case for one-night stands and flings, in which a partner appears only for sex and disappears right after sex. In such cases, one must take safety measures and practice only safe sex.

There are women who simply don't want a relationship at all; they don't want to deal with getting their hearts broken, involve their emotions or commit to another person. Perhaps such women just want to find a way to meet their sexual needs. Sex without commitment does not have the stigma that it used to have, since many people now feel that sex can be a pleasurable recreational act and not necessarily procreational. As long as everyone uses proper protection, these types of relationships should not be dangerous. With adequate precautions taken, friends with benefits, one-night stands and flings are great ways to meet sexual needs while never having to invest in a full-fledged relationship.

AVOID PAST RELATIONSHIP MISTAKES

Divorced women are especially vulnerable to the peril of jumping into another unsuitable or unworkable marriage. It is as though the failure of their original marital unions promotes an excess of self-doubt and anxiety, resulting in the need to rush into another relationship in order to fix things as quickly as possible.

While 40 percent of marriages around the Western world end in divorce, the statistics are even more shocking for second and third marriages, with 67 percent and 74 percent respectively ending in divorce in the US.[12] If so many women are overwhelmingly miserable in married relationships today, why do some women seem desperate to remarry?

The unfortunate truth is that divorced women often feel compelled to make the same relationship mistakes, because they truly believe that they are doing the right thing. Some women are duped into believing that the "right person" will come along if they just try a little harder. Although logic tells them otherwise, they do not wish to give up on the fantasy of being swept off their feet by a knight on a white horse. On top of that is the extra pressure on divorced women in a society which fails to provide adequate childcare and discriminates against divorced women trying to survive on one income. It is easy to see why divorced women are susceptible to remarriage.

However, a woman does not need a man in order to become self-sufficient or fulfilled following a divorce. Actually, it can be far healthier for women who find themselves alone after a period of sharing their lives with partners to take the necessary time to look after themselves. Divorced women do not need to find new spouses in order to make right the wrongs of past relationships.

In the same way, a woman who has been widowed should take the necessary time to grieve her loss. Trying to replace a late husband right away is counterproductive and disrespectful of special memories together. Be aware that married women are not happier than their unmarried counterparts, whether single, divorced or widowed. The best gift a widow can give herself is one in which she cherishes her own special gifts.

As a woman, you are much stronger than you realize. The solution to your relationship needs actually lies within you, regardless of your circumstances or previous marital status. Living alone has nothing to do with feeling alone. And being unmarried, single or divorced does not mean you cannot or should not love someone. Listen to your heart. Never do what's good for someone else if it is bad for you.

If you happen to meet another special person, you can choose from a variety of different relationship options available to you. There is no need for any woman to feel pressured into accepting a marriage proposal that does not fit her lifestyle or plans for the future. Today you can choose to remain single if that is what feels right for you.

NEW PREGNANCY OPTIONS

As we've discussed earlier, science and technology have moved forward, so nowadays if a woman wants a baby, she can have one, even if unmarried. This once unimaginable phenomenon of single women conceiving without getting married or even without any commitment or bond is now a reality.

Women today have more options than ever before to fulfill their aspirations and truly take charge of their lives. New pregnancy options have opened up possibilities that allow women to remain resolutely in control of their reproductive systems. Thanks to scientific and technological advances, single women now have the ability to conceive a child according to their own specific requirements. They are no longer bound by their biological clocks or marital considerations as in the past. They can decide when and how they wish to conceive a baby and whether they wish to raise the child alone or involve others. Most importantly, a woman does not need a husband anymore in order to become a mother and raise a happy and healthy child.

You may feel that you have no need for the added complications of a man in your life at this time and yet still desire the experience of motherhood. Some women may wish to retain control of all aspects regarding the birth and upbringing of their child, whereas others may simply wish to retain their autonomy without the "help" of a man. Regardless of the reason, you have a number of options available that will enable you to bring a child into this world and experience the sense of joy and fulfillment that comes from being a mother.

If you are a single woman considering this route, there are groups and workshops available to help you in your decision as well as many women who have done this and are eager to share their experiences. These women are dedicated to helping you with this decision through networks and social communities, some online. Such groups share opinions about which doctors to consult, whom to avoid and which clinics and hospitals are good choices.[13] They can also help you screen the options available in order to help you make an informed decision about which is the right path for you. Most importantly, they are real women sharing their stories and offering words of encouragement to single women who are making the life-changing decision to raise a child.

CONCEIVING WITH A LOVER OR FRIEND

This option involves conceiving a baby with a trusted friend or lover. You can decide the extent to which you would like the father of your baby to be involved in your life as well as the life of the child. There are many exciting new family options to consider and you may opt for an arrangement in which you both raise the child together or apart; it's completely up to you.

There are several issues to address with the future father. You will need to talk with him to verify he is of the same mindset you are for conceiving and raising the child. Determine what rights the future father wants with the child. Does he want to participate in raising the child? Will he be a father figure? Is he willing to pay child support? Do you need to go to court to figure out custody arrangements? Is he going to sign away his paternal rights? If this last question is the choice that the father takes, then he will not be responsible for child support, but the child will belong to only you.

Conceiving can sometimes be complex, so you should visit your doctor and check with him or her about your fertility. You will need to have sex on days you ovulate during each month in order to get pregnant. Let your lover or friend know about it in advance and make him aware of the process. Don't expect to get pregnant on the first try; it can take several months to conceive a baby.

Conceiving a child with a friend or lover is a controversial issue, but an idea to consider. Never make the mistake of doing it unilaterally, without your lover's or friend's consent. You should not deceive your friend. That most likely will end badly.

ARTIFICIAL INSEMINATION

Artificial insemination allows a woman to use a sperm donor in order to become pregnant without having intercourse. The use of donor sperm also allows a woman a certain amount of choice regarding the father of her child-to-be, such as ethnicity, physical features, intelligence, health, personality traits and abilities. While there is no guarantee that the desired genetic traits will be passed down exactly as expected, those who use the sperm donor method have considerably more control over the outcome.

If artificial insemination is the chosen route, once a woman chooses her sperm donor, whether known or anonymous, a doctor inserts the sperm in the woman when she is ovulating for conception.

IN VITRO FERTILIZATION

Women who struggle to conceive or who may be physically unable to become pregnant naturally may opt for in vitro fertilization (IVF). Advances in health sciences and technology have made it possible for many women who would otherwise have been unable to experience the joy of motherhood to undergo pregnancy and birth.

Similar to artificial insemination, IVF uses donor sperm—and sometimes donor eggs—to help a woman become pregnant. With IVF, an egg is fertilized outside a woman's body and then the resulting embryo is placed in the woman's uterus. Like artificial insemination, the sperm can come from a known donor or an anonymous one.

IVF is an option for single women who want to have a baby. However, there are some downsides and risks to IVF. First, IVF does not always work and it can take several attempts to achieve a viable pregnancy. In many cases, women who choose IVF have had trouble getting pregnant through intercourse in the first place, so a woman who simply chooses IVF may also not conceive. Next, an IVF procedure is costly. In the United States, for instance, IVF can cost anywhere from ten thousand to fifteen thousand dollars per trial.[14]

Because an embryo does not always implant, several embryos are placed in the uterus to increase the chances of becoming pregnant. Consequently, there is a chance that more than one fetus will become viable and you will end up with multiple children. A famous case is that of Nadya Suleman, also known as the "Octomom," who employed IVF as a single woman to get pregnant and ended up having eight babies.

SURROGACY

Another option which is gaining popularity today involves the use of a surrogate mother. In this situation, a healthy woman agrees to carry another woman's child to term in order to allow a woman who is usually unable or unwilling to have children herself the pleasure of raising a child of her own.

ADOPTION

In some instances, a woman may be unable to conceive. In other instances, a woman missed the chance for conceiving. However, adoption is an altruistic choice for those who wish to reach out to a child in need. Regardless of the reason, adoption provides the means for any woman who desires a child to experience the joy of sharing her love and caring with another person. Marriage is no longer seen as a prerequisite for adoption and many agencies are now open to the idea of single women raising adopted children.

Adoption requires much preparation. A woman must determine the desired age of the adopted child. Most people choose babies, but there are many older children in foster care or orphanages who need homes. The future mother must also decide on the child's country of origin. Almost every country has adoption options available—China, Vietnam, Thailand and the continent of Africa, just to name a few—or the baby can come from the country in which the woman lives.

The next step is to visit an adoption agency or connect with a pregnant woman who is looking to give her child up for adoption and discuss the adoption. Be sure to demonstrate your financial and emotional stability. Afterward, a study of the future mother's home will be conducted. In most instances, a case worker will examine the house to make sure that the environment is healthy for a child. The social worker will ask the woman about her lifestyle, finances, background and many other personal questions, but this is in the best interest of the child. Social workers are especially interested in how a single woman plans to raise a baby and provide for him or her.[15]

Once the adoption is approved, the parties need to decide on the role of the biological parents, if they are involved, after the child is adopted. Do the biological parents want the adoption to be an open one, where they have contact and the child knows who his biological parents are? Or will it be a closed one, where the biological and the adopting parents have no contact at all and the records are sealed to prevent the child from finding his biological parents at a later date?

NEW FAMILY OPTIONS

Many women have been brought up to believe that marrying and having children is of paramount importance, regardless of their individual traits, values and aspirations. There is still huge pressure on most women around the world to create a traditional, monogamous nuclear family structure.

As we've discussed earlier, families today come in all shapes and sizes and single parents are on the rise. Families no longer require a man to be the head of the household. Everything from getting pregnant to raising a child can be done by a single woman if she chooses so. It is easier than ever before, because there are many more resources and options available.

EXTENDED FAMILIES AND COMMUNITY LIVING

The existence of extended families and community living offers women the opportunity to experience the benefits of participating in a group of likeminded people without the unnecessary legal commitment required by the institution of marriage. Indeed, an extended family can provide an amazing support system, while allowing a woman to maintain her independence and autonomy. In China, for example, grandparents play a major role as caretakers of a child for the first few years of the child's life so that the mother is available to return to work. In many cases, the grandparents move in with the family to offer childcare support.[16]

Community living has existed for many years, for instance in tribal Africa, Israel and the former Soviet Union. And yet North America and Western countries have been slow to take full advantage of its benefits. The biggest challenge for most women who participate in community living arrangements is finding the right balance between voluntary seclusion and fellowship in the group. There is no doubt that a group of people can achieve considerably more when working together constructively than a single person can. Other benefits include the feeling of camaraderie experienced through belonging to a special group of people. It has been noted that for some single women, meaningful communities ultimately become their families.[17]

NUCLEAR FAMILY WITH COHABITATION

Many women choose the arrangement of a nuclear family with cohabitation. In this family option, marriage is not the goal, nor should it be. Instead, both partners focus on living together without the need for being married. If they ultimately decide to have a child, he or she will be raised in much the same way as a child born to a married couple living in a traditional nuclear family setting. Sometimes couples create blended families in which children from different parental relationships come together under one roof to form a family.

LIVING APART TOGETHER

Women who have opted for a Living Apart Together relationship may also need to consider whether there are any children involved and how best to accommodate their needs. One possibility involves raising the children in two separate households. While some people may see this as a duplicate of the living arrangements imposed upon children affected by divorce or separation, there is a big difference. Children raised in LAT families experience none of the animosity and trauma that might exist between struggling spouses in the middle of a marital breakup.

GLBT RELATIONSHIPS

Children are also being raised successfully in gay, lesbian, bisexual and transgender households, a living arrangement that has caused controversy because of misplaced apprehension regarding the parents' sexual orientations and the effect it might have on a child.

But recent studies show that living in a household with two opposite sex parents is not the major factor for children doing well. A 2004 study involving twelve thousand adolescents and their families revealed that the most important factor for children to be well-adjusted and balanced is growing up in loving homes, regardless of their parents' sexual choices, who raised them or who was in relationships with their parents. Children raised in homosexual households grow up to engage in similar dating habits and romantic relationships as children of heterosexual parents.[18] So today a woman does not have to forfeit her desire to raise children in order to be true to herself and her sexual orientation.

SINGLE PARENTS

It is now generally understood and accepted that single parents are very capable of raising a child alone. In fact, 40 percent of children today are born to single mothers.[19] Women have come a long way from the days when society considered pregnancy outside of wedlock to be scandalous or shameful.

Unfortunately, childcare options within the workplace have not kept pace with the new reality of single parenthood today, so many women still struggle to obtain maternity leave and find good child-care. For instance, America is the only developed country in the world in which many women fail to receive adequate paid maternity leave. This is not the case in Israel, where a maternity leave of 3.5 months is fully covered by social security. And European nations provide generous family leave to new mothers. But compared to 1978, when American women could be fired by their employers for being pregnant or having a child, progress has been made.[20]

Despite limited leave, Americans continue to produce more chil-dren than many European nations which provide excellent benefits and state-run childcare facilities. As a matter of fact, 34 percent of American children live in households headed by a single parent.[21] That demonstrates that regardless of the challenges, the single parenthood lifestyle choice is enduring.

Women who are single by choice and financially sound should be able to provide a stable and loving home for a child. Children need a secure and stable environment to grow in, committed parental care, unconditional love and affection and a parent with the resources to offer them a good life filled with opportunities. These vital childhood needs can be satisfied by a dedicated single woman. Children whose physical and emotional needs are taken care of by single parents develop into healthy and well-adjusted adults.

If a single woman finds herself needing money to pay for neces-sities for her family, there are programs to which to apply for funds. One American example, the Women, Infants and Children Program (WIC), is for expectant and new moms. The program is designed to aid single mothers, especially in the areas they need it the most. There are several different WIC programs which a representative can help single mothers choose from in order to maximize benefits.[22] For example, single mothers who shop from a WIC-approved list will be reimbursed for the groceries, including milk, eggs, cereal, formula and other items needed for babies or children.[23]

Some European countries have excellent daycare facilities. The *écoles maternelles* in France and centers in Nordic countries provide inexpensive daycare. Finland guarantees daycare and for families with low incomes it is free. Also, there are many daycare centers in the United States that will work with single moms to accommodate their budgets and schedules. They set up payment plans and offer affordable choices. Some daycares are also willing to stay open to assist working mothers, though there might be associated costs.[24] Daycares are a useful tool available to help single mothers who need to or choose to work.

Many daycares provide children with new skills, learning tools and socialization with other children. Most children who are in daycares are very favorably affected by the experiences and seem to progress well in becoming ready for their next educational experiences.

There is no such thing as a perfect mother, although many moms feel pressure to be "supermoms." All moms, no matter single or not, make mistakes. Don't feel guilty for feeling overwhelmed at times by your children's needs. It is normal. Think about calling a sitter and taking a night off to do something just for you, because you deserve it. Sometimes mothers feel they are not doing or being all their children need. This is normal. Just do the best you can and love your children.

It is clear that although challenges, discrimination and stereotypical thinking still exist to an extent, women have gained a tremendous number of options when it comes to relationship opportunities, family alternatives and pregnancy choices.

Attitudes toward single women not only in the Western world but also in many other countries are changing to the benefit of single women. Recent articles about women in England, France and Australia indicate that many feel that love is more important than marriage and that it is love that should be celebrated, not the act of signing a binding contract.

I strongly believe that single women can be anything they want to be and no man should stand in their way. Women are becoming astronauts, politicians, governors, teachers, scientists, doctors, lawyers and so much more. They do not have to worry about whom their career choices have to benefit, except for themselves. Single women do not have to hold themselves back when their employers ask them to move across the country or the world for a promotion or a raise. They do not have to think about a spouse first or what might be best for the family. Additionally, within their freedom of options, they may want to create families, have children and raise them with or apart from partners.

Today many active and successful women are single by choice and do not want to cater to the needs and desires of a husband. Many single women have the time and the resources to realize what a great option singlehood can be. Many married women who miss the freedom, the time and the ability to choose for themselves envy powerful and free single women's lifestyles.

Many women are not afraid to speak up for themselves and are demanding that the patriarchal values of the past be laid to rest. I strongly feel, as do many single women today, that a woman does not have to sacrifice her life goals and heartfelt aspirations just to conform to a marital relationship that confines her to a hierarchical, monogamous and nuclear family setting. Remember, time is precious. Don't be tempted to sign binding contracts and spend your life with someone for the sake of something that you don't really want. Live your life freely; you deserve that kind of life.

Women in increasing numbers are managing to live on their own. By remaining single by choice, happily unmarried or happily divorced, I believe you are setting yourself up for a lifetime of personal satisfaction and joy. You are free to create your own personal piece of history in a world full of likeminded, unafraid single women.

Chapter 12

How Women Can Open Up

As a single, unmarried or divorced woman, you can experience the abundance of an extraordinary and wonderful life filled with purpose and possibility. The institution of marriage is no longer an inevitable rite of passage; today, many women around the world are choosing to remain unmarried or single by choice. These women do not see themselves as second-class citizens to their married peers. Instead, they are celebrating their single-by-choice status every day. You do not have to sacrifice your valued independence and happiness in order to fit into the traditional marital relationship. You can choose to live your own way: free and independent, successful and respected, with or without a man.

Julie's Story

Julie, a young designer, was in a troubled marriage. The romance had been missing for some time and there was little left in the way of togetherness and shared dreams. Julie and her husband drifted apart until they were nothing more than two people living in the same house. A combination of boredom and exhaustion led to a number of extramarital affairs and empty promises, leaving an emotional void. Eventually, Julie found herself going through her daily routine like a robot, a situation she found both demeaning and soul-destroying.

As often happens in life, a small incident usually delivers the final blow. In the case of Julie's marriage it was a movie: *The Bridges of Madison County*, starring Clint Eastwood and Meryl Streep. "It all seems a bit humorous now," Julie said to me, "but at the time, the love affair in that movie represented everything that was sorely missing in my own personal relationship." Julie remembers watching the excitement build and the passion unfold between the two on-screen lovers. She also found herself doing some necessary and long overdue soul searching. Reflecting on the movie helped Julie express what she had been unwilling to face for a number of years: No amount of hard work or good intentions can overcome an ill-suited partnership that is no longer meeting the needs of the persons involved; no amount of so-called security or stability is worth a lifetime of missed opportunity.

That night, Julie came to the undeniable conclusion that she was no longer willing to settle for an indifferent life of boring routine and monotonous monogamy just so she could call herself married. Julie longed to be inspired by all that life has to offer. She came to the conclusion she didn't need a man to look after her and she didn't want to be tied down in a mediocre relationship. "My whole being ached for the freedom of unfettered passion and truly meaningful romance that I had witnessed in the movie," Julie explained defiantly. "I felt like a prisoner in my own life and I was determined to do something about it."

Before that evening, Julie had been burying her feelings along with any hope of things changing for the better. Once she acknowledged her real feelings, years of tension lifted and she felt utter relief at the prospect of being an unattached woman again, once her ill-fated marriage was dissolved. The incredible exhilaration she experienced throughout her divorce turned out to be much greater than the infatuation she had felt during the original whirlwind romance which had swept her off her feet, leading to a hurried exchange of vows at the tender age of eighteen. "I felt reborn and ready to take on the world," Julie grinned while reflecting on her divorce.

As it began to sink in that her marriage was finally over, Julie encountered a sense of pride at her own accomplishments, along with a feeling of limitless freedom and independence to do as she truly wished in life. The implications of being a liberated single filled her with happiness and anticipation.

Best of all, she no longer needed to answer to anyone other than herself. "I was completely free to make my own life decisions, even if that meant making some mistakes along the way," she recalled. "I can honestly tell you that I had no regrets ending my marriage and, interestingly enough, neither did my husband. We had both separately come to the same conclusion that enough was enough and it was time to move on."

Not everything went smoothly in those first heady days of post-marital autonomy. While Julie had no regrets over ending an ill-conceived, mediocre marriage, she was shocked by the depth of feelings that she had repressed over so many years.

A person doesn't suddenly end a large portion of her life without needing to do some major readjustments. Practical things aside, it is more often the feelings and anxieties going on inside her mind that require the greatest work. Even the most confident and self-assured women find that the emotional upheaval from the collapse of a relationship can take its toll on their sense of well-being and balance. However, the energy required to remain in an unhappy relationship can leave a woman feeling consumed and depleted. This is the sad situation shared by thousands of women who are stuck in desperately unfulfilling marriages.

The fact that Julie acted on her own personal agenda to abandon her failed marriage was a major indication that she was more than ready to put her own needs first, for once. Many women are so culturally conditioned to be caregivers that dismantling relationships might make them feel guilty, even when they know it's for the best. Some may worry about being perceived as selfish or insensitive or that their intentions may be labeled counterproductive by outsiders who do not understand the crushing weight of deceit and depression experienced by women who are unable to be true to themselves.

When a woman considers the repercussions of pretending to be happy for the sake of something or someone when actually the reverse is true, she begins to realize the personal cost of staying in a miserable marriage. I strongly believe all women deserve to feel contented and fulfilled, regardless of their relationship choices. A woman should never concede to social pressure or justify her right to live her life as a strong, independent and self-determined woman.

If you have never been married or are recently separated or divorced, you may feel immense pressure to marry in order to appease your family and satisfy the cultural expectations of society. You may believe that you are inferior to married women or that somehow, without a marriage partner, you have missed out and been left behind. Some might try to sell you the idea that as a single woman by choice, your life cannot possibly be as fulfilling or as productive as those of married women. But nothing could be further from the truth. There are many amazing lifestyle options and incredible opportunities available to you in our postmodern era. Moreover, as I know, there is a personal sense of satisfaction that comes from achieving your goals, alone, as a woman who is single by choice.

SUCCESSFULLY SINGLE BY CHOICE

Many female public figures, business executives, doctors, lawyers, friends, neighbors, coworkers and family members around the world are both successful and single. Much has changed over the past fifty years. Strong, empowered, self-reliant women are both valued and respected in our society. Thanks to the hard-fought battles of the women's movements, there are more educational and career opportunities for women than ever before. As long as you are willing and able to put in the necessary time and effort to achieve the goals you set for yourself, you will succeed.

This is where I feel single, unattached women are ahead. There is no doubt that in order to be successful today in the field of one's choice, there is a huge commitment involved. Most would agree that it's easy to spread oneself too thin when trying to take care of multiple responsibilities simultaneously. Executive women employed in demanding, well-paid career positions admit that their work takes a lot of time and energy. Women who are single by choice have more time and resources to immerse themselves fully into whatever careers they want and can do so unapologetically. If you want to work long hours in order to develop or complete a job, your own initiative or a dream you have always dreamed, you can choose to do any or all of these. If you need to move because of economic necessity or to take advantage of an opportunity, there is no reason not to go. Employers know that they can count on unattached, committed women to get the job done and single women have the will and usually also the means to work as hard as they want in order to achieve success.

You can gain an enormous amount of personal pride, self-esteem and satisfaction from your life's work and accomplishments. Many people define themselves and their identities according to the jobs they do. Over the past ten years, women have generally performed better in the workplace than men, with three out of four people laid off due to the economic fallout from the recession being men, not women. There are now more female than male students attending university in America. And women make up the majority of professional workers in a number of countries, including the United States.[1]

By choosing to remain single, you are ultimately free to define your own priorities and follow your true calling in life. For each woman this means different things. You may want to develop your own initiative in your career or start a new business. You may have a vision of yourself making a difference in other people's lives or creatively expressing yourself through the fine arts. You may have a passion for scientific discovery, an appetite for studies or a desire to travel the world and explore exotic locations. Whatever you choose, it is essential to identify your strengths and talents and the things that are meaningful for you alone. Then go for it. Nurture your own dreams and fantasies and take in the wonders that our incredible world has to offer.

There are many amazing unmarried female role models to inspire you in your journey through life as a single-by-choice woman. You are not bound by the expectations of the past and you are free to discover your own unique destiny. Some famous single women who have forever changed the way we view our world include Coco Chanel, Martha Stewart, Joan of Arc, Susan B. Anthony, Temple Grandin, Mother Theresa and Helen Keller.

Lesser well-known but just as successful in their own ways are single women such as Agnes Martin (a minimalist painter), Molly Ivins (a liberal newspaper columnist and author), Moms Mabley (an African-American vaudeville entertainer and comedian), Janet Reno (the first female Attorney General), Sally J. Priesand (the first ordained female rabbi in America), Harriet Meiers (a lawyer to the White House), Dame Freya Stark (a British travel writer and cartographer), Golda Meir (Israeli Prime Minister) and Dr. Mae Jemison (an astronaut and physician and the first black woman to fly into space).[2]

Some of these women overcame enormous hardships and personal challenges as they refused to allow difficult circumstances and discrimination to dictate their roles in life. Others were determined to make a difference by excelling in their fields. None of these resourceful women defined themselves by a man and all of them remind us of the enormous talent and potential that lies in every one of us.

This list is by no means a definitive one. There are countless numbers of happy, successful, remarkable single women living incredible lives all over the world. It's time to lay to rest the assumption that unmarried women are merely waiting on the sidelines of life, desperate to "get a life" or become fulfilled by a man. The founder of the Grey Panthers, Maggie Kuhn, probably said it best when asked why she had never married; her response was simple: "Sheer luck!"[3]

Of course you do not have to be famous to lead an exceptional life as a single woman. Ordinary single women all across the world excel at what they do while remaining determined career women, devoted mothers, generous mentors and unequivocal masters of their own amazing lives. Outstanding women are everywhere. You probably know a few of them already.

By its very nature, the definition of success is an individual state of mind. Everyone has diverse ideas regarding what constitutes success and what motivates one person to act on her dreams may be quite different from someone else's passionate endeavor. You alone have the ultimate control over the direction your life takes. Everyone is free to make important life choices, whether they see it that way or not. Single women are especially privileged in that they can act unilaterally on their life goals without having to worry about the potential impact on spouses or partners. Remaining single by choice allows you to focus on your own personal growth and heartfelt aspirations. Relationships may come and go, but it is your strength of character, talents and accomplishments which ultimately touch the lives of others and define you as a person.

THE VALUE OF FRIENDSHIP

In her book *The Single Girl's Manifesta*, author Jerusha Stewart points out the simple truth that single women are by no means sentenced to a life of aloneness. Close friendships provide an essential means of support and emotional pleasure. Most treasure the time spent with good friends, whether they are male or female. Both married and single women rate hanging out with their friends higher than time spent with their boyfriends, spouses or partners.[4] It seems that there is no substitute for the unique bond women share with close friends and maintaining these special relationships is a fabulous way to ensure that a single woman is never alone unless she truly wishes to be.

In the past, extended families helped when women needed a little extra support, but in today's mobile society it is more likely to be close friends who fulfill this important role. Keeping in touch with good friends is a wonderful way for women to surround themselves with people who care about them and can share in their lives on their terms. A comfortable sense of togetherness is best achieved through a strong network of like-minded friends who appreciate a woman for who she really is.

Single woman need and value the members of their chosen social communities. They can prioritize valuable friendships when single, because usually they have more time to keep in touch with these all-important relationships. The beauty of being single is that women can choose to nurture these friendships by sharing in activities together. There are endless options for having a good time with wonderful friends, such as participating in social events, sports, traveling or hiking. Single women may want to establish new traditions by joining with great friends to celebrate holidays and birthdays, lend a hand by working on a volunteer project together or just hang out together for the sake of old times.

The perception that single women are lonely and sitting at home waiting for the phone to ring is nothing more than a myth. Most singles are too busy enjoying themselves! Many single women lead interesting lives filled with a variety of exciting social events and a large circle of captivating and gregarious friends. The only difference between single women and their married peers is that singles are more in control of how much time they spend in the company of others. Single women remain in touch with their own important needs and goals as well as connected to the wider community.

However, for many, having to contend with the well-meaning intentions of overly-concerned family members is one of the most annoying aspects of being single. There are some who may view your choice to remain single with a mixture of morbid curiosity and pity. There will always be people who struggle to understand the attraction of the single lifestyle, believing instead that marriage represents the pinnacle of achievement for all women. While the benefits of a single-by-choice lifestyle may be lost on some, let me reassure you that you are in excellent company. There are thousands of amazingly contented single women who choose not to marry and are wholeheartedly satisfied with their lifestyle choice.

This truth may be lost on some worried relatives and friends who forget that what is right for one person may be wrong for someone else, including you. Marriage works well for some but is a very poor fit for many modern women. Allowing yourself to be impacted by someone else's relationship anxiety is ultimately damaging to your own sense of self-worth. Remember, you owe it to yourself to make the right choice for your life, not for anyone else. You don't have to convince anyone but yourself.

Just because a woman is single, it does not preclude her from enjoying intimate relationships should she desire them. The beauty of being single by choice is that the woman determines how and when she enjoys sexual relationships, without the fear of becoming unnecessarily tangled in a complicated and limiting set of obligations to another person. As long as a single woman is honest and upfront about her intentions and uses the best safety measures, she can enjoy all the benefits of an intimate sexual encounter without any fear of becoming tied down. If you choose to remain single, it's completely up to you whom you date and how often you enjoy their company. You may want to have great sex with someone and nothing else. It's up to you. The joy of being single is about seizing the moment, increasing options in life and taking advantage of the right opportunities when they occur.

Remaining single does not remove the possibility of enjoying a relationship with a person for whom you care deeply. You can be happily unmarried yet in a lasting relationship with someone special. As we discussed earlier, many women are opting for Living Apart Together arrangements with their significant others. In this case, you retain the autonomy to make your own decisions in life, maintain your separate residence and control your personal finances. At the same time, you enjoy the benefits of sharing an intimate relationship with another person. In my opinion, LAT allows both parties the freedom to develop their own important goals while avoiding the pitfalls of dependency and enmeshment. You are still the number one person in your life and your greatest commitment belongs to yourself.

Beyond your relations with lovers or friends, it is important to be your own best friend. Many women find it easier to spend their precious time and energy supporting and encouraging others rather than extending the same respect to themselves. Even though you may be aware of the anxiety and depression which you can suffer when you ignore your own emotional and physical requirements for too long, you may still find yourself culturally conditioned to overlook the warning signs and place your own needs last. But you cannot afford to turn your back on yourself. You owe it to yourself to ensure that your needs are taken care of. Allow yourself the time it takes to restore yourself to optimal health, whether that means making time for reading a book or e-book on your digital device, beauty treatments, physical exercise, relaxation, meditation or some much-needed personal introspection.

Most women recognize the signs of exhaustion, depletion and burnout that occur when they lose sight of their priorities. It's time to do something about these issues and one of the best ways involves placing oneself right at the center focus. Single women are in the unique position of being able to take action to look after themselves. Don't you deserve the same care and consideration that you provide for others? Of course you do. An investment in befriending yourself is the best gift of all.

INVESTING IN YOURSELF

Stay positive and take good care of yourself. You are absolutely worth the time and energy it takes to nurture yourself, look after your special needs and ensure that you maintain your physical health and emotional well-being. You don't even need to leave your home or apartment in order to spoil yourself. You are perfectly situated to create your ideal relaxing retreat right within your own living space.

Set up a comfortable spot in your home which will be just for your relaxation purposes. You can use this place however you wish. Some suggestions include reading a favorite novel, listening to soothing music, taking time to meditate and relaxing with aromatherapy.[5] The important thing about this area in your home is that it is yours alone and used only for this purpose. This calm, peaceful and restful spot will become your favorite escape when you need to take some well-deserved time out to boost the way you feel about yourself, both physically and mentally.

Other fun activities to relax include trying some new recipes and cooking a wonderful meal or snack, tackling home renovation projects, having a chick flick movie night, indulging your passion for arts and crafts, yoga or tai chi, planning a fabulous vacation, connecting with others through social networks, training your body with the help of an exercise videos or equipment, creating a scrapbook or indulging in an at-home beauty spa experience with exotic hair and body treatments with which to pamper yourself. These are just some of the leisure pursuits that are yours to enjoy without leaving your home.

There are also wonderful options that are waiting for you in the community. Participating in exercise classes such as aerobics, Pilates or modern dance or training regularly in a gym are great methods to keep yourself in optimal condition while having fun at the same time. Swimming is an excellent workout for your entire body and is quite relaxing at the same time. You may enjoy going to a gym and trying out the exercise equipment or bicycling to work in order to enjoy the fresh air and sunshine. Some people are committed to an enjoyable daily routine of walking a dog, while others prefer more solitary activities such as jogging, skating or rollerblading. Some health benefits of keeping fit include strengthening your muscles, controlling your weight, improving your cardiovascular fitness and taking advantage of the flood of natural endorphins following a great workout—the same endorphins that keep you happy. There are so many ways to exercise and relax. The way you choose to exercise depends on you. The only firm rule is that it should be an activity you enjoy or you won't want to continue doing it for very long.

For those who prefer more sedentary pursuits, try attending a compelling theatre production or going to the movies. Learn a new skill just for fun: sign up for art classes, learn a new language, take up a musical instrument or join your local library. Some women have a passion for amazing hobbies such as skydiving, scuba diving or horseback riding, whereas others prefer quieter activities such as gardening or photography.

All such fun activities can be enjoyed by you completely alone. You may choose to involve a friend, but it's really not necessary and in some cases you may prefer to do it solo because you find it more enjoyable. There is no lack of rewarding activities to do and you do not need a man or marriage in order to have a great time.

There will be times when you crave the company of others. Here again, your single status puts you at an advantage. Most single women have no trouble surrounding themselves with a crowd of like-minded individuals when they want to socialize. A little advance planning or "future think" is required, according to author Jerusha Stewart.[6] She notes that successful single women are more likely to engage in the practice of actively ensuring that their datebooks are full and that they have numerous social events available from which to choose. You just need to be a little bit proactive in order to ensure that your time is spent how you wish.

There are many fun ways to satisfy your desire to mingle with interesting people during your free time. You may enjoy meeting with a group of close friends for an enjoyable meal at a restaurant or you may find dancing in the local club to be more your style. Some single women find it easier to join an activity-oriented group with a common interest, such as a photography or gourmet cooking class. Others choose to participate in volunteer work or fundraising.

Nichole's Story

Nichole is a thirty-six-year-old single woman whose life ambition is to visit every continent of the world. She refuses to wait until she is in a relationship with someone before indulging in her passion for travelling. Instead, she makes herself available to various non-profit organizations stationed in different countries. The organizations benefit from Nichole's skills and expertise and Nichole gains wondrous lifetime experiences and a life well lived, according to her desires.

FINANCIAL FREEDOM AS A SINGLE WOMAN

Most women are paid less than their male counterparts in executive and other positions and both single men and women often find themselves receiving less financial compensation and fewer benefits than their married counterparts for doing the same work.[7] Though equality in the workplace still has a way to go, there is a new reality taking place for many women who are single by choice and it's a very positive one.

While financial equality may be somewhat elusive for women, there is
no shortage of opportunities in America and around the industrialized Western world for those who wish to excel in their fields.[8]

As women have entered the workforce in increasing numbers,
there is a newfound recognition that talented and capable women
have an enormous contribution to offer. The gifts and abilities of
these women are no longer wasted in menial, dead-end jobs and many
women are leading the way by creating new inroads in fields such as
science, technology and business. The ability to control one's own
financial future is becoming a reality for many single women as they
work hard and prosper in their chosen fields.

CHOOSING ALTERNATE PATHS

As always in society, there is an unspoken drift toward the "one size
fits all" mentality which dictates that everybody should desire the
same thing and be striving for the same goals. But we are all uniquely
different. Successful, self-determined women have a wide variety of
hopes, dreams and aspirations. Never allow yourself to be talked into
doing something that does not feel right for you and don't let yourself
be talked out of trying something that truly ignites your passion.

Single women are freer to take risks in life. If you are unmarried and childless, it is completely up to you how you decide to spend
your time and money and you alone stand to reap the benefits or learn
from your mistakes. You may be tempted to break down barriers in
adrenaline-pumping activities such as sky diving, mountain climbing,
horse racing or back country skiing, pushing through your fear and
mastering the challenges ahead. At work, you may be determined to
enter areas that have previously been dominated by men.

Today, women join the military, pilot aircraft, sign up as reporters
and are deployed to hostile environments, work in correctional institutions, serve their communities through the police force or operate
heavy equipment in the fields of construction and engineering. Not
only have single women proven themselves to be excellent workers in
non-traditional fields, but also they offer additional commitment and
perseverance, driven by their desire to prove themselves and excel.

Women who own their own homes usually maintain their properties and manage their investments well. Renovation projects are a
great way to learn new skills and save some money too. And you don't

need a man to do the renovation. Some construction firms are run by women or you can do it yourself with the aid of some friends. Once again, women have proven themselves to be enthusiastic and capable as they live out their lives single by choice and with no regrets.

Many women are attracted to the idea of travelling to exciting places around the world. There are some who may feel that single men and women are at a disadvantage when it comes to booking vacation packages, which are often designed for double occupancy. This is where your ability to do advance planning is important. Some of the best travel experiences can be taken with a good friend whom you invite to share in the fun. You may also decide to visit your friends who live in different and fascinating parts of the world or swap your house or apartment with other singles around the world who might be interested in visiting your location.

Spending time with a group of people with similar relationship statuses and interests can be a fabulous way to meet new friends while you learn about the history and culture of new and exotic places. There are a number of different tours, travel clubs and organizations that cater to singles who are interested in exploring the world. The great thing about many of these single travel clubs is that they provide many activities as well as the social benefits of discovering new friends with whom to share your experiences.

There are so many single travel clubs available that many of them offer unique travel experiences based upon different vacation themes, such as adventure-focused travel, discount holidays or single parent travel clubs.[9] Others provide vacations geared for certain age groups. It is always a good idea to check the references of singles travel clubs before signing up. That way, you can be confident that you have chosen the best possible travel arrangement to suit your needs and tastes.

What are some ways that you can fill your time? The best thing to do is start a list, if you haven't already taken the time to write one down. List at least one hundred things that you would love to do or accomplish before you die. It might seem hard at first, but stay with the exercise. If you can push past the mental block, you will find that you give yourself the permission to think big for yourself.

J.M. Power put it succinctly when he said "If you want to make your dreams come true, the first thing you have to do is wake up."[10] This list-making exercise is a way for you to wake yourself up, to let all of those dormant dreams that you hold inside of you come alive and gather momentum. You will start to see how many things there actually are that you want to do in your life and that there is no one but yourself standing in your way of actually doing them.

Try to think way outside of the box for what you believe is realistic. Who cares if you want to surf, yet don't know how to swim? Put "learn to swim" on your list, with "learn to surf" right after it! You want to garden, yet don't have space at your city apartment? Start a community garden and beautify a vacant lot, while bringing your neighbors together. Don't make up any excuses why you can't accomplish something, no matter how farfetched it may seem at the time.

When you have your list completed, put it somewhere that you will see it often, for example on your refrigerator. Then get to work on one item. Soon, you will start checking items off and within a year you will be surprised when you see how many amazing things you have managed to accomplish for yourself, while many of your married friends have done little but complain they don't have any time for themselves anymore. And who knows, while you are out and about living life, you are likely to meet other vivacious and spirited people with whom you have a lot in common and you will have the time to hang out with them and enjoy their company. Remaining single by choice increases possibilities in life and does not limit your options.

Dian's Story

Dian, a businesswoman who is happily single at the age of forty-six, never lacks for an interesting vacation when she decides to take a break from her demanding job. She is a generous and entertaining guest who has so far visited locations as diverse as Argentina, New Zealand, Spain, Nigeria and Thailand. Dian is quick to return the favor, providing a welcoming home for her international friends when they visit her country.

SHARING YOUR LOVE OF CHILDREN

The decision to remain unmarried and single by choice does not prevent you from taking pleasure in the amazing experience of enjoying children, whether it be your own baby or sharing your love with someone else's children. While some women profess no desire to parent children, others associate childbearing with a fundamental part of what it means to be a woman.

As we've discussed earlier, some women greatly desire the experience of giving birth and/or raising their own children. With ever-increasing self-sufficiency and financial prosperity for women, many find that this is a realistic choice for them to make without a man. Thanks to advances in reproductive technology, women no longer even need to have sex in order to become pregnant and give birth.

As we've discussed, today's technology means that older women can choose the option of motherhood if they desire. Women are no longer bound to their biological clocks and many choose to delay childrearing until they have established careers and are financially stable. Other arrangements such as surrogate mothers and adoption are available for those who would prefer not to carry a child themselves or for those who are unable to become pregnant.

Single parents are no longer the victims of stigma in our society and old-fashioned contempt is slowly being replaced with a level-headed recognition that what children need above all else is love. Women who are single by choice and financially sound are able to provide stable and loving homes for children, should they wish to do so. Children whose physical and emotional needs are met by single parents often develop into well-adjusted adults who possess desirable qualities of independence and responsibility at a much younger age compared to their peers from two-parent families. In addition to this, many children of single parents develop close relationships with their extended family, a win-win situation for everyone involved.

The most potentially damaging environment for raising a child is one in which there is ongoing fighting, domestic violence or abuse. With high divorce rates and dysfunctional marriages, many children today are exposed to damaging disputes and contentious friction within their families. Here, single women are in a perfect position to nurture their children in safe and secure environments, free from childrearing disagreements or marital conflicts.

Single women who want children will ensure that their children's needs are well looked after. Close friends or extended family members may take on important roles in the child's life. Good parents from every walk of life recognize the significance of effective community support in order to offer the richness of experience that is characteristic of healthy and well-balanced children.

Our children want and need secure and stable environments, committed parental care, unconditional love and affection and parents with the resources to offer them good lives, filled with opportunity. I strongly believe these childhood needs can be satisfied by a stable and dedicated single woman.

For some women, the desire to spend time with children and play a role in their upbringing does not translate into becoming parents themselves. But that does not mean that they have to miss the opportunity to make a real difference for a child. There are many possibilities to become involved in a child's life either as a favorite aunt, relative, mentor or as a volunteer in the community.

Ella's Story

Ella, a fifty-year-old single woman, cannot imagine living her life without children. However, she is a committed single and not about to give up her fast-paced existence, travelling between several major cities around the world as a sales executive for a large firm. "I'm just too happy with my life the way it is," she said to me. "Not to mention the fact that I could never give up my great-paying job in order to raise a child full-time." Ella decided to get involved in her nieces' lives a few years ago and it has become immensely rewarding for everyone involved. "I get to spend as much time with the girls as I want and we do all sorts of fun activities together," she explained. Ella is happy to spend time nurturing her nieces as a favorite aunt and has even surprised herself at the depth of feelings she has while providing comfort and care for the girls in her free time.

THE TRANQUILITY OF BEING ALONE

Much has been said about being single and surrounding yourself with fabulous friends and other kindred souls. However, there is no doubt that the best thing about living as a single-by-choice woman is the effortlessness of being alone. While it is great to share your time with others, sometimes nothing beats the peace and quiet of a lazy evening spent in the company of yourself.

There is something almost magical about entering your house after a hard day at work and realizing that the evening belongs to you and only to you. You can choose to spend your time exactly as you want. After all, the only person you need to consider, for now, is yourself. Being single gives you the means to determine exactly what you need to do in order to release the cares of the day and replenish your body and soul. You can cook yourself something tasty, order takeaway or choose not to eat if you're not in the mood. You can watch a quality movie, read a good book or listen to relaxing music to soothe your mind while you enjoy a bubble bath sipping a glass of wine. You may decide to indulge in a well-deserved nap and then take a walk outside to watch the sun disappear below the horizon or you may prefer the warm glow from a crackling fire. If you take a few moments to imagine how your life as a single woman contrasts with women who are living in partnership with their boyfriends or spouses, you can be sure that they are not enjoying the same level of serenity as you, while they try to accommodate their own needs as well as the expectations and desires of other household members.

Many single women are rarely lonely. In fact, it is possible to feel extremely alone even when surrounded by a large group of people. There is a major difference between the isolation experienced by someone who feels disconnected from those around them (something that can easily happen during the strained dynamics of marital breakdown) and people who treasure their quality time alone, unapologetically comfortable with their solitude.

This has nothing to do with single women being antisocial. It is, instead, a simple recognition that everyone needs to spend time reconnecting with themselves. The busy, often frantic nature of women's public lives inevitably takes its toll and causes them to retreat into the sanctity of their inner selves. Women need this time to restore their balance, process the day's events and actually function better when they allow themselves periods of aloneness. The ability to balance the amount of time spent in the company of others with alone time is yet another benefit to the single lifestyle enjoyed by many modern women.

STAYING SINGLE AND LOVING EVERY MINUTE

The number of single people around the world is increasing every year. There are approximately ninety-two million people in America who are eighteen years or older and who are either widowed, divorced or never married. Women can now expect to spend the majority of their adult years unmarried.[11] With these startling statistics, not only in the United States but also around the industrialized world, it quickly becomes apparent why the failure to enjoy being single is nothing more than a futile waste of a woman's time and precious life energy. Every woman can expect to be single at some point during her lifetime, so women should to make the most of the situation and enjoy it to the fullest.

Why, then, do some single women still feel that their lives are empty or lacking something? A lot of these negative thoughts have to do with cultural conditioning which tells them that the covenant of marriage is the pinnacle of achievement for all women. But as the divorce rate reveals, it isn't. Living alone has nothing to do with feeling alone. Women who choose to remain single do so because they see the awesome personal benefits of maintaining their autonomy and avoiding dependency upon another human being. They are not single because they can't find a man; they base the decision on a lifestyle choice that feels right for them.

Today, many strong and self-reliant single women recognize that searching for Mr. Right is no guarantee of future happiness. Contrary to popular opinion, married women are not any happier than their single friends are. Unfortunately, this misleading belief contributes to an enormous amount of distress and dissatisfaction for some single women.

As psychologist and author Bella DePaulo points out in her book *Single with Attitude*, society has not kept up with the new reality of millions of single women living fulfilling lives without being attached to men.[12] Hurtful and demeaning stereotypes persist and may cause some single women to second guess their decisions and doubt their good fortune. A single woman today may still find herself being asked why she hasn't married, an intrusive and unnecessary attempt to pry into the private business of another with the unspoken intent of passing critical judgment upon a woman's preferred lifestyle choice.

As a consequence of the social pressure to marry, many impressionable young women still experience a feeling of panic when they realize that they are likely to remain single for the rest of their lives. Instead of celebrating their wonderful single lives, they put everything on hold, waiting for the perfect man to turn up for them to marry. But when the fairy-tale romance and subsequent marriage fails to materialize, they are left with the crushing feeling that they have somehow failed and that their current lives do not measure up.

You do not have to internalize the inaccurate and outdated values of those who would have you believe the myth that single women are doomed to be loveless, rejected or lonely. These mistaken labels and stereotypical thoughts often come from insecure people who may feel threatened by perceived changes to traditional relationship patterns or those people who are uncomfortable with their own marriage choices.[13]

There is no greater blow to a woman's self-esteem than feeling inadequate because she is trying to measure up to an unrealistic and non-existent ideal; an ideal that is perpetuated through popular culture. Women should strive instead to rejoice proudly in the fabulous possibilities contained within their amazing life potential.

Chances are, you already have some strong opinions regarding relationships and partnerships that work for you, and if your vision docs not include marriage, so be it! You do not need to justify your choice of marital status in order to gain recognition and approval from other people. It's your life that you are living, not theirs, so don't succumb to their pressure.

Single women are acutely aware of their personal traits and preferences and this self-awareness forms a large part of their strengths and personalities. Single women can be strong, confident and independent. It is their choice to be so. They do not choose to form their identities from vicarious associations with other people but instead celebrate their own personal gifts and achievements.

Single-by-choice women are overwhelmingly content with their decision to remain unattached. Such empowered women thrive on living constructive and meaningful lives filled with creativity, yet grounded in integrity and respect for themselves and for others.

There is tremendous freedom to gain from allowing yourself to be totally honest and truthful about what works best for you and the direction you wish to take in life. You should not have to spend energy convincing yourself that someone else's priorities are number one. You do not have to settle for second best nor do you have to live with regrets about missed opportunities because you were placing someone else's needs above your own. You don't have to marry just because society sends you the message that married life is the high point of a woman's existence and you don't need to enter an unsuitable and potentially destructive relationship just because you're worried about getting left behind.

By remaining single, you join thousands of other independent and self-assured women around the world who, day after day, live authentic lives as happily unmarried and divorced women by choice.

Making the Right Choice for Yourself

D o you think less of your closest friends based on whether they are in relationships or not? Of course not! The things that you love and respect about your friends, whether it is the way they make you laugh, the way they understand and inspire you or the way they listen, have nothing to do with their relationship statuses. Would you consider your brother a failure because he was single? No! Would you turn your back on your sister if, after years of marriage, she confided in you that she felt empty and unhappy and wanted a divorce? No! You would want to help her do whatever it takes to find happiness again. So why are you holding yourself to more rigid and stricter standards than everyone else whom you love? Why don't you become your own cheerleader?

Former gymnastic world-champion and author Dan Millman, in his bestselling book *Way of the Peaceful Warrior*, shares that "Our sense of self-worth is the single most important determinant of the health, abundance and joy we allow into our lives."[1] If you begin to doubt your self-worth, whether it be on a conscious or subconscious level, you will severely limit the good things you allow to enter your life. It is well worth the effort to get rid of as many self-imposed limits as possible. Then choose, attract and go after the circumstances and goals you deserve.

Some societies continue to inundate women with messages that they should be married with children if they are to be deemed respectable, fulfilled women. Mix in possible judgmental comments or opinions from good-intentioned yet sometimes ignorant and insensitive family members and women may feel a lot of pressure to let go of their single ways and marry the first man who comes along. But it is so important for your sense of self-worth to come from within; you should never have to rely on the opinions of others to validate yourself.

Remember, the purpose of a relationship is not to make you feel better about yourself. Especially if a woman goes through a difficult divorce or breakup, her first reaction may be to feel undesirable or unwanted, causing her to want to run into the open arms of any person whom she thinks can make her feel better about herself. Oftentimes, in the throes of a bad breakup, a woman questions her ability to survive on her own. She may even mistakenly think that her innate fabulousness is somehow tied to her ex and without him, she is nothing. However, the reality is that it just isn't true.

The worth of going through several breakups is in discovering your ability not only to survive, but also to thrive on your own. In realizing your own resilience, you discover how fabulous you really are.[2] Take note of Dawn French, a fifty-three-year-old actress in the United Kingdom. After being married to her husband for twenty-five years, she went through a very public divorce. While many women in their fifties would look at the future apprehensively, Dawn has become proactive and has since lost over seventy pounds and written a novel—things that she said that she never would have been motivated to do had she stayed in her relationship. Says Dawn, "I am doing the opposite to what I have done for the past 30 years and just taking life as it comes. It's good; it's very exciting but quite frightening, but good frightening and every day is a new thing. I'm really relishing it."[3]

Look at being single, unmarried or divorced as a great chance to stabilize your emotions so that you can see yourself, your situation and your opportunities clearly. Oftentimes in a relationship, women tend to get sucked into the emotional ups and downs of their partners. On your own, you can realize that you alone are responsible for your emotions and for what you create in life. You'll start to recognize more clearly the criticism and self-judgment that you sometimes inflict on yourself. Consciousness is the first step to moving away from these negative and destructive behaviors to head toward a more empowered and authentically happy life. By avoiding all of the energy-sucking, stupid trivialities that tend to run through your mind in a relationship, such as *Does he secretly hate my flannel pajamas?* or *I wish I could go red with my hair, but his ex was a redhead so he won't like that*, you can direct your energy toward figuring out and going after exactly what it is that *you* like.

When you really reach a state of being content with yourself, you will realize that you never want to go back. You will wonder why anyone would give up that exhilarated feeling. If you do choose to date or cohabit with someone, nothing that your new partner does or says should be able to shake you off center, nor should anyone be able to lessen your self-worth.

Having a solid sense of self-worth means that you will never settle, no matter how badly you want to attach yourself to someone someday. One blog writer who goes by the name "Redacted Guy" wondered how his gorgeous, intelligent, funny and successful female friend could possibly be single. Then he realized, "Although she gets sad and feels lonely occasionally, and although she wants a family one day, she won't fake-laugh her way through life with a genuinely unfunny man because he's pretty swell otherwise and *it's time*...[My friend] has remained single due to not settling for the cavalcade of men she's had in her life who weren't right and also because she hasn't let the pressure of society, family and friends constantly asking her 'Why are you still single?' get to her. She won't choose Mr. Good Enough...because she's acutely aware of the epic chasm between Good Enough and Truly Good."[4]

All women should know that if they choose to be in a relationship, they deserve nothing but the very best. And they should also remain aware that even the very best men do not have the power or responsibility to maintain women's true self-worth for them. That job is the responsibility of all individuals for themselves and should be seen as an opportunity.

WHY IT'S GREAT TO BE SINGLE

For many women, it's culturally okay to be single in their twenties, as that is a time to explore, date, have one-night stands and get to know themselves and what it is that they are looking for. But with that comes an unspoken belief that it is something to "get out of your system," that it is all fun and games, but by the time a woman turns thirty or forty, she should have found the person she was looking for and if not, she should settle.

Hopefully you have not bought into that lame idea, because, as we've explored, your thirties and beyond are amazing times to be single. Older women are more secure in themselves and have the experience to recognize more clearly what it is that they want out of life. Then they spend their time accordingly, without wasting a moment. The older women get, the more they realize that life is too short to settle or to compromise. Women tend to get more fabulous with time, exactly like red wine.

Many single women in their thirties, forties and fifties also express how liberating it is not to be tied down. While they watch their friends suffering through heart-wrenching divorces or, perhaps worse, staying in depressing, dysfunctional and mediocre marriages, they are busy living life to the fullest on their own terms.

For some women this means having time to go back to school, without the added pressure of having to take care of a relationship or family. They can focus on work or leisure without having energy sucked out of them by spouses who want their needs to come first. For others, they enjoy dating a broad spectrum of men, both younger and older. Culturally, it is becoming much more acceptable for a woman of any age to date a man of any age. Most older single women are at a point in their careers where they are either financially stable or are heading in that direction and the money that they earn is used toward whatever they choose without having to get permission. If that means weekend shopping on clothing that makes them feel good, so be it. If that means going on a singles' cruise to the Mediterranean, then why not? No one is telling them they can't or shouldn't.

Sex as an older woman seems to get better with age and single women have the freedom to enjoy it to the maximum if they choose to, which many of their married friends envy.

BEING SINGLE DOES NOT MEAN BEING LONELY

Your attitude about your single, unmarried or divorced status is probably the single most important factor about the type of people whom you attract to yourself. Be careful you don't set yourself up for loneliness and rejection. How? When people feel bad about themselves they tend to project that energy to others. Just as confidence inspires confidence, negativity invokes negativity. If you walk around slump-shouldered with a scowl on your face and frown lines on your fore-head, it's easy for other people to be put off by you. They prefer to talk to a person emitting confidence with a smile on her face. Also, feelings of low self-worth over your single status might cause you to withdraw from the world, cutting yourself off from the very company and activities that can make your life fun and fulfilling. This behavior can reinforce negative feelings. If *you* are not comfortable being with you, why would anyone else be?

As you've learned in earlier chapters, by being more active and more positive you'll reinforce your new perspective on aloneness and begin to create a new reality in your life. This same recipe can infuse every aspect of your life, not just your plans for an open Saturday, but also your plans for your future, where to focus your energies and how you approach the challenges you routinely face. Mastering the art of aloneness is about treating yourself well and shedding the old beliefs and stereotypes that limit your ability to realize your greatest potential. It's about becoming your own and no one else's cherished "soul mate."

SINGLE CELEBRITIES

You may still have the archaic notion in your head that single women are middle-aged, frumpy and washed up. However, all it takes is a look at some of the most gorgeous, rich and talented female celebrities who choose to love the single life to get that idea out of your head.

One famous single actress is Jennifer Aniston. Although she was married to Brad Pitt and has had relationships with Vince Vaughn and John Mayer, she has also been through a series of very public break-ups. Even so, Jennifer "has remained remarkably upbeat and optimis-tic" about the benefits of being single. In an interview with Oprah Winfrey, another successful and happily-unmarried woman, Aniston "dismissed the notion that she has been unlucky in love, insisting instead that she has been 'unbelievably lucky' and that she is genu-inely happy for all of her exes...Perhaps the key to Jennifer's resiliency is her solid sense of self and self worth...'I have a really great rela-tionship with myself and that's a lifelong process.'"[5] For women, that surely is an attitude that deserves some respect.

It looks like excitingly hot yet voluntarily single Cameron Diaz is in full agreement with Aniston. "I've been in relationships since I was 16 years old. In the past three years, I've made a conscious decision not to be in a relationship for as long as I want...I've stayed away from all the traps out there for me to just fall into something that will potentially lead me down the same road...I want to have a relationship with myself right now."[6]

Lauren Conrad, who has not only become a successful actress but also an entrepreneur and designer, has chosen to focus on herself as opposed to men. Lauren's main concern is establishing her career: "I'm a fan of labels, but 'girlfriend' doesn't always look good on me. I've been in relationships where I literally felt guilty for not having enough time for that person, but I don't ever want to have to make excuses for working hard and wanting a career."[7] Why should anyone ever have to make an excuse for wanting success for themselves?

A famous woman from history who paved the way by inspiring talented future females to go the solo route was the remarkably accomplished Impressionist artist Mary Cassatt. According to author Nancy Mowll Mathews, Cassatt, born in America, lived and worked in France. While she was a "classically trained artist, she preferred the company of radicals." She never married, but this is not an attribute that defines her life or her work, which work speaks for itself.[8] She led a fabulous single life while making her mark on history, much like her modern day counterpart, the single (although once engaged) former United States Secretary of State Condoleezza Rice, who has also found a way to make her mark on history without a man by her side.

Among the famous and fabulous couples who have not seen any need to marry are Angelina Jolie and Brad Pitt. As two of the world's most recognizable faces, with success both on and off-screen, they have juggled raising a family of six, working with refugees and human rights groups and maintaining a stable relationship, all without a marriage certificate.

Oprah Winfrey has been with her partner Stedman Graham for over twenty years without marrying and she has no intention to do so. In a September 2001 interview with Larry King, Oprah said, "I think the relationship as it is works really, really solidly well." Two years later, in an interview with *TV Guide,* she had a similar view of her relationship and marriage: "People look at me and think, 'She *must* be unhappy, something *must* be missing.' But that's because they're looking at my life from their perspective. Stedman and I have a great relationship that allows me to be me in the fullest sense, with no expectations of wifedom and all that would mean."[9]

So, if some of the world's most gorgeous, wealthy and talented women are proud of being single, why shouldn't you be?

BE TRUE TO YOURSELF

Around the world, there are many thriving subcultures that have never bought into the idea that marriage is necessary for society as a whole to function. Among them are gay couples, polygamy and the Mosuo people of southwest China.[10]

As we've explored, single women in our era have more options than ever before for how they want to live their lives. Want a live-in boyfriend whom you have no intention of marrying? Want an open relationship that includes men and/or women? Want to date a man twenty years older than you? All these and more are now options for single-by-choice women. *The Atlantic* writer Kate Bolick spoke about this topic with Stephanie Coontz, a social historian at Evergreen State College and author of *Marriage, A History: From Obedience to Intimacy or How Love Conquered Marriage*, who opined: "We are without a doubt in the midst of an extraordinary sea change...When it comes to what people actually want and expect from marriage and relationships and how they organize their sexual and romantic lives, all the old ways have broken down."[11]

Decide exactly what type of situation fulfills you, one that you are comfortable with, no matter what society, your family or your friends say. There are many ways to know love in this world, including love directed at yourself and love to be shared with others. Love yourself first. It is your life and it is time you take responsibility for your personal happiness, however that manifests itself.

CREATE A POWERFUL, MORE FULFILLED YOU

Arnold H. Glasow said, "Success isn't a result of spontaneous combustion. You must set yourself on fire." As a single woman, you should relish the free time that you have and make the most of it! Being single can give you a deeper awareness of who you really are at your core and not someone defined by a relationship.[12]

During the initial stages of a relationship, a woman tries to make herself look as good as possible to impress the other person and she often finds herself saying and doing things she normally wouldn't. Being single allows you both the time and the space to be yourself and develop who you really are.

We live in a busy society. People complain on a daily basis that they never have enough time. These people probably aren't single. When single, you have more time for yourself and the things that you like to do. You can set your own schedule. Stay aware, as we've discussed, that being single may give you more time to develop your business and career, to devote to hobbies, to spend with friends and family and to travel.

Being single gives you more time to better yourself. You can use the extra time to advance your career, volunteer in your community, take classes for job advancement or study for a degree, just because you have always wanted to. Relationships, especially marriages, require a significant amount of time, as anyone who is married or in a relationship will tell you.

Kate Bolick, in her article "All the Single Ladies," cites a report published by sociologists Naomi Gerstel and Natalia Sarkisian in which they conclude that "unlike singles, married couples spend less time keeping in touch with and visiting their friends and extended family, and are less likely to provide them with emotional and practical support," a relationship they termed "greedy marriages." Bolick comments that it is possible to see "how couples today might be driven to form such isolated nations—it's not easy in this age of dual-career families and hyper-parenting to keep the wheels turning, never mind having to maintain outside relationships as well." Yet society continues to place high value on marriage.[13]

Remember, being single is a time to understand yourself. It isn't using the time to obsess about meeting someone else but an opportunity to enjoy your own life. You learn to challenge yourself and you grow. It's a special experience and one you couldn't possibly have inside a relationship. It is an opportunity to focus on yourself from a mature standpoint, which can only make for a healthier, more secure relationship the next time around, if that is the route you choose. And if not, you will enjoy your own company that much more and be a stronger and more centered friend to those whom you care about the most.

SHARE YOUR EMPOWERMENT

In this book we've focused on how you are stronger and more capable than you may think. Are you convinced at last that the single life is a good choice? Do you now look at other singles who are moping about their relationship statuses and wish that they could just realize that being single is a huge advantage? Well, get out there and do just that. Inspire other women!

For instance, get involved in your community by working with abused women. Teach these women that they can stand on their own and show them that a single life is one that they can look forward to. Find a local non-profit organization that works with young female refugees, many of whom have been rescued from the sex trade industry. Be a role model for these young girls so that they have a strong example and can grow up to be independent, self-assured women.

Often, ambitious single women are so passionate about their purpose in life that they can't imagine the idea of sacrificing it in order to give exaggerated time and energy to a relationship (as one must in a marriage). That is not to say that singles of this type don't enjoy positive and rewarding romantic relationships; it's just that they are so filled with dedication and passion for their missions that they refuse to sacrifice them because these goals are an integral part of who and what they are.[14] Kim Calvert, editor of *Singular Magazine,* describes her never-married aunt who was dedicated to her career, passionate about civil rights and intent on sharing this with others. "So next time," Calvert says, "you hear someone say, with disdainful judgment, that so-and-so never married, look beyond the 'what's wrong with them?' knee-jerk response, and look for the passion and purpose they are 'married' to."[15]

The example that you set has the power to resonate with and inspire many future generations of strong, independent women and that is no small thing.

WHY MARRIED WOMEN ENVY SINGLE YOU

By now you should be aware that I feel strongly that a walk down the aisle and a ring on your finger cannot compare to the amazing life that you have in store for you as a single, unmarried or happily divorced woman. Many of your married girlfriends are probably thinking, *Wow,*

I would give anything for a day in her life. There are so many reasons why your life as a single woman is going to be the envy of all of your married friends! Here are just a few:

You don't have to justify or explain to anyone the expense of a new pair of shoes nor do you need to wait for a reason to wear them. If no one asks you out, you ask someone out or you take yourself out, knowing that you are worth it. The same goes for any new purchase that is expensive but makes you feel great. You never have to hide receipts, because it's your money and you are free to spend it exactly as you like.

You can spend all weekend on the couch with a pile of movies and not have to share the television with someone.

You can shamelessly and guiltlessly flirt with any man you want without hurting anyone's feelings. You can, if you want, have great sex with a different gorgeous man every week.

You can take singles cruises to exotic islands instead of spending your vacation time with your husband's family.

Perhaps best of all, you will not face a painful, ugly and very costly divorce.

If, as a single, unmarried or divorced woman, you choose to have a monogamous relationship with a man you love (without marriage!) all the while holding your ground that you are an individual, you can.

The time has come for you not to be ashamed of your single status, but to be proud of it. You are more than a title that someone bestows upon you, through some piece of paper that a government official signs. You are an empowered woman who can do anything to which you set your mind and heart.

You are not the "crazy cat lady" who secretly wants love yet is too scared to go out. And you're not regretting anything. You live your single life to the fullest and see the abundance of new options and opportunities that come your way. There will be challenges, but these should not scare you. The adventures of the single life dwarf the mediocre life that you could have in the traditional tailor-made setting upon which society seems to insist. There are so many alternatives to the kinds of relationships, family structure, children, study, work, play and career that you can have that it would be foolish not to seize all those benefits available to you as a brave single woman.

I hope by reading this book you have learned that you are a vivacious, fun-loving, independent woman who knows there is too much you want to accomplish to give up so much of that precious time for an old-fashioned marriage. You can be the type of single woman who makes married women second guess their decisions to walk down the aisle. You are a woman with unlimited possibilities who has the time, desire and self-worth to take classes, travel, date, dance, dine, wine, kiss or make love to anyone you want. Remember, your options are boundless today and your happiness is in your own hands, exactly where it should be!

Notes

Introduction

1. Les Brown, "Les Brown Motivational Quotes," Lesbrown.com, December 2011, http://www.lesbrown.com/lesbrown.com/english/motivational_quotes.html.
2. Conor Dougherty, "New Vow: I Don't Take Thee," *The Wall Street Journal*, September 29, 2010, http://online.wsj.com/article/SB10001424052748703882404575519871444705214.html.
3. Mark Mather and Diana Lavery, "In U.S., Proportion Married at Lowest Recorded Levels," Population Reference Bureau, September 2010, http://www.prb.org/Articles/2010/usmarriagedecline.aspx.
4. "Selected Data for International Women's Day 2011," Central Bureau of Statistics of Israel, March 6, 2011, http://www1.cbs.gov.il/hodaot2011n/11_11_050e.pdf.
5. Ibid.
6. Sharon Jayson, "Nearly 40% say marriage is becoming obsolete," *USA Today*, November 18, 2010, http://www.usatoday.com/yourlife/sex-relationships/marriage/2010-11-18-1Amarriage18_ST_N.htm.

Part I: Married Women

Chapter 1: Pros and Cons of Marriage

1. Carol Morello, "Number of long-lasting marriages in U.S. has risen, Census Bureau reports," *The Washington Post*, May 18, 2011, http://www.washingtonpost.com/local/number-of-long-lasting-marriages-in-us-has-risen-census-bureau-reports/2011/05/18/AFO8dW6G_story.html.

2. "The Decline of Marriage and Rise of New Families", The Pew Research Center, November 18, 2010, http://pewresearch.org/pubs/1802/decline-marriage-rise-new-families.
3. Margarita Tartakovsky, "What You Need to Know Before Living Together," PsychCentral.com, 2011, http://psychcentral.com/lib/2011/what-you-need-to-know-before-living-together/all/1/.
4. Corey Dade, "Data On Same-Sex Couples Reveal Changing Attitudes," NPR, September 30, 2011, http://www.npr.org/2011/09/30/140950989/data-on-same-sex-couples-reveal-changing-attitudes.
5. Joseph Chamie and Barry Mirkin, "Same-Sex Marriage: A Global Perspective," The Globalist, September 20, 2011, http://www.theglobalist.com/StoryId.aspx?StoryId=9343.
6. Andrew Cherlin, The Marriage-Go-Round: The State of Marriage and the Family in America Today (New York: Knopf, 2009), 11.
7. "Single? You're not alone", CNN Living, August 19, 2010, http://articles.cnn.com/2010-08-19/living/single.in.america_1_single-fathers-single-mothers-single-parents.
8. Nellie Andreeva, "23 Million Americans Watch Royal Wedding, Beating U.S. Audience for Charles and Di's," Deadline.com, April 30, 2011, http://www.deadline.com/2011/04/so-how-were-the-royal-wedding-ratings/.
9. Cele Otnes and Elizabeth Pleck, Cinderella Dreams: The Allure of the Lavish Wedding (Los Angeles: University of California Press, 2003).
10. Michelle Langley, Women's Infidelity: Living in Limbo: What Women Really Mean When They Say "I'm Not Happy," (St. Louis: McCarlan Publishing, 2005).
11. Ibid.
12. Cherlin, The Marriage-Go-Round, 5.
13. CDC/National Center for Health Statistics, "New Report Sheds Light on Trends and Patterns in Marriage, Divorce, and Cohabitation," Centers for Disease Control, updated January 13, 2010, http://www.cdc.gov/nchs/pressroom/02news/div_mar_cohab.htm.
14. Heather Boushey, "The New Breadwinners," in A Woman's Nation Changes Everything ed. Heather Boushey and Ann O'Leary, October 2009, http://www.americanprogress.org/issues/2009/10/pdf/awn/a_womans_nation.pdf.
15. Ibid.
16. Kimberly Palmer, "Why Women Should Manage Their Own Money," US News & World Report, October 18, 2011, http://money.usnews.com/money/personal-finance/articles/2011/10/18/why-women-should-manage-their-own-money; Marissa Calligeros, "Financial stress 'main cause of divorce' for women," Brisbane Times, October 12, 2008, http://www.brisbanetimes.com.au/news/queensland/financial-stress-main-cause-of-divorce-for-women/2008/10/14/1223749983243.html#.
17. Monty and Sarah Don, The Jewel Garden (London: Hodder & Stoughton, 2005), 17.

Chapter 2: Why Women and Men Cheat

1. Parents Television Council, "Happily Never After," Parents Television Council, August 2008, http://www.parentstv.org/ptc/publications/reports/sexontv/main.asp.
2. David M. Buss and David P. Schmitt, "Sexual Strategies Theory: An Evolutionary Perspective of Human Mating," *Psychological Review* 100, no. 2 (1993): 204-232.
3. Ibid.
4. Ibid.
5. Ibid.
6. Ibid.
7. Ibid.
8. Ibid.
9. Ibid.
10. Saul L. Miller and Jon K. Maner, "Sex Differences in Response to Sexual Versus Emotional Infidelity: The Moderating Role of Individual Differences," *Personality and Individual Differences* 46 (2009): 287–291.
11. Shirley P. Glass, *Not 'Just Friends': Rebuilding Trust and Recovering Your Sanity After Infidelity* (New York: The Free Press, 2003).
12. Ibid.
13. Ibid.
14. Ibid.
15. Willard F. Harley Jr. and Jennifer Harley Chalmers, *Surviving an Affair* (Grand Rapids, MI: Revell, 1998).
16. Ibid.
17. Michael J. Formica, "Gender Differences, Sexuality and Emotional Infidelity," *Psychology Today,* January 8, 2009, http://www.psychologytoday.com/blog/enlightened-living/200901/gender-differences-sexuality-and-emotional-infidelity.
18. Ibid.
19. Ibid.
20. Patricia Potter-Efron and Ronald Potter-Efron, *The Emotional Affair: How to Recognize Emotional Infidelity and What to Do About It* (Oakland, CA: New Harbinger Publications, 2008).
21. Ibid.
22. Ibid.
23. Ibid.
24. Glass, *Not 'Just Friends.'*
25. Ibid.
26. Langley, *Women's Infidelity.*
27. Ibid.
28. Sean Elder, "Our Cheatin' Hearts," WebMD, June 1, 2007, http://men.webmd.com/guide/our-cheatin-hearts.
29. "Do social media sites make cheating easier?" *Chicago Tribune,* August 17, 2010, http://articles.chicagotribune.com/2010-08-17/news/sc-fam

-0817-facebook-cheating-20100817_1_facebook-andrew-noyes-social-media-sites.

30. Elisabeth LaMotte, "Is Facebook Causing Us To Cheat?" Your Tango, September 10, 2009, http://www.yourtango.com/200936849/facebook-causing-us-to-cheat.

31. Glass, *Not 'Just Friends.'*

32. Rick Nauert, "Online Cheating Usually Leads to Physical Encounters," PsychCentral.com, June 21, 2011, http://psychcentral.com/news/2011/06/21/online-cheating-usually-leads-to-physical-encounters/27109.html.

33. Janis Abrahms Spring and Michael Spring, *After the Affair: Healing the Pain and Rebuilding Trust When a Partner Has Been Unfaithful* (New York: HarperCollins, 1997).

34. Ibid.

35. Harley and Chalmers, *Surviving an Affair.*

36. Ibid.

37. Ibid.

38. Ibid.

39. Glass, *Not 'Just Friends.'*

40. Ibid.

41. Ibid.

42. Ibid.

43. Ibid.

Chapter 3: Unhappily Married Women

1. Timothy S. Grall, "Custodial Mothers and Fathers and Their Child Support: 2007," US Census Bureau, November 2009, http://www.census.gov/prod/2009pubs/p60-237.pdf.

2. "Single-Parent Families on the Rise," WatchTower.org, October 8, 2002, http://www.watchtower.org/e/20021008/article_01.htm.

3. "As Marriage and Parenthood Drift Apart, Public Is Concerned about Social Impact," Pew Research Center, July 1, 2007, http://pewsocial trends.org/2007/07/01/as-marriage-and-parenthood-drift-apart-public-is-concerned-about-social-impact/.

4. M. Gary Neuman and Patricia Romanowski, *Helping Your Kids Cope with Divorce the Sandcastles Way* (New York: Random House, 1999).

5. "Women in the Labor Force: A Databook," US Bureau for Labor Statistics, December 2010, http://www.bls.gov/cps/wlf-databook-2010.pdf.

6. Catherine Rampell, "Single Parents, Around the World," *The New York Times,* March 10, 2010, http://economix.blogs.nytimes.com/2010/03/10/single-parents-around-the-world/.

7. Sheila Weinstein, "Loneliness: Use It...And Lose It," *Psychology Today,* June 23, 2011, http://www.psychologytoday.com/blog/what-do-i-do-now/201106/loneliness-use-it-and-lose-it.

8. Richard Fry and D'Vera Cohn, "Living Together: The Economics of Cohabitation," The Pew Research Center, June 27, 2011, http://pew research.org/pubs/2034/cohabitation-rate-doubled-since-mid-90s-only -more-educated-benefit-economically.

9. "New Marriage and Divorce Statistics Released," The Barna Group, March 31, 2008, http://www.barna.org/barna-update/article/15-familykids/42 -new-marriage-and-divorce-statistics-released.

10. "Domestic Violence Facts," National Coalition Against Domestic Violence, http://www.ncadv.org/files/DomesticViolenceFactSheet(National).pdf.

11. Joan D. Atwood and Limor Schwartz, "Cyber-Sex: The New Affair Treatment Considerations," *Journal of Couple and Relationship Therapy* 1, no.3 (2002): 37-56.

12. Frank Pittman, *Grow Up! How Taking Responsibility Can Make You a Happy Adult* (New York: St. Martin's Griffin, 1998).

13. Sinead McIntyre, "Rise of the wandering wives," *Daily Mail,* http://www .dailymail.co.uk/femail/article-200766/Rise-wandering-wives.html.

14. Felicia R. Lee, "Influential Study on Divorce's Impact Is Said to Be Flawed," *The New York Times,* May 9, 1996, http://www.nytimes.com/1996/05/09/ garden/influential-study-on-divorce-s-impact-is-said-to-be-flawed.html.

15. Ed Sherman, *Making Any Divorce Better! Specific Steps to Make Things Smoother, Faster, Less Painful, and Save You a Lot of Money* (Santa Cruz, CA: Nolo Press Occidental, 2007).

16. Ibid.

17. Carl E. Pickhardt, *Everything Parent's Guide To Children And Divorce: Reassuring Advice to Help Your Family Adjust* (Avon, MA: Adams Media, 2005).

18. Ibid.

19. Ibid.

20. Ibid.

21. Ibid.

22. Ibid.

23. Ibid.

24. Susan B. Garland, "Claiming Social Security After a Divorce," *Kiplinger,* May 1, 2010, http://www.kiplinger.com/features/archives/krr-claiming -social-security-after-a-divorce.html.

25. Kay Moffett and Sarah Touborg, *Not Your Mother's Divorce: A Practical, Girlfriend-to-Girlfriend Guide to Surviving the End of a Young Marriage* (New York: Broadway, 2003).

26. Ibid.

27. Ibid.

28. Ibid.

Part II: Unmarried Women

Chapter 4: Marriage Deliberations

1. Laura Kipnis, *Against Love: A Polemic* (New York: Pantheon Books, 2003), 56.
2. "Domestic Violence Facts."
3. Cherlin, *The Marriage-Go-Round*, 5.
4. Ibid., 11.
5. Ibid., 10.
6. Kipnis, Against *Love*, 60.
7. Sandra Tsing Loh, "Let's Call the Whole Thing Off," *The Atlantic,* July/August 2009, http://www.theatlantic.com/magazine/archive/2009/07/let-8217-s-call-the-whole-thing-off/7488/.
8. "Achievements in Public Health, 1900–1999," Centers for Disease Control, *Morbidity and Mortality Weekly Report* 48, no. 29 (July 30, 1999), http://www.cdc.gov/mmwr/PDF/wk/mm4829.pdf.
9. Elizabeth Arias, "United States Life Tables, 2006," *National Vital Statistics Reports* 58, no. 21 (June 28, 2010), http://www.cdc.gov/nchs/data/nvsr/nvsr58/nvsr58_21.pdf.
10. "Women's Health USA 2010: Life Expectancy," Health Resources and Services Administration, http://mchb.hrsa.gov/whusa10/hstat/hi/pages/207le.html.

Chapter 5: Unmarried Women in Happy Relationships

1. Kahlil Gibran, *The Prophet* (New York: Alfred A. Knopf, 1973).
2. Rose M. Krieder, "Number, Timing, and Duration of Marriages and Divorces: 2001," US Census Bureau, February 2005, http://www.census.gov/prod/2005pubs/p70-97.pdf.
3. Craig G. Kallen, "My Divorce is Going to Cost How Much?," womansdivorce.com, http://www.womansdivorce.com/cost-of-a-divorce.html.
4. Cherlin, *The Marriage-Go-Round*.
5. Boushey and O'Leary, " The New Breadwinners."
6. Warren Farrell, *Why Men Earn More: The Startling Truth Behind the Pay Gap--and What Women Can Do About It* (New York: AMACON, 2005).
7. Jeff Schnepper, "7 tax reasons not to get married," msn.com, December 13, 2011, http://money.msn.com/tax-planning/7-tax-reasons-not-to-get-married-schnepper.aspx.
8. "Dave Ramsey, *More Than Enough: The Ten Keys to Changing Your Financial Destiny* (New York: Penguin, 2002).
9. Glenn Setzer, "Single Women Home Buyers Finding A Home Of Their Own," *Mortgage News Daily*, July 17, 2006, http://www.mortgagenewsdaily.com/7172006_Woman_Home_Buyers.asp.

10. "Bridal Market Overview," *The National Mail Order Association* http://www.nmoa.org/articles/dmnews/bridalandweddingmarketoverview.htm.
11. Brian Alexander, "Is monogamy dead?," msnbc.com, September 7, 2005, http://www.msnbc.msn.com/id/9117931/ns/health-sexual_health/t/monogamy-dead/.
12. David Brown, "Wait until marriage? 'Extremely challenging'," *Washington Post*, December 21, 2006, http://archive.sltrib.com/article.php?id=4872498&itype=NGPSID&keyword=&qtype=.
13. "What Some Celebrities Think of the 'M' Word," *Singular Magazine*, August 15, 2010, http://singularcity.com/singular-lifestyle/674-what-some-celebrities-think-of-the-m-word.
14. Belinda Luscombe, "Who Needs Marriage? A Changing Institution," *Time*, November 18, 2010, http://www.time.com/time/magazine/article/0,9171,2032116,00.html.
15. Ibid.
16. "Wedding Money: What Does the Average Wedding Cost?" theknot.com, http://wedding.theknot.com/wedding-planning/wedding-budget/qa/what-does-the-average-wedding-cost.aspx.

Chapter 6: Unmarried Women in Unhappy Relationships

1. "What Some Celebrities Think of the 'M' Word."
2. Leanne Coffman, "Why Some Women Prefer to Be Single," livestrong.com, March 7, 2011, http://www.livestrong.com/article/155594-why-some-women-prefer-to-be-single/#ixzz1Y7tlhCKr.
3. "Too many suits," *The Economist*, November 26, 2011, http://www.economist.com/node/21539924.
4. "Living arrangements of children," OECD Family Database, Organisation for Economic Co-operation and Development, updated January 7, 2010, http://www.oecd.org/dataoecd/63/5/41919559.pdf.
5. "Custodial Mothers and Fathers and Their Child Support: 2007", U.S. Census Bureau, November 2009, http://www.census.gov/prod/2009pubs/p60-237.pdf.
6. Grall, "Custodial Mothers and Fathers and Their Child Support."
7. Sharon Jayson, "Free as a bird and loving it: Being Single has its benefits", *USA Today*, December 4, 2007, http://www.usatoday.com/life/lifestyle/2007-04-11-being-single_N.htm.
8. " Facts for Features: Unmarried and Single Americans Week", US Census Bureau, September 11, 2008, http://www.census.gov/newsroom/releases/archives/facts_for_features_special_editions/cb08-ff16a.html.
9. Jayson, "Free as a bird and loving it."
10. Bella DePaulo, "Single and Happy," mysinglespace.org, http://www.mysinglespace.org/images/Bella_DePaulo-Single_and_Happy.pdf.

238 NOTES

Chapter 7: Divorced Women

1. Jacob C. Toews, "Is Marriage Outdated?" *The Real Truth*, February 22, 2011, http://www.realtruth.org/articles/110222-002-marriage.html.
2. Sharon Jayson, "Cohabitation is Replacing Dating," *USA Today*, July 17, 2005, http://www.usatoday.com/life/lifestyle/2005-07-17-cohabitation_x.htm.
3. Boushey and O'Leary, "The New Breadwinners."
4. "Closing the gap," *The Economist*, November 26, 2011, http://www.economist.com/node/21539928.
5. "Here's to the next half-century," *The Economist*, November 26, 2011, http://www.economist.com/node/21539930.
6. Deirdre Bair, *Calling It Quits: Late-Life Divorce and Starting Over* (New York: Random House, 2007).
7. Ibid.
8. Ibid.
9. Ibid.
10. "The cashier and the carpenter," *The Economist*, November 26, 2011, http://www.economist.com/node/21539932.
11. Moffett and Touborg, *Not Your Mother's Divorce*.
12. Vicki King and Jennifer O'Connell, *The Divorced Girls' Society: Your Initiation into the Club You Never Thought You'd Join* (Avon, MA: Polka Dot Press, 2007).
13. Ibid.

Chapter 8: Single by Choice

1. Liz Weiss, Ellen-Marie Whelan and Jessica Arons, "Unmarried and Uninsured: Single Women Face Additional Health Insurance Barriers," Center for American Progress, October 27, 2009, http://www.americanprogress.org/issues/2009/10/unmarried_uninsured.html.
2. "Issues Affecting Single People," unmarriedamerica.org, http://www.unmarriedamerica.org/issues.html.
3. Boushey and O'Leary, "The New Breadwinners."
4. Grall, "Custodial Mothers and Fathers and Their Child Support."
5. Ellen Kay Trimberger, *The New Single Woman* (Boston: Beacon Press, 2005), 116.
6. Ibid., 5.
7. Carol M. Anderson, Susan Stewart and Sona Dimidjian, *Flying Solo: Single Women in Midlife* (New York: W.W Norton & Company, Inc., 1995), 133.
8. Trimberger, *The New Single Woman*, 115.
9. Anderson, Stewart and Dimidjian, *Flying Solo*, 134.

Part III: Today's Women

Chapter 9: Women's Education and Careers

1. "A world of bluestockings," *The Economist*, November 26, 2011, http://www.economist.com/node/21539926.
2. Tamar Lewin, "At Colleges, Women Are Leaving Men in the Dust," *New York Times*, July 9, 2006, http://www.nytimes.com/2006/07/09/education/09college.html?pagewanted=all.
3. Ibid.
4. Ibid.
5. Jenna Goudreau, "Best-Paying Jobs For Women," *Forbes*, May 3, 2010, http://www.forbes.com/2010/05/03/best-paying-jobs-women-salary-forbes-woman-leadership-careers.html.
6. Ibid.
7. Ibid.
8. Ibid.
9. Dennis Cauchon, "Women gain as men lose jobs," *USA Today*, September 3, 2009, http://www.usatoday.com/news/nation/2009-09-02-womenwork_N.htm.
10. "The cashier and the carpenter."
11. Joelle Schmitz, "Women in Politics? The U.S. is failing," *USA Today*, October 12, 2010, http://www.usatoday.com/news/opinion/forum/2010-10-13-column13_ST_N.htm.
12. Ibid.
13. "Closing the gap."
14. "A world of bluestockings."
15. Ibid.
16. "Baby blues," *The Economist*, November 26, 2011, http://www.economist.com/node/21539925.
17. Barbara Stanny, *Secrets of Six-Figure Women* (New York: HarperCollins, 2002).
18. Ibid.
19. Ibid.
20. Ibid.
21. Ibid.
22. Ibid.
23. Ibid.
24. Ibid.
25. Ibid.
26. "Here's to the next half-century."
27. Ibid.
28. Ibid.
29. "Too many suits."
30. Ibid.

31. "The sky's the limit," *The Economist*, November 25, 2011, http://www.economist.com/node/21539931.

32. Ibid.

33. Ibid.

34. ??.

35. Richard R. Peterson, *Women, Work, and Divorce* (Albany, NY: State University of New York Press, 1989) 13.

36. Ibid., 23.

37. Ibid., 40.

38. Jayson, "Nearly 40% Say Marriage is Becoming Obsolete."

39. Sabrina Tavernise, "Study Finds Women Slower to Wed, and Divorce Easing," *The New York Times*, May 18, 2011, http://www.nytimes.com/2011/05/19/us/19marriage.html.

40. Harry Wallop, "Average age for women to marry hits 30 for first time," *The Telegraph*, March 30, 2011, http://www.telegraph.co.uk/news/8415852/Average-age-for-women-to-marry-hits-30-for-first-time.html.

41. Jayson, "Nearly 40% Say Marriage is Becoming Obsolete."

42. Ibid.

43. Barbara Brotman, "Happily Unmarried," *Chicago Tribune*, December 20, 2000, http://articles.chicagotribune.com/2000-12-20/features/0012200390_1_single-women-national-marriage-project-chicago-sociologist-linda-waite.

44. Susan Maushart, *Wifework: What Marriage Really Means for Women* (New York: Bloomsbury, 2001).

45. Ibid.

46. Susan Hirshman, *Does This Make My Assets Look Fat?: A Woman's Guide to Finding Financial Empowerment and Success* (New York: St Martin's Press, 2010).

47. "Baby blues."

48. "Table 3.13, Fertility Rates by Age and Religion," Statistical Abstract of Israel, CBS.gov, 2011, http://www.cbs.gov.il/shnaton62/st03_13.pdf.

49. "Baby blues."

50. Carol Fishman Cohen and Vivian Steir Rabin, *Back on the Career Track: A Guide for Stay-at-Home Moms Who Want to Return to Work* (New York: Warner Business Books, 2007).

51. Ibid.

52. Ibid.

53. Ibid.

54. Ibid.

55. Ibid.

Chapter 10: The Sexual Revolution: Stage for New Options

1. Landon Y. Jones, *Great Expectations: America and the Baby Boom Generation* (New York: Coward, McCann and Geoghegan, 1980).

2. Aine Collier, *The Humble Little Condom: A History* (New York: Prometheus Books, 2007).

3. William Strauss and Neil Howe, *Generations: The History of America's Future, 1584 to 2069* (New York: Harper Perennial, 1992), 324.

4. Andrea Tone, *Devices & Desires: A History of Contraceptives in America* (New York: Hill and Wang, 2001); Lara V. Marks, *Sexual Chemistry: A History of the Contraceptive Pill* (New Haven, CT: Yale University Press, 2001).

5. Bernard Asbell, *The Pill: A Biography of the Drug That Changed the World* (New York: Random House, 1995).

6. Barbara L. Tischler, *Sights on the Sixties* (New Brunswick, NJ: Rutgers University Press, 1992).

7. Theodore Roszak, *The Making of a Counter Culture: Reflections on the Technocratic Society and Its Youthful Opposition* (Berkeley, CA: University of California Press, 1995).

8. Wendy McElroy, "The Free Love Movement and Radical Individualism," *The Libertarian Enterprise*, December 1, 1996, http://www.ncc-1776.org/tle1996/le961210.html.

9. "Teen Sexuality and Pregnancy in Nevada," University of Nevada, Las Vegas, December 25, 2005, http://cdclv.unlv.edu//healthnv/teensex.html.

10. Andrea Sachs, "Happily Unmarried," *Time Magazine*, March 3, 2003, http://www.time.com/time/magazine/article/0,9171,1004360,00.html.

11. Carrie Sloan, "Living Apart Together," *Elle*, August 12, 2009, http://www.elle.com/Life Love/Sex Relationships/Living Apart Together.

12. Ibid.

13. Leigh Dyer, "I'm a single mother...by choice," newsobserver.com, July 6, 2010, http://www.newsobserver.com/2010/07/06/563301/im-a-single-mother-by-choice.html.

14. Sharon Jayson, "What does a 'family' look like nowadays?" *USA Today*, November 25, 2010, http://www.usatoday.com/yourlife/sex-relationships/marriage/2010-11-18-pew18_ST_N.htm.

15. Dyer, "I'm a single mother...by choice."; "The Decline of Marriage and the Rise of New Families."

16. Rachel Sarah, "Surviving (and Thriving) as a Single Mom," parents.com, http://www.parents.com/parenting/dynamics/single-parenting/surviving-and-thriving-as-a-single-mom/.

17. Caroline Wilbert, "Nontraditional Families: How Kids Fare," WebMD, August 7, 2008. http://www.webmd.com/parenting/news/20080807/nontraditional-families-how-kids-fare.

18. Ibid.

19. "The cashier and the carpenter."

20. Jessica Knoll, "Are You on the Fence About Kids?" *Cosmopolitian*, October 2011.

21. Ibid.

22. Emily Bazelon, "2 Kids + 0 Husband= Family," *The New York Times*, January 29, 2009, http://www.nytimes.com/2009/02/01/magazine/01Moms-t.html?pagewanted=all.

23. Ibid.
24. Mikki Morrissette, "Why Single Women Make Great Parents," HuffingtonPost.com, December 11, 2006, http://www.huffingtonpost .com/mikki-morrissette/why-single-women-make-gre_b_36056.html.
25. Brette McWhorter Sember, *The Complete Adoption & Fertility Legal Guide* (Illinois: Sphinx Publishing, 2004).
26. Ibid.
27. Ibid.
28. Ibid.
29. Ibid.
30. Ibid.
31. "Here's the next half-century."

Chapter 11: New Roles Women Can Play in Relationships

1. "Marriage and Divorce," Centers for Disease Control and Prevention, October 5, 2010, http://www.cdc.gov/nchs/fastats/divorce.htm.
2. Amy DePaul, "An Interview with Andrew Cherlin," Bookslut, September 2009, http://www.bookslut.com/features/2009_09_015093.php.
3. Anderson, Stewart and Dimidjian, *Flying Solo,* 84.
4. Stephanie Coontz, *Marriage, a History: From Obedience to Intimacy, How Love Conquered Marriage* (New York: Viking, 2006).
5. Cherlin, *The Marriage-Go-Round,* 100.
6. Ibid., 104.
7. DePaul, "An Interview with Andrew Cherlin."
8. Julie Cwikel, Helen Gramotnev and Christina Lee, "Never-married Childless Women in Australia: Health and Circumstances in Older Age," *Social Science & Medicine* 62, no. 8 (2006), Abstract.
9. "The Decline of Marriage and Rise of New Families."
10. Anderson, *Flying Solo,* 142.
11. "The cashier and the carpenter."
12. "Marriage and Divorce in America," Real Relational Solutions, 2007, http:// www.terryreal.com/press/pdfs/marriage_divorce_in_america-FS.pdf.
13. Rosanna Hertz, *Single by Chance, Mothers by Choice: How Women are Choosing Parenthood Without Marriage and Creating the New American Family* (New York: Oxford University Press, 2006), 22.
14. "A Comparison of the IVF Cost Worldwide," ivfcost.net, August 27, 2008, http://www.ivfcost.net/ivf-cost/a-comparison-of-the-ivf-cost-worldwide.
15. "Single Parent Adoption," Adopting.org, October 2011, http://www .adopting.org/adoptions/single-parent-adoption.html.
16. "The sky's the limit."
17. Victoria Jaycox, "Communal Living: Wave of the Future?" in *Single Again: A Guide for Women Starting Over* (New York: W.W. Norton & Company, Inc., 1999).

18. Kathy Belge, "Children of Lesbian Parents Study: Teen Children of Lesbian Parents Study," About.com, http://lesbianlife.about.com/od/families/a/ParentStudy.htm.

19. Kate Bolick, "All the Single Ladies," *The Atlantic,* November 2011, http://www.theatlantic.com/magazine/archive/2011/11/all-the-single-ladies/8654/?single_page=true.

20. "Baby blues."

21. National Kids Count Program, "Children in single-parent families," The Annie E. Casey Foundation, October 2011, http://datacenter.kidscount.org/data/acrossstates/Rankings.aspx?ind=106.

22. "Benefits and Services," Food and Nutrition Service, USDA, modified November 30, 2011, http://www.fns.usda.gov/wic/benefitsandservices/foodpkg.HTM.

23. Ibid.

24. "Baby blues."

Chapter 12: How Women Can Open Up

1. "We did it!," *The Economist*, December 30, 2009, http://www.economist.com/node/15174489?story_id=15174489.

2. Jerusha Stewart, *The Single Girl's Manifesta: Living in a Stupendously Superior Single State of Mind* (Sourcebooks Inc., 2005), 18–19.

3. "Famous Unmarried People, Past and Present," Alternatives to Marriage Project, March 19, 2010, http://www.unmarried.org/unmarried-people.html.

4. Stewart, *The Single Girl's Manifesta*, 24.

5. Christyann Anderson, "Strategies for a Happier Single Life," BellaOnline, http://www.bellaonline.com/articles/art171982.asp.

6. Stewart, *The Single Girl's Manifesta*, 30.

7. Bella DePaulo, *Single with Attitude: Not Your Typical Take on Health and Happiness, Love and Money, Marriage and Friendship* (CreateSpace, 2009), 8.

8. Jamal Simmons, "Genders Full of Question Marks," in *A Woman's Nation Changes Everything* ed. Heather Boushey and Ann O'Leary, October 2009, http://www.americanprogress.org/issues/2009/10/pdf/awn/a_womans_nation.pdf.

9. Gail Cohen, "About Single Travel Clubs," ehow.com, http://www.ehow.com/about_4688637_single-travel-clubs.html.

10. Lollie Barr, "Suddenly Single: What It's Like to Go It Alone," *Marie Claire,* October 14, 2008, http://au.lifestyle.yahoo.com/marie-claire/features/sex-relation/article/-/5877841/suddenly-single-what-its-like-to-go-it-alone.

11. DePaulo, *Single with Attitude*, 7.

12. DePaulo, *Single with Attitude*, 8.

13. Bella DePaulo, "When Do Women Cling to Mythologies about Marriage and Coupling?," *Psychology Today*, February 5, 2011, http://www.psychologytoday.com/blog/living-single/201102/when-do-women-cling-mythologies-about-marriage-and-coupling.

Conclusion

1. Dan Millman, *Way of the Peaceful Warrior: A Book That Changes Lives* (Tiburon, CA: H. J. Kramer, 2006).
2. Chief Woohoo Woman, "The Benefits of Breaking Up,"OneMinuteU, http://www.oneminuteu.com/default.taf?page=content&id=5522.
3. Sanchez Manning, "Dawn French reveals svelte new figure after dramatic weightloss,"*Mirror*, June 11, 2011, http://www.mirror.co.uk/celebs/news/2011/11/06/dawn-french-reveals-svelte-new-figure-after-dramatic-weight-loss-115875-23542436/.
4. Redacted Guy, "Its OK to Be Single in Your 30s...Unless You're a Girl" lemondrop.com, June 30, 2010, http://www.lemondrop.com/2010/06/30/its-okay-to-be-single-in-your-thirties-unless-youre-a-gir/.
5. "Celebrities Who Are Single, Fabulous & Loving It!" starpulse.com, January 19, 2010, www.starpulse.com/news/index.php/2010/01/19/celebrities_who_are_single_fabulous_aamp?page=1.
6. "'I'm attracted to girls and like animalistic sex': Cameron Diaz shocks fans with graphic confession," *Daily Mail Reporter*, June 18, 2010, http://www.dailymail.co.uk/tvshowbiz/article-1287475/Cameron-Diaz-shock-confession-Im-attracted-girls-like-animalistic-sex.html#ixzz1eLvdPoRX.
7. "Celebrities Who Are Single, Fabulous & Loving It!"
8. Nancy Mowll Mathews, *Mary Cassatt: A Life*, (New York: Villard Books, 1994).
9. "Famous Unmarried People, Past and Present."
10. Bolick, "All the Single Ladies."
11. Ibid.
12. Barr, "Suddenly Single."
13. Bolick, "All the Single Ladies."
14. Barr, "Suddenly Single."
15. Kim Calvert, "Those Who choose to Stay Single," *Singular Magazine*, November 29, 2009, http://singularcity.com/those-who-choose-to-stay-single/.